Transforming Preschool Storytime

Transforming Preschool Storytime

A Modern Vision and a Year of Programs

Betsy Diamant-Cohen

Melanie A. Hetrick

Illustrations by Celia Yitzhak

Neal-Schuman

An imprint of the American Library Association

Chicago | 2013

Dr. Betsy Diamant-Cohen is an independent library trainer/consultant specializing in children's programming, early literacy, and partnerships. Diamant-Cohen received her master's degree in library and information science from Rutgers University and a doctorate in communications design from the University of Baltimore. She was named a *Library Journal* Mover and Shaker in 2004 for developing the Mother Goose on the Loose early literacy program. Visit her website at www.mgol.org.

Melanie Hetrick is the children's librarian in Tillamook County, Oregon. She focuses on early literacy, reading difficulties, and learning differences in children. Her other passion in life is collection development. While at work, Hetrick can often be found in storytimes. She also enjoys working with teachers, tackling summer reading, and finding books for kids who swear they have read everything or don't want to read anything.

© 2013 by Betsy Diamant-Cohen and Melanie A. Hetrick. Any claim of copyright is subject to applicable limitations and exceptions, such as rights of fair use and library copying pursuant to Sections 107 and 108 of the U.S. Copyright Act. No copyright is claimed for content in the public domain, such as works of the U.S. government.

Printed in the United States of America
17 16 15 14 13   5 4 3 2 1

Extensive effort has gone into ensuring the reliability of the information in this book; however, the publisher makes no warranty, express or implied, with respect to the material contained herein.

ISBNs: 978-1-55570-805-4 (paper); 978-1-55570-870-2 (PDF). For more information on digital formats, visit the ALA Store at alastore.ala.org and select eEditions.

Library of Congress Cataloging-in-Publication Data

Diamant-Cohen, Betsy.
  Transforming preschool storytime : a modern vision and a year of programs / Betsy Diamant-Cohen and Melanie A. Hetrick ; illustrations by Celia Yitzhak.
    pages   cm
  Includes bibliographical references and index.
  ISBN 978-1-55570-805-4
  1. Children's libraries—Activity programs—United States. 2. Libraries and preschool children—United States. 3. Storytelling—United States. I. Hetrick, Melanie A. II. Yitzhak, Celia, illustrator. III. Title.
  Z718.3D537 2013
  027.62'51—dc23
                                                                    2013006362

Cover design by Rosemary Holderby/Cole Design and Production.
Text design by Kimberly Thornton in Miller Text and Interstate.

♾ This paper meets the requirements of ANSI/NISO Z39.48-1992 (Permanence of Paper).

To my parents for the first 34 and to Chris for the 35th
—*Melanie*

To the most creative, hard-working, fun-loving, and dedicated team of all—
the Education Department of Port Discovery Children's Museum
—*Betsy*

WEB
Supplemental
materials, including
flannelboard patterns,
can be found online at
www.alaeditions.org/
webextras

contents

PART I

Preschool Storytime, Learning Theories, Research, and Practical Applications

figures

preface

While I was the children's programming specialist at the Enoch Pratt Free Library in Baltimore, some of my colleagues questioned if it was time to rethink the traditional structure of preschool storytime. Given that children learn best through repetition, the best way to forge new connections in the brain is by building on something already learned. Since a child who loves a book will listen to it repeatedly without getting bored, we reasoned that incorporating the same book into multiple storytimes would enhance learning. In fact, since repetition with variety expands an experience, if the same book was used in different ways for a succession of storytimes, the experience with that particular book could become much richer than it might if the book was read aloud only once. The question became "Would using repetition with variety help increase the school readiness and reading readiness skills of preschoolers in Baltimore?"

This theory of repetition with variety made sense, and I began looking for ways to use books repetitively but creatively in preschool storytimes. Repeating a book in different, fun ways shows children that reading is fun, which builds print motivation. As children understand the meaning of a story, connections are made between concepts and the words describing them, increasing vocabulary and enhancing comprehension. Paying attention to printed words increases concepts of print (also called *print awareness*). Exploring their connection with a story helps children learn the nuances of language and life experiences. Examining illustrations in a story's context increases comprehension while enhancing visual awareness. Dialectic reading or taking a story walk (asking questions about the story, giving children time to form thoughts and the opportunity to respond) allows children to expand their comprehension while developing and improving communication skills. Reciting poetry or reading rhyming texts that end with the same sounds heighten phonological awareness and sensitivity. Playing with words by singing them, engaging in call-and-response games, using intonation during fingerplays (funny voices for funny words, LOUD voices for LOUD words, and soft voices for soft words), and inviting children to chime in during repeated story phrases or rhyming parts also reinforce vocabulary and comprehension. Playing games with stories that involve interaction with other children introduces social skills; following directions helps build self-regulation skills. These skills all set the scene for reading success and increase the likelihood of school completion.

Of course, it would be impossible to incorporate all of these activities in relation to one particular book read during just one storytime session. Using the same storytime book repeatedly over the course of a few weeks, though, could emphasize the development of different skills each time. Therefore, wouldn't preschool storytime best serve its clients as a purposeful learning experience if repetition rather than themes became the basis for planning programs? Or—for those librarians who prefer themes when planning their programs—if themes were incorporated into the repetition, with the main emphasis being on new ways to present the repeated book?

Melanie, also a former children's librarian at Pratt, joined me in the quest to discover answers to these questions and find out more about repetition, variety, and themes in preschool storytimes. While there is a large amount of professional library literature on preschool storytimes based on themes or lessons, there is not much on using the same book numerous times while presenting it in different ways. Librarians who have tried to incorporate repetition of specific books in their preschool storytimes have found it difficult. Questions have arisen regarding the amount of times a book should be repeated, what exactly constitutes "new ways of using the book," and how librarians who enjoy using themes can continue to do so. Parents accustomed to different books being presented at every preschool storytime have questioned why one particular book is repeated from session to session.

Melanie and I have both presented preschool storytimes that use repetition with variety. Because of our personal experiences as well as the theoretical background, we wanted to share our findings with other librarians. This book hopes to answer many questions while helping librarians, child care providers and parents to plan transformed preschool storytimes.

The Purpose of This Book

This book provides the rationale for repetition with variety. Within its pages you will find explanations, outlines, examples, and templates all designed to make it easy for librarians to experiment with repetition in preschool storytime. Taking brain research, domains of school readiness, multiple intelligences, constructivism, and best practices for early literacy into mind, it encourages rethinking the traditional preschool storytime model.

Transforming Preschool Storytime is based on the premise that children learn best through repetition. Children enjoy hearing the same beloved books read aloud repeatedly, and repetition with variety not only expands an experience but enhances brain development as well. Presenting the book in different ways enables the experiences to develop and strengthen a variety of skills. For instance, programs that involve following directions and taking turns help strengthen self-regulation skills. Singing and playing are also essential for the development of early literacy skills: singing builds vocabulary, and playing involves interacting socially with others. Science, math, and art activities can be woven into the presentation of a book in ways that make the story richer while also broadening children's horizons. Life skills such as empathy, persistence, and being able to put oneself in another person's shoes can also be tied into activities.

Scope of the Book

Transforming Preschool Storytime is a manual for using repetition creatively in preschool storytimes. With sample sessions, book and activity recommendations, resource lists, and extension suggestions, this book serves as a guide for librarians who are interested in expanding their repertoire and transforming their storytimes.

Part 1 contains background information on preschool storytime, along with an explanation of ways that traditional preschool storytimes can be transformed. Information about early literacy and school readiness, multiple intelligences, life skills, and constructivism are supplemented with theories supporting repetition with variety. Detailed explanations of both theory and research are presented in plain English, including practical real-world examples that will help explain changes to parents and administrators. Two researchers—Klaus Libertus of the Kennedy Krieger Institute and Melissa Libertus of Johns Hopkins University—share their research findings on how children learn. Finally, part 1 includes "The Nitty Gritty," a chapter containing specific details regarding planning and presenting successful preschool storytimes. It includes a planning template, a list of resources, information about keeping records, ways to modify programs based on personal style, and tips for presenting preschool storytime including the use of big books, puppets, nonfiction, and poetry.

Part 2 provides planning aids to make your job easier with outlines of storytime sessions that can be used as fill-in-the-blank planning sheets. It also includes scripts to facilitate an easy transformation from traditional preschool storytime to ones where the same book is repeated in different ways. There are also booklists and questions for evaluation. Most important, we highlight eight selected books that are proven preschool storytime favorites. Two scripts are complete, with lyrics to all fingerplays, titles of books to be used, and simply stated directions. Repeated materials are clearly marked; suggestions for alternative activities and lists of other recommended books are also given. In a series of six consecutive storytime sessions in later scripts, selected books are paired with activities that touch on different skills.

Chapter-by-Chapter Organization and Different Ways the Book Might Be Used

Supplying background information about preschool storytime, summaries of learning theories, and current research provides an explanation to librarians who have taken on the challenge of this new way of planning rather than continuing to present the same type of storytime they have been doing for years. It also provides a reasonable response for librarians to give to parents who ask, "Why are you reading that same book again?" by explaining the value of repeating a book with variation.

The first two scripts in part 2 of this book can be used word for word. Ideas for the following six books (with six sessions each) are presented as part of a script; librarians can "fill in the blanks" with books and activities of their choosing. Together, these chapters provide a full year's worth of preschool storytimes.

These outlines are simply a guide suggesting different ways the selected books can be used; it is fine for readers to come up with their own ideas. Lists of alternative activities, media, and books provide substitute items for scripts, yet even these are replaceable. This guide is meant to make programming with repetition using variety easy and fun. Thus, this book intends to show by example how to create transformed storytimes and to build knowledgeable librarians who feel confident creating these new kinds of storytime on their own.

Developmental tips provide informal asides that librarians can use to explain the value of an activity to parents, to suggest ways to replicate or create similar activities at home, to reinforce the message that a parent is a child's first and best teacher, and to familiarize parents with the different domains of school readiness and the importance of life skills.

The end result, then, is a guidebook to help librarians easily transition into using a selected book repeatedly in numerous storytimes, through fun activities that inspire imagination, encourage creativity, and help children to exercise problem-solving skills.

acknowledgments

There are many people who need to be thanked for their role in the creation of this book. Our colleagues at the Enoch Pratt Free Library in Baltimore provided many wonderful ideas. Special thanks go to Selma Levi for her incredible knowledge of books and to Gloria Bartas for her endless supply of creative ways to present books. Kit Bloom, Carolyn Harnick, and Caitlin Huddleston also shared some favorite books and implementation ideas. Other helpful, creative librarians include Nancy Feierstein, Lori Guenthner, Summer Rosswog, and Dorothy Stoltz. Marisa Conner, from the Baltimore County Public Library, showed me the Read, Play, and Learn curriculum, which extends the theory of learning through repetition of chosen picture books in a wide variety of ways that touch upon different senses. It has become a great resource and provides validation for the theory of repetition with variety. Michele Presley enthusiastically shared many creative ideas and provided examples for the story signs in chapter 10 ("Series 8: *The Little Old Lady Who Was Not Afraid of Anything*"). Thank you to my fellow librarian Regina Wade who shared wonderful playful activities that have been incorporated in this book!

The Education Department at Port Discovery Children's Museum in Baltimore has been an invaluable resource; each staff member is a hard-working, thoughtful, fun-loving, and creative person, dedicated to helping children become the best they can be while encouraging learning through play. We've had many stimulating discussions and together have designed programs that include books, drama, art, music, STEM, and much more. Jennifer Bergantz, Sarah Draude, Daveed Korup, and Nora Moynihan all played an important part in the creation of this book. In addition, while discussing a Talking about Tots program at Port Discovery, Drs. Klaus and Melissa Libertus offered to share some valuable supporting research, which has been included in chapter 1, "An Overview of Preschool Storytime."

I would also like to thank the ladies who sat next to me on a plane ride coming back from a Mother Goose on the Loose workshop; they asked what I was writing and began offering suggestions once the subject matter was described! Fran Glushakow supplied Friday-night dinner for weeks as the deadline for the manuscript was getting closer; Shira Glushakow-Smith and Elinor Naor helped with technical details. Thank you to Stuart, who lovingly brought me many cups of tea and gave plenty of moral support!

A big thank-you goes to Jan Fabiyi, who is not only a terrific friend but a wonderful editor as well. I appreciate the time she took to read early drafts of my books and steer me in the right direction. Kathy Buchsbaum, our Neal-Schuman editor, showed remarkable patience, kindness, and understanding during the writing process. She has been an important member of our team; we are very lucky to have had the opportunity to work with her.

Celia Yitzhak is an absolutely incredible artist, and we greatly appreciate all the wonderful flannelboard templates she created for this book.

And thank you to Melanie, a terrific librarian, who agreed to write this book with me!

—*Betsy*

I couldn't have done this book without the help, support and encouragement, understanding and patience of many people. First off, I'd like to thank Chris for his unfailing support, promising over and over again that yes, there is light at the end of the tunnel, and for letting me take over his dining room table for months on end. Thanks also to Irene for helping me go through many, many song and fingerplay books to find ideas. To Barbara Scott for allowing us to reprint rhymes from her book. To Kathy Buchsbaum for answering the same questions over and over again! To the staff (especially Lynette) of the Tillamook County (Oregon) Libraries for physically handling the hundreds and hundreds of holds I placed on materials for this book. Thanks also to the staff of the Tillamook branch libraries and the Driftwood, Newport, Siletz, Toledo, and Waldport libraries for pulling many of those material holds and sending them on. And, of course, many hugs to the children of Tillamook County who came to many a storytime and let me try out ideas on them.

And finally, to Dr. Betsy Diamant-Cohen for inviting me into this project. Your support and faith in me throughout this process has been amazing—thank you!

—*Melanie*

Preschool Storytime, Learning Theories, Research, and Practical Applications

chapter 1

An Overview of Preschool Storytime

What Is Preschool Storytime?

Preschool storytime is generally a thirty-minute program offered in a public library for children ages 3 to 5. A librarian, staff person, or volunteer reads several picture books aloud, using props and activities between books to keep children attentive. There are variations on this; some libraries extend the thirty-minute program and offer crafts or films as part of the preschool storytime. Others offer a family-based storytime that includes a larger age range. However, this book will refer to preschool storytime as the thirty-minute picture book–based program geared for children from ages 3 to 5.

The first programs for children in public libraries were geared toward school-age children. In the 1930s, they were expanded to include programs for preschoolers. Today, a significant responsibility for most children's librarians is programming for children of all ages, which often includes planning and presenting lap-sit programs for caregivers with babies and toddlers, picture book–based storytimes for preschoolers, extended-book programs for early elementary children, and booktalk programs for school-age children.

When presented enthusiastically, good books can hold any audience spellbound. Although a program may be aimed at one specific age group, it is not unusual to have a few older or younger siblings attend. Family storytimes are planned to appeal to everyone, despite varying ages. Through hearing stories read aloud from books, children are exposed to new vocabulary and concepts. Presenting high-quality storybooks helps to develop critical thinking skills, and can instill a lifelong love of reading. It makes sense, then, that books are the basis of most public library programs for children, including preschool storytime.

The main goal of preschool storytime is to help children develop a positive connection with books and illustration, which will later translate into a positive attitude toward books in general. It gives them (and the parents or child care providers who attend) a chance to become familiar with the library, to feel as though it is their place. Additionally, a positive relationship with the person regularly presenting the storytime is fostered. Preschool storytime introduces children and their caregivers to a wide range of books with a variety of authors and illustrators, providing exposure to numerous vocabulary words and artistic techniques. It brings books and people together, hopefully inspiring program attendees to borrow books from the public library and look at them together at home. It creates a community of program attendees; children who do not attend preschool can interact with other children and adults. Preschool storytime becomes a place where adults who may feel isolated at home can socialize with other adults in the same situation. Book-reading behavior is modeled, and children are given the opportunity to learn how to become part of a group.

Benefits of Preschool Storytime

Specific areas related to school readiness (often referred to as *domains of school readiness*) are personal and social development, language and literacy, mathematical and scientific thinking, approach to learning, cognition and general knowledge, physical development and health, and the arts.[1]

SCHOOL READINESS DOMAINS

Personal and social development includes emotional health; it involves self-confidence, caring for others, having trust in others, and self-regulation skills such as the ability to pay attention, follow directions, and show empathy.

Language and literacy involves print motivation (liking books and thinking that reading is fun), vocabulary (knowing the names of things), print awareness (recognizing print and being familiar with the format of books), letter knowledge (knowing that letters have corresponding names and sounds), narrative skills (being able to tell stories or give descriptions), and phonological awareness (being able to hear the sounds in words).

Mathematical and scientific thinking involves recognizing shapes and patterns, understanding sequences, forming hypotheses and testing them out, and recognizing cause and effect.

Approach to learning is a positive attitude characterized by curiosity, the desire to learn, willingness to problem solve, and courage to try new things.

Cognition and general knowledge refers to knowledge about the surrounding world. It includes a very basic understanding of social studies, geography, and the natural world.

Physical development and health includes both fine and gross motor development. It involves knowing the names for body parts and what they do.

The arts involves appreciating and using creative expression through fine art, music, and drama.

In an effort to help more children enter school ready to read, storytime planning sheets for librarians were developed by Elaine Czarnecki, a reading specialist from Johns Hopkins University. Since the purpose of the sheets was to help children develop skills that "kindergarten teachers expect children to be familiar with when they enter school,"[2] librarians who were planning programs were asked to include developmentally appropriate, language-related activities for 3-to-5-year-old children that complemented the books being read aloud. These planning sheets gave librarians language and literacy goals to keep in mind when planning programs in order to promote age-appropriate school readiness skills.

In addition to language and literacy skills, activities and games that take place in preschool storytime can help develop a child's social and emotional skills. Self-regulation is important in a classroom; children need to know how to think before they act, to express their emotions through words, to wait their turn, and to be sensitive to others. Preschool storytime can help children develop self-regulation skills through simple activities that require both interaction and patience. Inviting children to take turns coming up to the front of the room, performing a specific task, and then receiving applause from the group is one way to build up their sense of self-confidence. At the same time, the children doing the applauding are learning how to show appreciation to others. Research has found that improved self-regulation skills combined with a broad academic basis are most effective in helping children succeed in school.[3]

LIFE SKILLS

Based on years of research on the changing workforce and the changing family, Ellen Galinsky, president and cofounder of the Families and Work Institute, compiled a list of seven essential life skills that children need.[4]

Focus and self control include remembering rules, paying attention, and thinking flexibly. It is essential in today's world where there is an overload of information and sensory stimulation.

Perspective taking is being able to put yourself in someone else's shoes. Being able to figure out what other people think and feel enables children to understand the intentions of the people around them. Whether they agree or disagree, children who can see things from another person's perspective are less likely to get into conflicts.

Communication involves knowing your thoughts well enough to know precisely what you want to say, understanding people and situations well enough to determine how to communicate, and correctly assessing how others will interpret that communication.

Making connections between ideas is like a lightbulb going off in the brain. Creative thought is spurred by determining what is the same and what is different and then finding ways to connect them. This enables people to use information they already know.

Critical thinking is wondering about the world, forming questions, looking for obvious and alternative solutions, and discovering accurate answers. A solution that has been tried and determined to be reliable can then help guide beliefs, decisions, and actions.

Taking on challenges is a mind-set that involves embracing a problem and choosing to tackle it rather than ignore it. As a tool for managing stress, it is proactive rather than reactive.

Self-directed, engaged learning builds on a child's already existing interests and desire to explore. Combining facts with experiences that are meaningful and purposeful results in an increased desire to learn and to grow based on what has been learned.

Read It Again!

In the late 1990s, scientific research demonstrated that the first three years of life are a crucial time for the formation of pathways in the brain that affect learning, behavior, and successful participation in adult society. Children's librarians then began designing programs for infants and toddlers. Many of these early childhood library programs incorporate knowledge of how children learn by repeating songs, rhymes, and books on a weekly basis. Infants and toddlers respond with great enthusiasm to familiar rhyming activities as joyful learning takes place through repetition. Research on children's learning strongly supports the importance not only of repetition, but of repetition with variation in learning situations. Dr. Klaus Libertus from Kennedy Krieger Institute and Dr. Melissa Libertus from Johns Hopkins University describe research findings below for this book:

At some point in our lives, all of us have experienced that learning something new is not easy. Learning requires practice, or put differently, learning requires repetition. This statement is fundamentally true and has been studied extensively by researchers across fields. For example, neurobiologists have uncovered how repetition shapes and enhances the connections between neurons in our central nervous system.[5] We now know how learning works on a biological level. But in order to make things really stick, in order to facilitate learning and improve our memory, we do not just need repetition—we also need variation. Psychologists have shown that repetition with added variation in context or task demands can strongly enhance learning and memory.[6] Indeed, several lines of research starting in early infancy and spanning the entire lifespan support the concept of learning through repetition with variation. Here, we offer a brief review of a few of these research findings in the domains of

Dr. Klaus Libertus

Dr. Klaus Libertus received his MA and PhD in psychology and neuroscience from Duke University in 2010 and is currently a post-doctoral fellow at the Kennedy Krieger Institute in Baltimore, Maryland. His research focuses on the connections between motor and social development and embodied cognition in infancy. In his work, Dr. Libertus applies behavioral and eye-tracking assessments to study the development of infants and toddlers at risk for autism spectrum disorders (ASD). His goals are to identify early signs of ASD in infancy, and to develop motor-training interventions to facilitate healthy development in infants and toddlers at risk for poor developmental outcomes.

Dr. Melissa Libertus

Dr. Melissa Libertus received her MA and PhD in psychology and neuroscience from Duke University in 2010 and is currently a postdoctoral researcher in the Department of Psychological and Brain Sciences at Johns Hopkins University. Her research focuses on the development of numerical thinking in infants and children and the relationship between basic numerical skills and later math abilities. Dr. Libertus combines behavioral and brain imaging techniques to investigate these issues from a behavioral and neural perspective.

visual perception, language, and motor skills learning to illustrate the value of repetition with variation in instruction and in game or play routines.

When an infant repeatedly observes the same event, this event will become boring and the infant will stop looking at it. Conversely, if something new or surprising happens, infants' attention rebounds and they start to look for a longer time again. These looking preferences can be used to study what infants remember. Bomba and Siqueland[7] made use of this technique and repeatedly showed 3-month-old infants a display where dots were arranged to form a shape such as a triangle. Following repeated exposure to one shape (e.g., a triangle), infants looked longer at a display of dots arranged in a different shape, but only if they had seen twelve different examples of the triangle shape before. Showing them just six different examples of the triangle repeatedly was not sufficient to facilitate learning in these infants.

In a study with 5-month-old infants, Needham, Dueker, and Lockhead[8] looked at how infants learn about object categories. To do this, they showed the infants an ambiguous object that may consist of either one piece or two pieces (a box with a hose attached). Without any prior experience, most infants at this age think that the object is one big piece. However, when given prior exposure to three similar (but different) boxes alone, infants seem to learn a category "box" and are more likely to judge the box-hose display as being composed of two objects. Critically, for this learning to take place infants had to be exposed to three or more boxes that were similar but not identical to the box used on the test object. Neither exposure to only two similar boxes, nor exposure to three boxes that were identical to the test object facilitated infants' learning in this case.

Similar benefits of repetition with variation have been found for learning a new motor skill in older children. Kerr and Booth[9] gave 8- and 12-year-olds practice in throwing a ball to hit a target either from a fixed distance of three feet or from variable distances. Children were subsequently tested in their ability to hit the target from three feet. Surprisingly, the children who practiced throwing the ball from variable distances were better at hitting the target than the children who had practiced from the exact same distance. Thus, varying the distance to the target proved to be better than practicing exactly the motor skill that was eventually tested.

Another domain in which repeated exposure to variable input has been found to be critical is the domain of language. For example, Gomez[10] examined how infants and adults learn syntactic dependencies between words that are not next to each other (e.g., subject-verb agreement as in "the *tree* behind the house *is* green . . ."). To this end, infants and adults listened to an artificial language that had such rules embedded. Adults and 18-month-old infants were able to learn these rules better if they were exposed to 24 different sentences than when they were only exposed to two, six, or twelve different sentences. Again, this shows that variability is essential to learn the underlying structure—in this case of the linguistic input.

Together, these studies show that starting at a very young age, both repetition and variation seem to strongly facilitate learning and memory across a variety of contexts and ages. Most important, these studies show that repetition with variation is a very powerful learning mechanism that should be harnessed to teach young children, for example, to enhance preschool-aged children's literacy.

Previous research has shown that young children develop a better understanding of a story through re-reading the same story multiple times.[11] But even more so, children's story comprehension increases through reading and active participation in the literary experience. For example, 4- to 6-year-old children who repeated each sentence that was read to them instead of only passively listening were significantly better at recalling the content of the story and its semantic content.[12] Moreover, Morrow[13] showed that frequent retelling of a story with guidance by an adult significantly improves story comprehension in kindergarten children. One particular area that seems to benefit immensely is the ability to correctly recall the sequence of events in a story, a task that is often very difficult for young children.[14]

Very young children love picture books and often like to hear them read aloud over and over; parents often tire of a book well before their children. When favorite bedtime stories are read aloud, the most common response is "Read it again!" In recognition of this, some libraries have started issuing special library cards for children under the age of 5 or 6 that allow books to be borrowed for extended periods of time without charging overdue fines. Three weeks is often not long enough for a child to hear a favorite book. After children have heard a story read aloud a number of times, they know what is going to happen next. This ability to predict correctly builds their self-esteem, gives them a sense that they are smart, and boosts their confidence to tackle tough tasks.[15] The extended circulation period allows adults to read a book again and again until the child is finally ready for some new reading material.

Rather than getting bored by hearing the same story multiple times, children enjoy being able to anticipate what will happen. In some cases, they memorize the entire story and then delight in being able to recite it word for word along with the reader. This makes sense; even adults learn easily through repetition.

When searching for songs on your car radio, which radio station do you prefer—the one that plays songs that you already know or one whose music is totally new to you? The Listen, Like, Learn approach developed by Barbara Cass-Beggs suggests that people like repetition; listening to something they already know stimulates their enjoyment of the piece and enables them to learn something new from it each time it is repeated.[16] This assertion correlates with findings in brain research that learning is comprised of connections made within the brain. A single piece of information that is not repeated is eventually pruned away, but repeated activities create new experiences that build upon one another, increasing the synapses and the actual weight of the brain. In essence, "What fires together wires together."[17] Curiously, when children begin attending library preschool programs at around the age of 3, this emphasis on repetition disappears. But is that really a best practice?

Constructivism

Jean Piaget understood that children learn best through their experiences, and he called the ideas that children get from these personal experiences "constructivism."[18] *Social constructivism* is when learners discover principles, concepts, and facts for themselves by making sense of their own experiences. When trying to draw children's attention to paintings in museums, instead of using factual labels, museum curators today often write labels that ask questions to help the child personally relate to the picture. For instance, the Dutch artist Frans Hals (1581–1666) painted "Portrait of a Woman with a Lace Collar and Bonnet." This woman is wearing a high collar that is both wide and thick; it looks as if it might be difficult to swallow when wearing such a collar. A constructivist approach to this painting might be to ask children questions such as "Do you have any clothing that looks like that? Would you enjoy playing outdoors wearing something like that? Why or why not? Do you think it would be easy to eat pizza wearing such a high collar?"

After thinking about these questions, the children are able to look at the painting from a personal perspective. This type of active technique connects children to the painting, encouraging them to think about it and share their comments. As the children are guided through reflecting and talking about their experience of the painting, their understanding of it grows. In addition to seeing the painting with their eyes, they are able to put themselves in the subject's place, to imagine wearing the same clothes, and to think about what it might be like to play while wearing such a restricting outfit. Thus, their experience of the painting is not simply visual but draws from all the senses. An experience involving multiple senses becomes more personal; this particular experience becomes richer because it has made the painting more meaningful for the child. As children become active in their own learning process, curiosity about the world around them grows and interest in how things work is generated.

Scaffolded Learning

Lev Vygotsky, a Russian child psychologist, promoted "scaffolded learning."[19] It begins with a child who knows something and an adult who engages with the child at his level. The adult assists the child to accomplish something he could not do on his own, engaging him in activities that raise his level of knowledge. Due to the support and mentoring of the adult, the child eventually is able to accomplish the same thing independently. Programs that include repetition with variety that are designed to expand children's experiences give librarians a way to put this type of scaffolded learning into action.

Multiple Intelligences

People learn in many different ways. Some learn best by hearing, and others by seeing. The majority of people, however, learn best by actually doing. When planning programs for children, it is important to keep the wide range of learning styles in mind. Preschoolers have not yet entered formal schooling and may not have had the opportunity to experiment with different learning styles. Introducing a book in ways that involve a variety of senses and experiences provides an opportunity to help awaken or strengthen a child's particular learning style.

Howard Gardner calls these styles "intelligences."[20] He asserts that there are multiple intelligences and each one of them is valuable. Although it may seem that our culture places greater importance on cognitive rather than other skills, society benefits from having a world full of people with a variety of intelligences. For instance, while it is important for surgeons to have strong kinesthetic intelligence (good eye-hand coordination), composers benefit from having strong musical intelligence. NASA scientists might be most successful if their logical-mathematical intelligence was strongest, yet psychologists would do well if their strengths were interpersonal skills.

GARDNER'S LIST OF INTELLIGENCES

It is helpful to keep Gardner's list of intelligences in mind when planning new ways to present a book; you can appeal to a different intelligence each time the same selected book is used in your preschool storytime sessions.

> **Linguistic intelligence** connects learning with words.
> **Logical-mathematical intelligence** connects learning with numbers or logic.
> **Spatial intelligence** connects learning with pictures.
> **Bodily-kinesthetic intelligence** connects learning with the body or a physical experience.

Musical intelligence connects learning with music.

Interpersonal intelligence involves learning through social experiences.

Intrapersonal intelligence connects learning with self-reflection or knowledge of oneself.

Naturalist intelligence connects learning through an experience in the social world.

ADDITIONAL INTELLIGENCES

Psychologist Daniel Goleman expanded Gardner's list:

Emotional intelligence (similar to Gardner's *intrapersonal intelligence*) uses self-awareness, confidence, and empathy for others to manage disturbing emotions and inhibit disruptive emotional impulses.[21]

Social intelligence (similar to Gardner's *interpersonal intelligence*) involves connecting with others in a deep way that influences mood and brain chemistry.[22]

Ecological intelligence connects awareness of and appreciation for our environment with decisions regarding what we buy, sell, make, and discard.[23]

Using multiple intelligences to teach goes beyond conventional and logical methods.[24] Introducing a particular book in preschool storytime and then presenting it a variety of ways that builds on different types of intelligences can expand a child's horizons. After having listened to a storybook, if children have the opportunity to re-create the story themselves by acting, singing, making something, and talking about it, they are bound to have a much richer appreciation of it. And, if linguistic or spatial intelligence are not their strong points, they will still be able to connect strongly to the story.

Every Child Ready to Read @ your library

Every Child Ready to Read® (ECRR) @ your library is a research-based early literacy outreach program centered on the principle that a parent is a child's first and most valuable teacher. The program was developed by a task force including representatives from the Association for Library Service to Children (ALSC) and the Public Library Association (PLA) and based on research from the National Institute of Child Health and Human Development of the National Institutes of Health.[25] This program originally focused on language skills but now highlights five practices as being essential for helping children develop reading readiness.[26] It provides workshop materials for librarians to present to parents and caregivers that teach ways to incorporate these five practices into their daily interactions with their children. While ECRR uses the five practices to promote six essential language skills, the program also assists in the development of the whole child.

THE FIVE PRACTICES

Talking: Speaking with children introduces them to new words. Asking questions, then listening and responding to answers, strengthens communication skills and increases bonding between children and their adults. Talking with an adult about books and illustrations expands a child's understanding of the story and can translate into greater understanding about the world around them.

Singing: Words set to music are easier to remember than spoken words. Notes and rhythms in music help define sounds, and when syllables in words are sung, more attention is focused on the syllables in those words. That, as well as clapping to the words of songs, helps to develop phonological awareness. Additionally, singing together creates community. Songs with movements strengthen fine and gross motor skills.

Reading: Adults who read joyfully with their children help to instill a lifelong love of books and reading. ECRR states, "Reading is an essential life skill"; positive reading experiences in childhood set the stage for a love of reading and appreciation of books. When an adult reads the same book a number of times, children see that the story remains the same and understand that reading is a way to decode the written word.

Writing: Although preschoolers may not be able to write words, they can understand that there is a connection between letters, the written word, and the spoken word. By seeing print in their environment and experiencing the many ways that words can be used, children learn that reading is important. Scribbling is a precursor to writing; it involves fine motor skills and eye-hand coordination, and allows children to express themselves via print.[27] Fingerplays help to develop fine motor skills needed for writing, as well as eye-hand coordination.

Playing: Play is essential for the healthy development of children.[28] Physical play involves coordination of muscles (gross motor skills for large muscles and fine motor skills for small ones). Playing matching games that compare shapes, colors, and sizes helps children develop cognitive skills that are precursors to reading and learning numbers. Dramatic play encourages social and emotional development as children act out various roles, create narratives, and discover the cause and effect of different behaviors. Scenarios during dramatic play are often stories that have a beginning, middle, and end. During group play, children experience the sharing of toys and the building of relationships. Playing with others improves social awareness and sense of self.[29] Team play teaches cooperation while allowing children to experience dependency. Talking during play strengthens oral language skills.[30] Play provides an emotional outlet and can become a vehicle for expression. Organized play teaches teamwork, taking turns, and following directions. Creative play sparks the imagination, encouraging children to see beyond the concrete and explore unknown possibilities, fostering understanding of abstract concepts.[31]

Since children learn through play, it stands to reason that by presenting books in a playful manner children will learn more from them. Instead of simply addressing the content of the book, the reenactment and related activities unleash the imagination, engage children in problem solving, and provide opportunities for peer interactions.

Incorporating Technology into Programs

Many librarians are uncomfortable with the idea of incorporating technology into their preschool storytimes on a regular basis. We know that there is nothing quite like physically holding a book in your hands and sharing it enthusiastically with children. The American Medical Association has recommended that children under the age of 2 have no screen time at all and that children between ages 3 and 5 limit television viewing to a maximum of two hours.[32] Studies have shown that children under the age of 5 who are prolonged television watchers have fewer social skills and a higher risk for behavior problems than children who do not watch much television.[33]

However, technology does not just mean television, and technology abounds in today's world. Computers, televisions, smart phones, DVD players, MP3 players, and Wii games have become part of a shared vocabulary. It is likely that more technological tools that have not yet been invented will be become everyday items in the near future for our youngest learners. Exposure to technology can be beneficial even for children from ages 3 to 5 if carefully designed. Computer play can involve exploration and discovery; it can help improve nonverbal skills, structural knowledge, long-term memory, manual dexterity, verbal skills, problem solving, abstraction, and conceptual skills.[34] Use of computers can provide a creative approach to science and math and "encourage debate, adaptation, analysis, and celebration."[35] If public libraries aim to help improve literacy and narrow the digital divide, including some sort of technology into preschool storytimes might thus be considered.

DIGITAL LITTLES
Digital Littles, a technology-rich preschool storytime experience, is offered on a regular basis at the main Indianapolis Public Library as well as in several of its branches. It includes laptops and a robotic dinosaur![36] During these programs, storytimes are combined with hands-on technology activities. For instance, after reading the book *Where's Tumpty?* by Polly Dunbar,[37] children use a flip camera to make a movie of the subsequent hide-and-seek game they play in the library. The movie is then uploaded to the computer and projected on a big screen for all storytime participants to see. This provides a good opportunity for an exciting variation that expands the experience of a book presented at storytime. It also gives children a chance to work as a team, to experience sequencing of events, and to develop their vocabulary. Handouts for parents describe the day's activities, the skills practiced and learned, related books, and follow-up activities that can be done at home both with and without a computer.

Abby Brown, early literacy specialist, explains that children enjoy extending their storytime experiences by drawing digital pictures related to a book featured in storytime using programs such as KidPix or Microsoft Paint and participating in other programs offered via the PNC-sponsored Digital Littles Mobile Lab. Tami Edminister, program specialist at the Indianapolis Marion County Public Library, has found that many librarians who originally did not want to use technology in their storytimes became supporters once they had tried it.

THE INTERNATIONAL CHILDREN'S DIGITAL LIBRARY

The International Children's Digital Library (ICDL)[38] is a database that contains picture books from around the world. Books can be "read" in many different formats, including typical two page spreads, comic book format, and spiral reader. Through ICDL, librarians have access to books that are hard to find, out of print, or in different languages. Digital storytimes using ICDL require a computer (laptop is fine), a projector, and a projection screen. The book is located on ICDL via the computer and projected onto the screen, and pages are turned with the click of a mouse. A study comparing traditional storytimes with digital storytimes found that preschoolers were less fidgety in the digital storytimes.[39] In the traditional preschool storytimes, the presenter sat in front of the children, held the book open, and turned book pages manually. In the digital storytime, the presenter sat *with* the children and viewed the stories on a large screen with them while turning pages with a click of a wireless mouse.[40] In these examples, the presenter seemed to be part of the activity rather than directing it.

In "Creative Ways to Use Digital Group Storytimes in the Classroom or Library,"[41] Lauren Collen presents a number of ways that ICDL can be integrated into storytimes. Large images on a screen are much easier to view than illustrations constrained to book size only. Wordless books projected on a bigger screen (with technology that can enlarge the pages even more, if desired) allow children to see small details they might otherwise miss. This benefit enables children to decode storylines for themselves via the illustrations and helps them experience narrative skills long before they have learned to read words. After holding a digital storytime, librarians can give the online address of books read aloud to parents, and children can then be encouraged to explore the book on their own on a computer in the library or at home, on an iPad, a netbook, or even a smartphone.[42]

Since possibilities for integrating technology into preschool storytime will only increase in the future, suggestions for incorporating a digital aspect will be included in some of the storytime scenarios in the following pages.

Themes

Most library literature on programming for preschoolers focuses on themes. Librarians are encouraged to choose a topic for each session and then build programs around the theme by utilizing picture books, songs, finger plays, music, and crafts. A program on teddy bears will include a rhyme such as "Teddy Bear, Teddy Bear, Turn Around," while the next week's program on hot drinks may include "I'm a Little Teapot." This means that none of the bear rhymes or books are repeated, since everything now focuses on hot drinks. Although there may be standard opening and closing rituals used in every program, the core of traditional preschool theme-based storytimes includes mostly new material; there is little continuity from week to week.

Building circle times around themes makes sense for day care centers, since their daily schedules are often based on curriculum-coordinated themes. If children are studying colors for a month, they may have one week focusing on green, one week focusing on red, and one week focusing on yellow. Their circle times will then include material related to a colors theme. This makes sense because the theme continues for more than one hour—it is usually mentioned each day for an entire week, enabling the children to attach new information to something they have already learned. The circle-time theme is just part of a larger curriculum theme that might also include art projects, role-playing activities in the dress-up corner, science activities, playground games, snacks, and much more. This type of learning takes place on an ongoing basis within a specific context, enabling the children to build multiple connections.

Preschool storytimes at the public library, however, generally take place only once a week, and there is often little repetition from program to program. The theme is a tool for the librarian to help make programming easier, but generally has little relevance to the participants because it was used only on a one-time basis. Once the preschool storytime has ended, the theme may be extended via a handout to parents, or with a follow-up craft activity. But generally, as soon as the storytime ends, the theme is forgotten.

Another problem inherent in building a program around a randomly chosen theme is that the librarian often can find only one or two good books on the topic. In order to incorporate other books, the librarian generally has to comb the collection. While the original book might be great, the rest of the books might not have similar literary merit but are picked anyway because of their content. The same might be said about related songs and fingerplays. Thus, storytimes built on randomly chosen themes have a small likelihood of songs, rhymes, and books being repeated from week to week, and by virtue of the desire to connect everything to an arbitrary theme, the quality of the material presented may be compromised.

Presenting a Book in Multiple Ways

The idea of using a picture book with children on a repeated basis and expanding the experience of the book into other areas is already an accepted practice in the field of early childhood education. "Read, Play, and Learn!", a transdisciplinary, play-based, storybook-oriented curriculum designed by Toni W. Linder, provides a wonderful example of ways to help children develop skills in all the developmental domains.[43] Designed for use in inclusive classrooms to help build the skills of children with a wide range of abilities, this curriculum is comprised of a series of sixteen instructional modules, each built around a particular picture book. In addition to using a book in circle time every day for two weeks, an entire environment in the classroom is created around the book, which greatly extends the story. Children are challenged in playful, fun ways to build on already existing skills through art, science, math, movement, and drama-based activities.

Each module includes planning sheets that explain ways to encourage learning across the developmental domains. A literacy-rich environment based on that particular story-book is created that includes "an area to dramatize the story; a literacy center; areas for sensory and motor play, an art area; and sites for science and math activities, floor play, table play, outdoor play, woodworking, and snack"[44] with the intent of building levels of understanding and learning on the sensorimotor level, the functional level, and the symbolic level. The sensorimotor level, also called the *exploratory level*, addresses the beginning stages of learning through sensory exploration, physical manipulation of the environment, social interactions, and concrete labels and meanings. The *functional level* of learning is attained when children use functional objects and actions to sequence ideas and actions. They watch and listen, imitate and relate. The *symbolic level* is when children move beyond the concrete and represent their understanding of the story through fantasy play, dance, music, art, storytelling, drawing, and print.[45]

> Vocabulary, actions, and information related to the themes contained in the storybooks are expanded into activities that enhance cognitive (problem-solving), social-emotional, communication and language, and sensorimotor skills. Emerging literacy development is also encouraged through the child's familiarity and comfort with the storybook and the activities and environment developed for the module.[46]

In *Picture Books Plus*,[47] Sue McCleaf Nespeca and Joan B. Reeve provide a wealth of art, drama, music, math, and science activities that can be used to extend picture books beyond simply reading them aloud. And, although it is geared toward preschool teachers, the Story Stretchers books[48] contain picture book expansion activities that involve art; music and movement; cooking and snack time; creative dramatics; dress-up; science fun; block building; nature study; and math games.

Incorporating Repetition into Preschool Storytime

Read once, a book may leave a small impression on a child. Storytime becomes a much richer learning experience when repetition is incorporated in a way that involves many senses and extends children's experience of the book, enhancing cognitive, social, emotional, and problem-solving skills while promoting literacy and creative thinking. Reading a book during an initial storytime session introduces it to children; using the book in subsequent weeks by reading it again, telling it, acting it out, running an activity that relates to some aspect of the book; and finding ways to involve different senses expand children's connection with and appreciation for that book. It also enhances early literacy skills. Creative ways can be found to tie the content or the book illustrations to fields such as math, science, social studies, art, and music.

Although there is not much published research on repetition in preschool storytime, there is a fair amount of research on related topics such as the value of preschool storytime, the value of play, early literacy, child care activities for preschoolers, child development, reading books aloud, engaging children with disabilities, expanding books beyond their cover, and book illustration for children. When combined, these sources make a strong case for using a book repeatedly in preschool storytime, and, it is optimally beneficial if the book is *repeated in a different way* each time.

Preparing for these programs can be hard work. Instead of simply reading the book, the presenter has to think of a few different creative ways to present the book that reinforce the story while stimulating a variety of intelligences and senses. Is it really worth the effort?

Leveling the Playing Field

Studies suggest that children who live in poverty have low literacy skills and often are not "ready to learn" when they enter kindergarten.[49] Interacting with caring adults and observing appropriate behavior can make a difference; through guided, playful activities in the library, children living in difficult circumstances have opportunities to speak, think, and behave in literate ways.[50] Learning how to retell stories provides the "narrative techniques that they [preschoolers] have absorbed from their experiences of hearing written language" and the syntax necessary for complex thinking; both are powerful and important tools for children.[51]

Programs in public libraries are open to children from all economic, racial, religious, and cultural backgrounds. One reason for providing these programs is to give equal opportunity to access good early literacy skills and therefore, give every child better opportunities to succeed in school and in life. What better reason could there be to experiment with using repetition with variety during your preschool storytimes and see for yourself if it makes a difference?

NOTES

1. Maryland State Department of Education. 2009. "Maryland Model for School Readiness (MMSR): Framework and Standards for Prekindergarten." 6th ed. Revised Summer. Maryland State Department of Education. http://mdk12.org/instruction/ensure/MMSR/MMSRpkFrameworkAndStandards.pdf.
2. Martinez, Gilda. 2007. "Partnering for Reading Readiness: A Case Study of Maryland Public Librarians." *Children and Libraries* 5, no. 1: 34.

3. Blair, Clancy, and Rachel Peters Razza. 2007. "Relating Effortful Control, Executive Function, and False Belief Understanding to Emerging Math and Literacy Ability in Kindergarten." *Child Development* 78, no. 2: 647–663.

4. Galinsky, Ellen. 2010. *Mind in the Making: The Seven Essential Life Skills Every Child Needs*. New York: HarperStudio.

5. Kandel, E. R., Schwartz, J. H., and Jessell, T. M. (Eds.). 2000. *Principles of Neural Science*. 4th ed. New York: McGraw-Hill.

6. See this for a review: Schmidt, R. A., Bjork, R. A. 1992. "New Conceptualizations of Practice: Common Principles in Three Paradigms Suggest New Concepts for Training." *Psychological Science* 3, no. 4: 207–217.

7. Bomba, P. C., Siqueland, E. R. 1983. "The Nature and Structure of Infant Form Categories." *Journal of Experimental Child Psychology* 35, no. 2: 294–328.

8. Needham, A., Dueker, G., and Lockhead, G. 2005. "Infants' Formation and Use of Categories to Segregate Objects." *Cognition* 94, no. 3: 215–240.

9. Kerr, R., Booth, B. 1978. "Specific and Varied Practice of Motor Skill." *Perceptual and Motor Skills* 46, no. 2: 395–401.

10. Gomez, R. L. 2000. "Variability and Detection of Invariant Structure." *Psychological Science* 13, no. 5: 431–436.

11. Yaden, D. 1988. "Understanding Stories through Repeated Read-Alouds: How Many Does It Take?" *The Reading Teacher* 41, no. 6: 556–560.

12. Blank, M., Frank, S. M. 1971. "Story Recall in Kindergarten Children: Effect of Method of Presentation on Psycholinguistic Performance." *Child Development* 42: 299–312.

13. Morrow, L. M. 1985. "Retelling Stories: A Strategy for Improving Young Children's Comprehension, Concept of Story Structure, and Oral Language Complexity." *The Elementary School Journal* 85, no. 5: 647–661.

14. Brown, A. L. 1975. "Recognition, Reconstruction, and Recall of Narrative Sequences by Preoperational Children." *Child Development* 46, no. 1: 156–166.

15. Kryczka, Cathie. 2008. "Again! Again!" *Today's Parent*, February 1. www.todaysparent.com/toddler/toddler-behaviour/again-again.

16. Cass-Beggs, Barbara. 1986. *Your Child Needs Music*. Mississauga, Ontario: The Frederick Harris Music Co.

17. National Scientific Council on the Developing Child. 2007. *The Science of Early Childhood Development: Closing the Gap Between What We Know and What We Do*. Cambridge, MA: National Scientific Council on the Developing Child.

18. Piaget, Jean. 1962. *Play, Dreams and Imitation in Childhood*. New York: W. W. Norton. http://developingchild.net/pubs/persp/pdf/Science_Early_Childhood_Development.pdf. Last accessed December 2011.

19. Vygotsky, Lev Semenovic, and Robert W. Rieber. 1993. *The Collected Works of L. S. Vygotsky*. New York: Plenum.

20. Gardner, Howard. 1983. *Frames of Mind: The Theory of Multiple Intelligences*. New York: Basic Books. Gardner, Howard. 1993. *Multiple Intelligences: The Theory in Practice*. New York: Basic Books. Gardner, Howard. 2000. *Intelligence Reframed: Multiple Intelligences for the 21st Century*. New York: Basic Books.

21. Goleman, Daniel. 1995. *Emotional Intelligence: Why It Can Matter More Than IQ*. New York: Bantam.

22. Goleman, Daniel. 2006. *Social Intelligence: The New Science of Human Relationships.* New York: Bantam.

23. Goleman, Daniel. 2009. *Ecological Intelligence: How Knowing the Hidden Impacts of What We Buy Can Change Everything.* New York: Broadway Books.

24. Armstrong, Thomas. 1999. *7 Kinds of Smart: Identifying and Developing Your Many Intelligences.* New York: Plume.

25. PLA and ALSC. 2011. "Every Child Ready to Read | Teaching Parents and Caregivers How to Support Early Literacy Development." American Library Association. www.everychild readytoread.org.

26. Every Child Ready to Read @ your library Sneak Peek Webinar. Originally presented May 4, 2011. Dr. Susan B. Neuman, Clara Bohrer, and Elaine Meyers, presenters. www.every childreadytoread.org/sneak-peek-webinar.

27. Schickedanz, Judith. 1999. *Much More Than the ABCs: The Early Stages of Reading and Writing.* Washington, DC: National Association for the Education of Young Children.

28. Rogers, Cosby S., and Janet K. Sawyers. 1988. *Play in the Lives of Children.* Washington, DC: National Association for the Education of Young Children.

29. Diamant-Cohen, Betsy, and Saroj Nadkarni Ghoting. 2010. *Early Literacy Kit: A Handbook and Tip Cards.* Chicago: American Library Association.

30. Ghoting, Saroj Nadkarni, and Pamela Martin-Díaz. 2006. *Early Literacy Storytimes @ your library: Partnering with Caregivers for Success.* Chicago: American Library Association.

31. Badegruber, Bernie. 2005. *101 Life Skills Games for Children: Learning, Growing, Getting Along (Ages 6 to 12).* Alameda, CA: Hunter House.

32. Brown, Ari, et al. 2011. "American Academy of Pediatrics: Policy Statement: Media Use by Children Younger than 2 Years." *portal: Pediatrics* 2011;128:1040–1045. doi; 10.1542/peds.2011-1753.

33. Mistry, Kamila B., Cynthia Minkovitz, Dona M. Strobino, and Dina L. G. Borzehowski. 2007. "Children's Television Exposure and Behavioral and Social Outcomes at 5.5 Years: Does Timing of Exposure Matter?" *portal: Pediatrics* 2007: 762–769. doi: 10.1542/peds.2006-3573.

34. Haugland, S. W. 1999. "What Role Should Technology Play in Young Children's Learning?" *Young Children* 55, no. 1: 26–31.

35. Long-Breipohl, Renate. 2001. "Computers in Early Childhood Education: A Jump Start for the Future?" *Gateways* Spring/Summer 40.

36. To find out more about Digital Littles, view this YouTube video: www.youtube.com/watch?v=285SzMgiVEk.

37. Dunbar, Polly. 2009. *Where's Tumpty?* Somerville, MA: Candlewick Press.

38. ICDL (International Children's Digital Library). 2011. *International Children's Digital Library: A Library for the World's Children.* Accessed December 15. http://en.childrens library.org.

39. Collen, Lauren. 2006. "The Digital and Traditional Storytimes Research Project: Using Digitized Picture Books for Preschool Group Storytimes." *Children and Libraries*, Winter 4, no. 3: 8–18.

40. Ibid., 12.

41. Collen, Lauren. 2008. "Creative Ways to Use Digital Group Storytimes in the Classroom or Library." http://laurencollen.com/Creative_Digital_Storytimes.pdf.

42. Tedeschi, Bob. 2010. "Top Picks for Apps to Help You While Away the Minutes." *New York Times*, December 22. www.nytimes.com/2010/12/23/technology/personaltech/23smart .html. ICDL's "StoryKit" Phone app was named as a "top pick" by the *New York Times* in this article.

43. Linder, Toni W. 1999. *Read, Play, and Learn! Storybook Activities for Young Children: Teacher's Guide*. Baltimore: Paul H. Brookes.

44. Ibid., 8.

45. Ibid., 9.

46. Ibid., 5.

47. Nespeca, Sue McCleaf, and Joan B. Reeve. 2003. *Picture Books Plus: 100 Extension Activities in Art, Drama, Music, Math, and Science*. Chicago: ALA Editions.

48. Raines, Shirley C., and Robert J. Canady. 1989. *Story Stretchers: Activities to Expand Children's Favorite Books*. Mt. Rainier, MD: Gryphon House; and Raines, Shirley C., and Robert J. Canady. 1991. *More Story Stretchers: More Activities to Expand Children's Favorite Books*. Mt. Rainier, MD: Gryphon House.

49. Landry, Susan H., Paul R. Swank, Karen E. Smith, Michael A. Assel, and Susan B. Gunnewig. 2006. "Enhancing Early Literacy Skills for Preschool Children: Bringing a Professional Development Model to Scale." *Journal of Learning Disabilities* 30, no. 4: 306–324.

50. Neuman, Susan B., and Kathy Roskos. 1993. "Access to Print for Children of Poverty: Differential Effects of Adult Mediation and Literacy-Enriched Play Settings on Environmental and Functional Print Tasks." *American Educational Research Journal* 30, no. 1: 95–122.

51. Fox, Carol. 1993. *At the Very Edge of the Forest: the Influence of Literature on Storytelling by Children*. London: Cassell.

Resources regarding Preschool Storytime, Theories of Learning, and Repetition

Adams, Marilyn Jager. 1990. *Beginning to Read: Thinking and Learning about Print*. Cambridge, MA: MIT Press.

Applebee, Arthur N. 1989. *The Child's Concept of Story: Ages Two to Seventeen*. Chicago: University of Chicago Press.

Armstrong, Thomas. 1999. *7 Kinds of Smart: Identifying and Developing Your Many Intelligences*. New York: Plume.

Arnold, R. 2003. "Public Libraries and Early Literacy: Raising a Reader: ALA's Preschool Literacy Initiative Educates Librarians on How to Play a Role in Teaching Reading to Children." *American Libraries* 34, no. 8: 49–51.

Badegruber, Bernie. 2005. *101 Life Skills Games for Children: Learning, Growing, Getting Along (Ages 6 to 12)*. Alameda, CA: Hunter House.

Bae, Ji-Hi. 2004. "Learning to Teach Visual Arts in an Early Childhood Classroom: The Teacher's Role as a Guide." *Early Childhood Education Journal* 31, no. 4: 247–254.

Barlin, Ann, and Paul Barlin (authors), and David Alexander (photographer). 1973. *The Art of Learning through Movement*. Los Angeles: Ward Ritchie.

Bennett-Armistead, V. Susan, Neil K. Duke, and Annie M. Moses. 2005. *Literacy and the Youngest Learner*. New York: Scholastic.

Bergen, Doris. 2002. "The Role of Pretend Play in Children's Cognitive Development." *Early Childhood Research and Practice* 4, no. 1. http://ecrp.uiuc.edu/v4n1/bergen.html.

Bergen, Doris, and Daria Mauer. 2000. "Symbolic Play, Phonological Awareness, and Literacy Skills at Three Age Levels." In *Play and Literacy in Early Childhood: Research from Multiple Perspectives*, edited by Kathleen A. Roskos and James F. Christie, 45–62. New York: Erlbaum.

Bettelheim, Bruno. 1987. "The Importance of Play." *Atlantic Monthly* March: 35–46. www.theatlantic.com/magazine/archive/1987/03/the-importance-of-play/5129/.

Blair, Clancy. 2002. "School Readiness: Integrating Cognition and Emotion in a Neurobiological Conceptualization of Children's Functioning at School Entry." *American Psychologist* 57, no. 2: 111–127.

Blair, Clancy, and Adele Diamond. 2002. "Biological Processes in Prevention and Intervention: The Promotion of Self-Regulation as a Means of Preventing School Failure." *Development and Psychopathology* 20, no. 3: 899–911.

Blair, Clancy, and Rachel Peters Razza. 2007. "Relating Effortful Control, Executive Function, and False Belief Understanding to Emerging Math and Literacy Ability in Kindergarten." *Child Development* 78, no. 2: 647–663.

Blank, M., and S. M. Frank. 1971. "Story Recall in Kindergarten Children: Effect of Method of Presentation on Psycholinguistic Performance." *Child Development* 42: 299–312.

Bomba, P. C., and E. R. Siqueland. 1983. "The Nature and Structure of Infant Form Categories." *Journal of Experimental Child Psychology* 35, no. 2: 294–328.

Bowman, David. 2011. "Read It Again, Sam." *New York Times, Sunday Book Review*, December 4: BR75. www.nytimes.com/2011/12/04/books/review/read-it-again-sam.html.

Brown, Ari, et al. 2011. "American Academy of Pediatrics: Policy Statement: Media Use by Children Younger Than 2 Years." *Portal: Pediatrics* 2011; 128: 1040–1045. doi; 10.1542/peds.2011-1753.

Brown, A. L. 1975. "Recognition, Reconstruction, and Recall of Narrative Sequences by Preoperational Children." *Child Development* 46, no. 1: 156–166.

Brown, Stuart, with Christopher Vaughan. 2009. *Play: How It Shapes the Brain, Opens the Imagination, and Invigorates the Soul*. New York: Penguin.

Bryant, P. D., M. MacLean, L. Bradley, and J. Crossland. 1990. "Rhyme and Alliteration, Phoneme Detection, and Learning to Read." *Developmental Psychology* 26, no. 3: 429–438.

Burns, M. Susan, Peg Griffin, and Catherine E. Snow, eds. 1999. *Starting Out Right: A Guide to Promoting Children's Reading Success*. Washington, DC: National Academy Press.

Bus, A. G., J. Belsky, M. H. van IJzendoorn, and K. Crnic. 1997. "Attachment and Bookreading Patterns: A Study of Mothers, Fathers, and Their Toddlers." *Early Childhood Research Quarterly* 12: 81–98.

Cahill, M. 2004. "Meeting the Early Literacy Needs of Children through Preschool Outreach Storytime Programs." *Knowledge Quest* 33, no. 2: 61–62.

Călinescu, Matei. 1993. *Rereading*. New Haven, CT: Yale University Press.

Cardoso, Silvia H. 2000. "Our Ancient Laughing Brain." *Cerebrum* 2, no. 4: 15–30.

Carlson, Frances M. 2011. *Big Body Play: Why Boisterous, Vigorous, and Very Physical Play Is Essential to Children's Development and Learning*. Washington, DC: National Association for the Education of Young Children.

Cass-Beggs, Barbara. 1986. *Your Child Needs Music*. Mississauga, Ontario: The Frederick Harris Music Co.

Celano, Donna, and Susan B. Neuman. 2001. "The Role of Public Libraries in Children's Literacy Development: An Evaluation Report." Harrisburg: Pennsylvania Library Association.

Christie, James, and Billie Enz. 1992. "The Effects of Literacy Play Interventions on Preschoolers' Play Patterns and Literacy Development." *Early Education and Development* 3, no. 3: 205–220.

Coles, Robert. 1993. Interview. "How to Look at a Mountain." *Artforum* 92, no. 3: 92–99.

Collen, Lauren. 2006. "The Digital and Traditional Storytimes Research Project: Using Digitized Picture Books for Preschool Group Storytimes." *Children and Libraries*, Winter 4, no. 3: 8–18.

———. 2008. "Creative Ways to Use Digital Group Storytimes in the Classroom or Library." http://laurencollen.com/Creative_Digital_Storytimes.pdf.

Conlon, Alice. 1992. "Giving Mrs. Jones a Hand: Making Group Storytime More Pleasurable and Meaningful for Young Children." *Young Children* 47, no. 3: 14–18.

Dennison, Paul E., and Gail E. Dennison. 1992. *Brain Gym: Simple Activities for Whole Brain Learning (Orange)*. Venture, CA: Edu Kinestheics.

Diamant-Cohen, B. 2004. "Mother Goose on the Loose: Applying Brain Research to Early Childhood Programs in the Public Library." *Public Libraries* 43, no. 1: 41–45.

———. 2007. "First Day of Class: The Public Library's Role in 'School Readiness.'" *Children and Libraries* 5, no. 1: 40–48.

Diamant-Cohen, B., E. Riordan, and R. Wade. 2004. "Make Way for Dendrites: How Brain Research Can Impact Children's Programming." *Children and Libraries* 2, no. 1: 12–20.

Diamant-Cohen, Betsy, and Saroj Nadkarni Ghoting. 2010. *Early Literacy Kit: A Handbook and Tip Cards*. Chicago: American Library Association.

Dickinson, David K., and Neuman, Susan B. 2006. *Handbook of Early Literacy Research: Volume II*. New York: Guilford.

Dunst, Carl. J., and Mary Beth Bruder. 1999. "Increasing Children's Learning Opportunities in the Context of Family and Community Life." *Children's Learning Opportunities Report* 1, no. 1.

Edmonds, Ernest, and Linda Candy. 2002. "Creativity, Art Practice, and Knowledge." *Communications of the ACM* 91–95.

Elkind, David. 2007. *The Power of Play: Learning What Comes Naturally*. Cambridge, MA: Da Capo Press.

Emery, D. W. 1996. "Helping Readers Comprehend Stories from the Characters' Perspectives." *The Reading Teacher* 49, 534–541.

English, W. *Brain Research and Music* (paper presented at the CMEA, Vancouver, B.C., 1979).

Every Child Ready to Read @ Your Library Sneak Peek Webinar. Originally presented May 4, 2011. Presented by Dr. Susan B. Neuman, Clara Bohrer, and Elaine Meyers. www.everychildreadytoread.org/sneak-peek-webinar.

Fader, Ellen. 2003. "How Storytimes for Preschool Children Can Incorporate Current Research." https://www.ala.org/ala/pla/plaissues/earlylit/storytimeapp/plastfader.pdf.

Fehrenback, Laurie, David P. Hurford, Carolyn Fehrenbach, and Rebecca Grove Brannock. 1998. "Developing the Emergent Literacy of Preschool Children through a Library Outreach Program." *Journal of Youth Services in Libraries* no. 1: 40–45.

Forencich, Frank. 2006. *Exuberant Animal: The Power of Health, Play, and Joyful Movement.* Bloomington, IN: AuthorHouse.

Fox, Carol. 1993. *At the Very Edge of the Forest: The Influence of Literature on Storytelling by Children.* London: Cassell. http://catalog.hathitrust.org/api/volumes/oclc/29635985 .html.

Fox, Mem. 2001. *Reading Magic: Why Reading Aloud to Our Children Will Change Their Lives Forever.* New York: Harcourt.

Fredrickson, B. L. 1998. "What Good Are Positive Emotions?" *Review of General Psychology* 2: 300–319.

———. 2000. "Cultivating Positive Emotions to Optimize Health and Well-Being." *Prevention and Treatment* 3, no. 1.

Galinsky, Ellen. 2010. *Mind in the Making: The Seven Essential Life Skills Every Child Needs.* New York: HarperStudio.

Gallagher, Kathleen Cranley. 2005. "Brain Research and Early Childhood Development." *Young Children* (July): 12–20.

Gardner, Howard. 1983. *Multiple Intelligences: The Theory in Practice.* New York: Basic Books.

———. 1993. *Frames of Mind: The Theory of Multiple Intelligences: The Theory in Practice.* New York: Basic Books.

———. 2000. *Intelligence Reframed: Multiple Intelligences for the 21st Century.* New York: Basic Books.

Gariepy, N, and N. Howe. 2003. "The Therapeutic Power of Play: Examining the Play of Young Children with Leukemia." *Child Care, Health and Development* 29, no. 6: 523–537.

Geist, Kamile, Eugene A. Geist, and Kathleen Kuznik. 2012. "The Patterns of Music: Young Children Learning Mathematics through Beat, Rhythm, and Melody." *Young Children* 67, no. 1: 74–79.

Geyer, Gessner. 2003. "The Optimal Brain." *Brain Energy: Optimal Learning.* www.brainergy .com.

Ghoting, Saroj Nadkarni, and Pamela Martin-Díaz. 2006. *Early Literacy Storytimes @ your library®: Partnering with Caregivers for Success.* Chicago: American Library Association.

Goleman, Daniel. 1995. *Emotional Intelligence: Why It Can Matter More Than IQ.* New York: Bantam.

———. 2006. *Social Intelligence: The New Science of Human Relationships.* New York: Bantam.

———. 2009. *Ecological Intelligence: How Knowing the Hidden Impacts of What We Buy Can Change Everything.* New York: Broadway Books.

Gomez, R. L. 2000. "Variability and Detection of Invariant Structure." *Psychological Science* 13, no. 5: 431–436.

Gopnik, Alison. 2011. *Why Preschool Shouldn't Be Like School.* www.thinkfun.com/content/ why-preschool-shouldnt-be-school.

Gopnik, Alison, Andrew N. Meltzoff, and Patricia K. Kuhl. 2001. *The Scientist in the Crib: What Early Leaning Tells Us about the Mind.* New York: Perennial.

Greene, Ellin. 1991. *Books, Babies, and Libraries: Serving Infants and Their Parents and Caregivers.* Chicago: American Library Association.

Greenough, William T., James E. Black, and Christopher S. Wallace. 1987. "Experience and Brain Development." *Child Development* 58: 539–559.

Gronlund, Gaye. 2010. *Developmentally Appropriate Play: Guiding Children to a Higher Level*. St. Paul, MN: Readleaf Press.

Grugeon, Elizabeth. 2005. *Teaching, Speaking, and Listening in the Primary School*. London: David Fulton. http://search.ebscohost.com/login.aspx?direct=true&scope=site&db=nlebk&db=nlabk&AN=125381.

Haines, B. Joan E., and Linda L. Gerber. 2000. *Leading Young Children to Music*. Upper Saddle River, NJ: Merrill.

Hart, Betty, and Todd Risley. 1995. *Meaningful Differences in the Everyday Experience of Young American Children*. Baltimore: Paul H. Brookes.

Haugland, S. W. 1999. "What Role Should Technology Play in Young Children's Learning?" *Young Children* 55, no. 1: 26–31.

Healy, Jane M. 2001. *Your Child's Growing Mind: A Practical Guide to Brain Development and Learning from Birth to Adolescence*. New York: Broadway Books.

Helm, Judy Harris, Stacy M. Berg, and Pamela Scranton. 2004. *Teaching Your Child to Love Learning*. New York: Teachers College Press.

Herman, Patricia A. 1985. "The Effect of Repeated Readings on Reading Rate, Speech Pauses, and Word Recognition Accuracy." *Reading Research Quarterly* 20, no. 5: 553–565.

Hirsch, E. D., and Linda Bevilacqua. 2008. *What Your Preschooler Needs to Know: Read-Alouds to Get Ready for Kindergarten*. New York: Bantam Dell.

Hirsh-Pasek, Kathy, and Roberta M. Golinkoff. 2007. *Celebrate the Scribble: Appreciating Children's Art*. Easton, PA: Crayola Beginnings.

———. 2011. *Play = Learning: How Play Motivates and Enhances Children's Cognitive and Social-Emotional Growth*. http://udel.edu/~roberta/play/index.html.

Hirsh-Pasek, Kathy, and Roberta M. Golinkoff, with Diane Eyer. 2003. *Einstein Never Used Flash Cards*. Emmaus, PA: Rodale.

Hughes, K. 2004. "PLA Early Literacy Research Demonstrates That Libraries Do Make a Difference." *Public Libraries* 43, no. 1: 58

Jalongo, Mary Renck. 2004. *Young Children and Picture Books*, 2nd ed. Washington, DC: National Association for the Education of Young Children.

———. 2008. *Learning to Listen, Listening to Learn*. Washington, DC: National Association for the Education of Young Children.

Johnson, Debra Wilcox. 1993. "Breaking the Cycle: The Role of Libraries in Family Literacy." *Reading Quarterly* 32, no. 3: 318–322.

Joseph, G. E., and P. S. Strain. 2003. "Enhancing Emotional Vocabulary in Young Children." *The Center on Social and Emotional Foundations for Early Learning*. University of Illinois at Urbana-Champaign. www.ecmhc.net/TTYC/documents/Folder8FeelingVocabulary/FileA%20EnhancingEmotVoc.pdf.

Juel, C., G. Biancarosa, D. Coker, and R. Deffes. 2003. "Walking with Rosie: A Cautionary Tale of Early Reading Instruction." *Educational Leadership* 60, no. 7: 12–18.

Kandel, E. R., Schwartz, J. H., and Jessell, T. M. (eds.). 2000. *Principles of Neural Science* (4th ed.). New York: McGraw-Hill.

Katims, David S. 1994. "Emergence of Literacy in Preschool Children with Disabilities." *Learning Disability Quarterly* 17, no. 1: 58–69.

Kerr, R., and B. Booth. 1978. "Specific and Varied Practice of Motor Skill." *Perceptual and Motor Skills* 46, no. 2: 395–401.

Kryczka, Cathie. 2008. "Again! Again! Read the Same Book 38 Times in One Sitting? Why Kids Love Repetition—and How to Keep Your Sanity." *Today's Parent* 25, no. 2: 47–48.

Lambert, Megan. 2010. "Gutter Talk and More: Picturebook Paratexts, Illustration, and Design at Storytime." *Children and Libraries* 8, no. 3: 36–46.

Landry, Susan H., Paul R. Swank, Karen E. Smith, Michael A. Assel, and Susan B. Gunnewig. 2006. "Enhancing Early Literacy Skills for Preschool Children: Bringing a Professional Development Model to Scale." *Journal of Learning Disabilities* 30, no. 4: 306–324.

Landy, Sarah. 2002. *Pathways to Competence: Encouraging Healthy Social and Emotional Development in Young Children*. Baltimore: Brookes.

Linder, Toni W. 1999. *Read, Play, and Learn! Storybook Activities for Young Children: Teacher's Guide*. Baltimore: Paul H. Brookes.

Long-Breipohl, Renate. 2001. "Computers in Early Childhood Education: A Jump Start for the Future?" *Gateways* Spring/Summer 40.

Lukehart, Wendy. 2010. "Playgrounds for the Mind: Drawn to Delight: How Picturebooks Work (and Play) Today." *Children and Libraries* 8, no. 3: 32–35.

MacLean, M., P. Bryant, and L. Bradley. 1987. "Rhymes, Nursery Rhymes, and Reading in Early Childhood." *Merill-Palmer Quarterly* 33, no. 3: 255–281.

Martinez, G. 2007. "Partnering for Reading Readiness: A Case Study of Maryland Public Librarians." *Children and Libraries* 5, no. 1: 32–39.

Martinez, Maria. 1985. "Read It Again: The Value of Repeated Readings during Storytime." *Reading Teacher* 38, no. 8: 782–786.

Maryland State Department of Education. 2009. "Maryland Model for School Readiness (MMSR): Framework and Standards for Prekindergarten." 6th ed. Revised Summer. Maryland State Department of Education.

McCathren, R. B., and J. H. Allor. 2002. "Using Storybooks with Preschool Children: Enhancing Language and Emergent Literacy." *Young Exceptional Children* 5, no. 4: 3–10.

McCord, S. 1995. *The Storybook Journey: Pathways to Literacy through Story and Play*. Upper Saddle River, NJ: Prentice Hall.

McCune, L. 1995. "A Normative Study of Representational Play in the Transition to Language." *Developmental Psychology* 31: 198–206.

McGee, Lea M., and Judith Schickedanz. 2010. "Repeated Interactive Read-Alouds in Preschool and Kindergarten." Reading Rockets. Posted May 3. www.readingrockets.org/article/16287/.

McKechnie, Lynne (E. F.). 2000. "Ethnographic Observation of Preschool Children." *Library and Information Science Research* 22, no. 1: 61–76.

Meyer, Marianne, and Rebecca Felton. 1999. "Repeated Reading to Enhance Fluency: Old Approaches and New Directions." *Annals of Dyslexia* 49, no. 1: 283–306.

Mistry, K. B., et al. 2007. "Children's Television Exposure and Behavioral and Social Outcomes at 5.5 Years: Does Timing of Exposure Matter?" *portal: Pediatrics* 2007: 762–769. doi: 10.1542/peds.2006-3573.

Morrow, Lesley Mandel. 1985. "Retelling Stories: A Strategy for Improving Young Children's Comprehension, Concept of Story Structure, and Oral Language Complexity." *The Elementary School Journal* 85, no. 5: 646–661.

National Center for Educational Statistics. 1993. "Public School Kindergarten Teachers' Views on Children's Readiness for School." *Kindergarten Teacher Survey on Student Readiness.* http://nces.ed.gov/quicktables/displaytableimage.asp?ID=QTFImage1280.

National Research Council. 1998. *Preventing Reading Difficulties in Young Children.* Washington, DC: National Academy Press.

———. 1999. *Starting Out Right: A Guide to Promoting Children's Reading Success.* Washington, DC: National Academy Press.

———. 2001. *Eager to Learn: Educating Our Preschoolers.* Washington, DC: National Academy Press.

National Scientific Council of the Developing Child. 2004. "Children's Emotional Development Is Built into the Architecture of Their Brains: Working Paper, no. 2." http://developingchild.harvard.edu/index.php/resources/reports_and_working_papers/working_papers/wp2/.

———. 2004. "Young Children Develop in an Environment of Relationships: Working Paper, no. 1." http://developingchild.harvard.edu/index.php/resources/reports_and_working_papers/working_papers/.

———. 2007. "The Science of Early Childhood Development: Closing the Gap between What We Know and What We Do." http://developingchild.net/pubs/persp/pdf/Science_Early_Childhood_Development.pdf.

Needham, A., G. Dueker, and G. Lockhead. 2005. "Infants' Formation and Use of Categories to Segregate Objects." *Cognition* 94, no. 3: 215–240.

Nespeca, Sue McCleaf. 1995. "Urban Head Start Mothers: Their Personal Reading Habits, Involvement in Sharing Books with Their Children, and Perceptions of Their Public Library." *Journal of Youth Services in Libraries* no. 8: 188–194.

Nespeca, Sue McCleaf, and Joan B. Reeve. 2003. *Picture Books Plus: 100 Extension Activities in Art, Drama, Music, Math, and Science.* Chicago: ALA Editions.

Neuman, Susan B. 1996. "Children Engaging in Storybook Reading: The Influence of Access to Print Resources, Opportunity, and Parental Interaction." *Early Childhood Research Quarterly* 11: 495–513.

———. 1999. "Books Make A Difference: A Study of Access to Literacy." *Reading Research Quarterly* 34, no. 3: 286–311.

Neuman, Susan B., and Donna Celano. 2001. "Access to Print in Low-Income and Middle-Income Communities: An Ecological Study of Four Neighborhoods." *Reading Research Quarterly* 36: 8–26.

———. 2004. "Save the Libraries!" *Journal of Educational Leadership* (March): 82–84.

Neuman, Susan B., and Kathy Roskos. 1993. "Access to Print for Children of Poverty: Differential Effects of Adult Mediation and Literacy-Enriched Play Settings on Environmental and Functional Print Tasks." *American Educational Research Journal* 30, no. 1: 95–122.

Paley, Vivian Gussin. 2005. *A Child's Work, the Importance of Fantasy Play.* Chicago: University of Chicago Press.

Pappano, Laura. "Kids Haven't Changed; Kindergarten Has." *Harvard Education Letter* September/October 2010.

Piaget, Jean. 1962. *Play, Dreams and Imitation in Childhood.* New York: W. W. Norton.

Posner, Michael I., and Mary K. Rothbart. 2005. "Influencing Brain Networks: Implications for Education." *Trends in Cognitive Sciences* 9, no. 3: 99–103.

Public Library Association (PLA), and Association for Library Services to Children (ALSC). 2011. "Every Child Ready to Read: Teaching Parents and Caregivers How to Support Early Literacy Development." American Library Association. www.everychildreadytoread.org.

Pullen, Paige C., and Laura M. Justice. 2003. "Enhancing Phonological Awareness, Print Awareness, and Oral Language Skills in Preschool Children." *Intervention in School and Clinic* 39, no. 2: 87–98.

Raines, Shirley C., and Robert J. Canady. 1989. *Story Stretchers: Activities to Expand Children's Favorite Books*. Mt. Rainier, MD: Gryphon House.

——. 1991. *More Story Stretchers: More Activities to Expand Children's Favorite Books*. Mt. Rainier, MD: Gryphon House.

Reif, K. 2000. "Are Public Libraries the Preschooler's Door to Learning?" *Public Libraries* 39, no. 5: 262–268.

Rimm-Kaufman, S. E., R. C. Pianta, and M. J. Cox. 2000. "Teachers' Judgments of Problems in the Transition to Kindergarten." *Early Childhood Research Quarterly* 15: 147–166.

Rogers, Cosby S., and Janet K. Sawyers. 1988. *Play in the Lives of Children*. Washington, DC: National Association for the Education of Young Children.

Roskos, Kathleen A., and James F. Christie (eds.). 2000. *Play and Literacy in Early Childhood: Research From Multiple Perspectives*. New York: Erlbaum.

Roskos, Kathleen, and Susan Neuman. 1998. "Play as an Opportunity for Literacy." In *Multiple Perspectives on Play in Early Childhood*, edited by Olivia N. Saracho and Bernard Spodek, 100–115. Albany, NY: State University of New York Press.

Russ, S. W. 1998. "Play, Creativity, and Adaptive Functioning: Implications for Play Interventions." *Journal of Clinical Child Psychology* 27, no. 4: 469–480.

Samuels, S. Jay. 1997. "The Method of Repeated Readings." *Reading Teacher* 50, no. 5: 376–381.

Schickendanz, Judith A. 1999. *Much More Than ABCs: The Early Stages of Reading and Writing*. Washington, DC: National Association for the Education of Young Children.

——. 2008. *Increasing the Power of Instruction: Integration of Language, Literacy, and Math Across the Preschool Day*. Washington, DC: National Association for the Education of Young Children.

Schiller, Pamela Byrne. 1999. *Start Smart*. Beltsville, MD: Gryphon House.

Schmidt, R. A., and R. A. Bjork. 1992. "New Conceptualizations of Practice: Common Principles in Three Paradigms Suggest New Concepts for Training." *Psychological Science* 3, no. 4: 207–217.

Shaffer, Sharon. *Preschoolers and Museums: An Educational Guide*. Washington, DC: Smithsonian Early Enrichment Center.

Sharapan, Hedda. 2012. "From STEM to STEAM: How Early Childhood Educators Can Apply Fred Rogers' Approach." *Young Children* 67, no. 1: 36–40.

Shedd, Meagan K, and Neil K. Duke. 2009. "The Power of Planning: Developing Effective Read-Alouds." In *Spotlight on Teaching Preschoolers*, edited by Derry Korlek, 26–31. Washington, DC: National Association for the Education of Young Children.

Shonkoff, Jack P. 2004. *Science, Policy, and the Young Developing Child: Closing the Gap between What We Know and What We Do*. Chicago: Ounce of Prevention Fund. www.ounceofprevention.org/downloads/publications/shonkoffweb.pdf.

Shonkoff, Jack P. (editor), Deborah Phillips (editor), and Youth and Families Committee on Integrating Board on Children, U.S. National Research Council, Committee on Integrating the Science of Early Childhood Development. 2000. *From Neurons to Neighborhoods: The Science of Early Childhood Development*. Washington, DC: National Academy Press.

Singer, Dorothy G., Roberta M. Golinkoff, and Kathy Hirsh-Pasek. 2006. *Play = Learning: How Play Motivates and Enhances Children's Cognitive and Social-Emotional Growth*. Oxford: Oxford University Press.

Smith, Peter K., and Susan Dutton. 1979. "Play and Training in Direct and Innovative Problem Solving." *Child Development* 50, no. 3: 830–836.

Strain, Phillip S., and Ronald Wiegerink. 1976. "The Effects of Sociodramatic Activities on Social Interaction among Behaviorally Disordered Preschool Children." *Journal of Special Education* 10, no. 1: 71–75.

Susina, Jan. 1998. "Children's Reading, Repetition, and Rereading: Gertrude Stein, Margaret Wise Brown, and *Goodnight Moon*." In *Second Thoughts: A Focus on Rereading*, edited by David Galef. Detroit, MI: Wayne State University Press.

Sylwester, Robert. 1995. *A Celebration of Neurons: An Educator's Guide to the Human Brain*. Alexandria, VA: Association for Supervision and Curriculum Development.

Teale, William H. 1999. "Libraries Promote Early Literacy Learning: Ideas from Current Research and Early Childhood Programs." *Journal of Youth Services in Libraries* no. 3: 9–16.

Tedeschi, Bob. 2010. "Top Picks for Apps to Help You While Away the Minutes." *New York Times*, December 22. www.nytimes.com/2010/12/23/technology/personaltech/23smart.html.

Trelease, Jim. 2006. *The Read-Aloud Handbook*. New York: Penguin.

U.S. Department of Education, National Center for Education Statistics. 1995. "Kindergarten Teacher Survey on Student Readiness." *Digest of Education Statistics Tables and Figures*. http://nces.ed.gov/quicktables/displaytableimage.asp?ID=QTFImage1280.

Vivas, Eleonora. 1996. "Effects of Story Reading on Language." *Language Learning* 46, no. 2: 189–216.

Vygotsky, Lev Semenovic, and Robert W. Rieber. 1993. *The Collected Works of L. S. Vygotsky*. New York: Plenum.

Walter, Virginia. 2001. *Children and Libraries: Getting It Right*. Chicago: American Library Association.

Watkins, Ruth V. 1996. "Natural Literacy: Theory and Practice for Preschool Intervention Programs." *Topics in Early Childhood Special Education* 16, no. 2: 191–212.

White, Dorothy. 1984. *Books Before Five*. Portsmouth, NH: Heinemann Educational Books.

Yaden, D. 1988. "Understanding Stories through Repeated Read-Alouds: How Many Does It Take?" *The Reading Teacher* 41, no. 6: 556–560.

Zero to Three. 2004. *The Power of Play: Learning through Play from Birth to Three*. Pamphlet. Washington, DC: Zero to Three Press.

Zigler, Edward, Dorothy G. Singer, Sandra J. Bishop-Josef, eds. 2004. *Children's Play: The Roots of Reading*. Washington, DC: Zero to Three Press.

Zimmermann, Susan, and Chryse Hutchins. 2003. *7 Keys to Comprehension: How to Help Your Kids Read It and Get It!* New York: Three Rivers Press.

chapter 2

The Nitty Gritty
A Step-by-Step Guide to Organizing a Storytime

Basics for Preschool Storytime Planning

The easiest way to plan preschool storytimes is to follow a few principles and use the following template for planning.

GET AN AUDIENCE

Without participants, there is no preschool storytime. Word of mouth is a great way to advertise. It can be done by talking to visitors when they are in the library, asking people to tell their friends, and asking child care providers to tell parents and other child care providers. If your library keeps a summer reading club database, you may want to use that for your initial publicity efforts.

When using flyers, circle or highlight the preschool storytime information. Bring flyers to neighborhood businesses, especially places where families go, such as stores that sell diapers, toy stores, ice cream parlors, and fast food restaurants. Target places where parents might go alone, such as nail or hair salons, and ask if you can leave some flyers there. Or, talk to the beautician and ask if she will pass on information to parents with upcoming appointments. Visit schools and churches; speak with office secretaries

Storytime Basics

- Get an audience!
- Like the book!
- Know the book!
- Think BIG!
- Practice name-dropping!
- Practice!
- Give credit!

and ask if they can give each child a flyer to take home. If you do not have flyers, print out your library's online events page and circle or highlight the program you want to publicize. Give this printed page to interested families. Details about programs can also be written and displayed on chalkboards, whiteboards, or flannelboard easels. They can be sent out via fax.

Build up a list of families with children who are the right age for preschool storytime. Ask these families for their contact information and put it in a preschool storytime file, online or off-line. Ask each family if they prefer phone calls or flyers. Then, when a program series is about to start, call the interested contacts to remind them of the upcoming program.

USE ONLY BOOKS THAT YOU LIKE

Enthusiasm breeds enthusiasm. If you like a book, your feelings will be communicated to your audience.

KNOW THE CONTENT OF THE BOOKS YOU PLAN TO READ

Although a colleague may have recommended a particular book, read it yourself before reading it aloud to children. What one person does not notice may be offensive to another. Be sure the material you plan on presenting publically is acceptable to you as well as to your audience.

LOOK AT THE PHYSICAL BOOK AHEAD OF TIME

Books from a circulating collection don't stay in pristine condition. Pulling books off shelves to use in programs is fine; however, you don't want the unexpected surprise of getting to the last page of the story and finding it torn out of the book!

CHOOSE BOOKS WITH ILLUSTRATIONS THAT ARE BIG ENOUGH FOR CHILDREN TO SEE

Familiarizing children with art via book illustrations is an important benefit of preschool storytime. Large colorful illustrations or big photographs work best with big groups. Some librarians prefer to use "big books" during their programs, but the selection of books is limited and they can be a bit unwieldy. An easel shelf can help hold a big book while the librarian reads aloud and turns the pages. Although using a big book occasionally is fine, using regular-sized picture books is a way to directly model book-use behavior such as turning pages.

ALWAYS INTRODUCE THE BOOK STATING TITLE, AUTHOR, AND ILLUSTRATOR

Show the cover of the book to your audience and, in addition to reading the title, mention the name of the author and illustrator. It is important to give credit where credit is due, as well as to familiarize children with the specific creators of the story that is being introduced to them.

General Structure of Preschool Storytime

Most Preschool Storytimes Follow a General Structure

Welcome

Opening Ritual

Book/Story 1: Present the longest book first

Activity 1: Sitting activity: fingerplay, song, puppet, flannelboard, or props

Book/Story 2: Read a shorter book

Activity 2: Sitting activity OR large motor activities: dance, creative dramatics, movement

Book/Story 3: Read a shorter book

Activity 3: Sitting activity or large motor activities

Book/Story 4: Very short book: interactive, very funny, lift-the-flap, counting

Closing Ritual

START WITH WELCOMING COMMENTS

Always introduce yourself and welcome everyone. Even if everyone in your audience has been to storytime before, stating your name and letting everyone know that you are glad to see them sets the tone for a friendly and welcoming program.

OPENING RITUALS

Start with an opening ritual. Choose a fingerplay, song, puppet interaction, or activity that you like to be part of every storytime. It should not be long and complicated, just a simple action that can be repeated on a weekly basis. You may decide to have one ritual for the beginning of storytime and one for the end or to use the same ritual for both beginning and end. (In this book, the same ritual is used both times.)

Always start your program with the opening ritual. Although you may be reciting it by yourself at the beginning of storytime, after the first week the children will be able to join in. By the third week, the repetition of the same activity will signify the beginning as well as ending of storytime to the children. Opening and closing rituals help define the storytime space and add extra meaning to the program. If you decide to skip the ritual one week, the children will let you know that you have forgotten and remind you to include it! The ritual provides a sense of safety; in defining the start and end of a program, the ritual tells children what to expect. In addition, they become partners in building up storytime and winding it down. Since they are familiar with the ritual, they can recite it too; rather than being a performance by the librarian, it becomes a community experience in which everyone takes part.

The ritual also impresses on memory. For instance, if the opening storytime ritual consists of singing "If You're Happy and You Know It" and a storytime participant hears that same song somewhere else, he or she will immediately be reminded of storytime at the library.

THE ORDER OF BOOKS

Choose the longest book for the first read-aloud. Three-to-five-year-olds have limited attention spans. The easiest time for them to sit still is at the beginning of your program. As your storytime progresses, choose books that are shorter and shorter.

NUMBER OF BOOKS PER SESSION

The length of the books you present will determine how many books to use in a session. Six books plus activities can fit into a preschool storytime if they are all extremely short. However, when programming for a sophisticated audience that can sit for longer books, two or three books plus activities may be all that fits into the thirty-minute structure. Don't be surprised if the number of books presented in a session varies from week to week; since it depends on their length (and the length of the accompanying activities), you may have some weeks with more books and others with less.

USING ACTIVITIES

Always place an activity between book readings. No matter how appealing your read-aloud books may be, a change of pace between each book helps keep the stories fresh and the children attentive. Activities can include singing songs, doing fingerplays, reciting poetry, interacting with puppets, doing stretching exercises, playing with musical instruments, listening to recorded music, dancing or marching, using colored scarves, including props such as plastic farm animals, using a flannelboard, playing call-and-response games, asking and answering questions, or participating in creative drama activities.

Include musical instruments. Popular percussion instruments for preschoolers are bells, maracas, chickitas, claves, rhythm sticks, and tambourines. Be sure that there are enough instruments to give one to each child and each adult. After passing them out, sing a song or two, play the instruments to a short piece of recorded music, or make a parade and march around the room. Sing a clean-up song inviting participants to drop their instruments back into a tote bag that you hold open as you walk around the room.

Include a movement activity in the middle of your program. Preschoolers are wiggly and cannot sit still for long periods of time. Break up your program with a creative drama activity or an action song that requires standing, jumping, shaking, or moving.

SHORT, SWEET, AND INTERACTIVE

Use an interactive short story for your final selection. Feel free to use board books, lift-the-flap books, pop-up books, or ABC books as your final selection. Books meant for younger audiences can be appealing to preschoolers if you turn it into a call-and-response activity or one in which children call out the name of an object, the name of a letter, names of colors, the sounds animals make, or what is under the flap. Even wordless books intended for babies can work as long as you make them interactive. Asking preschoolers to look at illustrations, to make connections between what they already know and those specific illustrations, and to call out their answers keeps them involved and enthusiastic.

VOTING

Before ending storytime, ask the children to vote on the books they liked best. Hold up each book one at a time with the cover facing the audience, reiterate the title, author, and illustrator, and ask the children to raise their hands if they liked the book. Children love raising their hands. Asking for their opinion empowers them while also reminding them of all the books that were read during storytime.

After voting for each story, say, "Everyone who liked every single book I read today, raise both hands, wave them around, and say 'WOO WOO WOO WOO WOO.'" This is so much fun that just about everyone in your storytime will do it. It leaves them with a great feeling about the storytime and provides a positive ending to your program.

END WITH A CLOSING RITUAL

Use a closing ritual. Just as the opening ritual identifies the start of preschool storytime, a closing ritual that is used at the end of each session helps children transition out of storytime mode. It signifies that the program is about to end, but does so in a comfortable, familiar way. Ending with the same rhyme each week prevents the librarian from having to indicate the program's end by an abrupt announcement, "Storytime is over now."

Invite participants to return for the next storytime and remind them to check out books from the library. Inviting people back makes them feel appreciated. Although families may be regular attendees at storytime, they may not know that library cards are free unless told. Use the closing minutes of storytime to give announcements, to mention special programs such as summer reading clubs, or to promote library cards (including special library cards for children under the age of the 6 that do not accrue overdue fees for late returns).

ADD DEVELOPMENTAL TIPS

Add two to three developmental tips to each session. Developmental tips are short asides for parents or caregivers that capitalize on their important role as their child's first teacher. They give information along with practical suggestions for implementation. For instance, these tips can be used to describe an aspect of child development, to explain the value of a storytime activity, to give an example of an activity that can be done with children outside of storytime, to describe a school readiness behavior and give an example of ways to nurture it, and to talk about early literacy and encourage dialectic reading.

Tips can be written on index cards and placed in the pile of books to be used in your program. When you have finished reading a book aloud, before picking up the next book, the index card in the pile will remind you of the tip you planned to share. If coming up with new developmental tips is difficult or time consuming, a great resource is *The Early Literacy Kit: A Handbook and Tip Cards* by Betsy Diamant-Cohen and Saroj Nadkarni Ghoting.[1] Tips from all domains of school readiness are paired with rhymes, songs, books, or activities and labeled by age (baby, toddler, or preschooler).

Another resource, *Early Literacy Storytimes @ your library: Partnering with Caregivers for Success* by Saroj Ghoting and Pamela Martin-Díaz[2] provides instructions for presenting an early literacy enhanced storytime. A skill that helps develop reading readiness in the domain of language and literacy is chosen. During the introduction to storytime, the librarian announces which tip topic will be featured during that program and will provide a definition of that topic. Sometime during the storytime, a tip from that topic will be cited. At the end of the storytime, before the closing ritual, the program facilitator gives a summary of the tip topic and a recap of the tip itself. While the tips are meant for the caregivers, they are concise enough not to divert the children's attention during storytime. Although the programs outlined in this book do not follow that specific model, it is easy to implement into these programs.

Planning Helpers

USE A PRESCHOOL STORYTIME TEMPLATE

Here is a general template for a preschool storytime session:

1. Introduce yourself and welcome everyone.
2. Start with an opening ritual.
3. Book 1: Read the longest book aloud.
4. Activity 1: Add a sitting activity: a fingerplay, song, puppet, flannelboard, or use of props.

Get Ready . . . Get Set . . . Go!

- Use a template!
- Fill in the blanks!
- Mold it to your style!
- Sing!
- Smile!
- Use a variety of books:
  > New and older books
  > Nonfiction
  > Poetry
  > Big books
- Enhance your storytime:
  > Puppets!
  > Sign language (ASL)
  > Crafts
  > Flannelboard
  > Script cards
  > Handouts

Top Ten Developmental Tips for Parents

1 Using books with children in a joyful manner while they are young motivates them to learn how to read. Reading good books aloud is not the only way to ignite a passion for books and reading; looking at book illustrations together, predicting what might happen while looking at the front cover of a book, talking about a story, describing favorite characters, or acting out scenes from a story are all good ways to connect children with books in a positive way.

2 An *illustrator* is the person who draws the pictures in a book. Try looking at different books by the same illustrator and see if you and your child can play an enjoyable game of finding things that are similar and things that are different. Then visit a local art museum or look at books by other illustrators and see if you can find pictures that remind you of the first illustrator's drawing. The ability to look at artwork and to get pleasure from looking is a skill that everyone can develop. It is never too early to start!

3 Your attitude rubs off on your children. If you are going to read a book to your child, make sure it is a book that you enjoy! If you are forcing yourself to seem interested, your child will notice. If you are enthusiastic, your child will be too.

4 One way to help your children develop early literacy skills is by giving them the opportunity to retell a story that they like. Gently guide them by asking questions such as *What happens in the beginning? What happens in the middle? And what happens in the end?* Understanding that a story has a beginning, a middle, and an end is called *narrative skills* and it is part of prereading skills.

5 Learning how to follow directions and take turns is essential for success in the classroom. Use a story that your child enjoys to play games that help develop these skills. For instance, if your child likes a character named Waldo, play games like Waldo Says instead of Simon Says. Playing games that use situations in a book your children enjoy spurs their desire to pay attention and follow directions.

5. Book 2: Read another book aloud.
6. Activity 2: Stand up and get the wiggles out with large motor activities: dance, creative dramatics, or movement.
7. Book 3: Read a shorter book aloud.
8. Activity 3: Include a sitting activity or large motor activities.
9. Book 4: Present a very short, interactive book: very funny, lift-the-flap, and/or counting.
10. Activity 4 (optional)
11. Vote.
12. End with a closing ritual.

FILL IN THE BLANKS

Answer these questions in order to successfully plan your first storytime.

Choose the book to be repeated. What book do I want to use and repeat for six consecutive sessions? Where do I want that book to be presented in my first storytime? (Once you have answered this question, write the title of the book in the appropriate space below.)

Plan welcoming comments. How will I introduce myself? What do I want to say in my welcoming comments? Are there any issues that need to be addressed (e.g., turn off cell phones, bathrooms are on the second floor, sign up for the summer reading club has started)? Are there any directions I need to give?

6 Imagination is a powerful tool. With imagination, people can see beyond what is already in existence to what might be possible. Help develop your child's imagination by extending a book beyond the actual story. Ask questions such as *What do you think happened a week later? What do you think happened a year later? What do you think could have happened in order to cause the story to end differently?*

7 Children often love to create things. Ask your children to draw a picture of something from a book read aloud in storytime, and then ask them to explain the picture to you. They will recount the story using different words. This activity can strengthen your children's ability to express themselves.

8 Nonfiction books for children are wonderful. Children are often fascinated by the animals in the natural world. They like imitating animal sounds, knowing animal names, and being able to mimic the different ways that animals move. If there is a storybook about an animal that your child particularly enjoys, see if the library also has a nonfiction book about that same animal and look at it together.

9 Singing together is loads of fun and creates a sense of closeness through a shared experience. Your voice produces your child's favorite sounds. Even if you don't think you are a great singer, your child will not notice! So rather than worrying about the quality of your singing voice, have fun and sing along with your child. Try to repeat some of the songs and rhymes that we have recited at storytime.

10 Rituals can ease the difficulty of transitions for children. Always starting and ending with the same song lets children know that storytime is about to begin or end, and gives them time to get used to the changes about to take place. The rituals serve as markers that notify children regarding what is about to happen; these familiar rituals ease the discomfort that some children feel when moving from one activity to another.

Reproducible Planning Template

- Beginning ritual
  - > Introduce yourself and give welcoming comments
  - > Opening fingerplay, song, or rhyme: _____

- Book/Story 1: _____

- Activity 1: _____

- Book/Story 2: _____

- Activity 2: _____

- Book/Story 3: _____

- Activity 3: _____

- Book/Story 4: _____

- Closing ritual
  - > Vote
  - > Closing fingerplay, song, or rhyme: _____

- Developmental Tip 1: _____

  _____

- Developmental Tip 2: _____

  _____

Choose the first book. What is the longest story I have to read today?

Activity. What activity should follow the reading of the first book?

Second book. Which is the second story I will read aloud?

Second activity. What activity can be done that gets the children up and moving?

Third book. Have I used up so much time that the third book is my final book, or is there time for one or two more books? What should my third book be? (Note: If this is the final book, it should be short and interactive with flaps to lift, or names of objects, letters, or colors to call out.)

Third activity. If there is time, what activity would go well here?

Final book. If there is time for a fourth book, what would it be? (Remember that it should be short and interactive with flaps to lift, or names of objects, letters, or colors to call out.)

Closing ritual. Will my closing ritual be the same as my opening ritual? If not, what closing ritual will I use? Are there any announcements I have to make? If so, what are they?

Add developmental tips. Once you have finished filling the blanks with your activities, choose your developmental tips (or early literacy asides) and add them into your program.

List all materials needed. Make a list of all the materials you will need for this particular storytime session (which books, puppets, instruments, tip cards, CD player, etc. you plan on using).

Prepare props in order. Put your books in a pile in the order in which they will be used during the program; slip tip cards and any flannelboard characters you plan to use into the appropriate places in the pile, as well. Place the pile in a big plastic storage tub with a tight lid. Keep bigger props in tote bags.

Storage. Keep the storage tub in your office until a few minutes before storytime. Then, place the tub next to your storytime chair. Just before the program starts, lift off the lid to find all of your materials in order, ready to be used.

MODIFY THE PROGRAM BASED ON YOUR PERSONAL STYLE

When it comes to library programs, there is no one size that fits all. Although templates and fully scripted programs can be extremely useful, there is always the unknown factor—you. Some people speak very quickly; others speak at a much slower pace. Some librarians zip right through activities while others linger with each song and fingerplay. Because of this, one librarian may be able to read five different books aloud during one storytime session while another may be able to fit only two or three into the thirty-minute time period. This does not mean that one way is right and the other is wrong! Both sessions are likely to be high-quality, enjoyable programs; they simply have been tailored to fit the personal style of the librarian presenting the program.

Both authors of this book tend to speak quickly and move at a rapid pace. Thus, the sample storytimes and templates that have been created contain a fair amount of material, suitable for people who speak relatively quickly. However, these storytimes are meant to last for thirty minutes. If you speak slowly, the programs presented here may be too long for you. In that case, try using fewer books and fewer activities. Feel free to edit anything in order to have just enough to fit into a thirty-minute time slot comfortably given your presentation style.

HOLD THE BOOK IN ONE POSITION

When presenting the storytime, hold the book being read aloud in just one position. With one hand, hold the bottom of the book open, facing the audience. Tilt it slightly toward yourself so that you can see the printed text and turn the pages from the bottom, using your other hand. Open the first book you plan on reading aloud and ask if everyone can see the pictures. If not, tell them to feel free to move into a position where the pages are visible. This way, everyone can see the pictures the entire time the story is being read aloud.

Tips for Presenting Preschool Storytime

SING

No one expects you to be a professional singer! Your job as the storytime librarian is to be a facilitator, not a performer. One of the five important practices that adults can use to help children build early literacy skills listed in the revised Every Child Ready to Read @ your library program is singing. Singing is an easy way for children to learn vocabulary. Words are divided into syllables when sung. This exposes children to the sounds in words—it is a great introduction to phonological awareness.

SMILE

If you look like you are enjoying what you are doing, your audience most likely will enjoy it too. A smile is infectious.

VARY BOOKS

Use New and Old Books

Since budgets are thin these days, some libraries keep the oldies but goodies, and other libraries try to keep only the most recent picture books on their shelves. There is no library that has an all-inclusive collection, so it does not make sense to give a list of specific books to use in each storytime; seeing booklists with titles not in one's collection leads to discouragement.

In order to make this book as useful as possible, alternative book selections are listed that include oldies but goodies as well as new materials. Keep in mind that all of the titles are optional, even the additional books listed for each of the storytimes. Any book that is appropriate for preschool audiences can be used; always feel free to substitute books that you love. Although the first two scripts are complete with words to all the fingerplays and titles of all supplemental books included, these books and activities can easily be replaced with substitutions.

Include a Nonfiction Book or Poetry

Try to include a nonfiction book and read a poem from a poetry book, if possible. There are many nonfiction books with fabulous photographs on topics of interest to preschoolers. Parents do not often look in the nonfiction section when selecting books for their children; using nonfiction books in storytimes alerts them to nonfiction borrowing possibilities.

Consider Using a Big Book

While using big books ensures that large crowds can see the book illustrations, handling them can be unwieldy. Some librarians use an easel to hold the big book while reading it aloud and turning the pages. Librarian Keri Ann St. Jean has tips for using big books: Glue a piece of cardboard or flattened cereal boxes to the inside front and back covers to make them sturdier. Paper clip the cover and first page together; when turning pages, slip them into the paper clip to keep them from flapping. Type the entire text of the book in a big font, adding marks to indicate the end of each page. Print out this text and glue it to the back cover of the big book. The text can then be read aloud and the pages turned while the illustrations remain facing the audience.

Consider Enhanced Storytimes

INCLUDE A PUPPET (OR PUPPETS!)

Puppets invite attention. Easily distractible children will often focus as soon as a puppet appears. If the puppet seems shy and will only speak if the children say hello first, almost all children respond by greeting the puppet. When the same puppet attends every story-time, children grow attached to it and feel that something is missing if it does not appear. Puppet kisses are a great reward for children who follow directions. They can be used in the middle of a storytime to encourage children to participate in an activity or at the end of a program to thank children for putting on their jackets and lining up in an orderly fashion.

USE SIGN LANGUAGE

To include sign language in your programs, choose a word related to the storytime session and visit the main dictionary at www.aslpro.com or the American Sign Language (ASL) dictionary at www.handspeak.com/word/index.php to view a video of the word being signed accurately. Another good resource is Kathy MacMillan's *Try Your Hand at This: Easy Ways to Incorporate Sign Language into Your Programs.*[3]

INSERT A CRAFT

Although craft activities traditionally take place at the end of storytime, simple crafts can be successfully incorporated into the actual session and then used as part of the program.

USE THE FLANNELBOARD

Using a flannelboard with creative flannel picture pieces is another way to tell a story. Flannel pieces are generally needed for each of the main characters in a story and for any settings that have a key role. Make them by cutting out illustrations that have been photocopied in color from discarded books (horrors!) or photographs from magazines. Or, cut out pictures from coloring pages and color them in, if needed. Glue the pictures to pieces of flannel using tacky glue (always use tacky glue—regular glue will not stick well). For longer-lasting pieces, spread glue over the entire paper figure and not just around the edges.

In addition to helping to retell a story, flannel pieces also serve as a visual represen-tation for a thought, poem, or story. For instance, a picture of one apple is sufficient to indicate that you are about to recite the rhyme "Two Little Apples in the Apple Tree."

USE SCRIPT CARDS IF NEEDED

If you're using a flannelboard/easel with a shelf in the middle, you can write script cards on index cards and keep them on the middle shelf where only you can see them. Similar to cheat sheets, script cards are meant to contain everything you need to know in order to retell a story without the book. You may decide to write out your entire script with a few sentences per card, or simply to have a few key words to remind you of what you want to say.

After making script cards, practice using them until you are comfortable telling the story aloud. If the script cards are intended for use with flannel pieces to help tell a flannelboard story, be sure to pile the flannel pieces in the order that they appear in the story.

USE HANDOUTS IF DESIRED

Some libraries provide families who have attended storytimes with handouts that include follow-up activities, developmental tips, literacy links, or other types of information. Suggestions for handouts are given in many of the sessions. You may want to ask storytime adults for their e-mail addresses during the first session of each series and e-mail the handout rather than printing it on paper. Since links to useful websites are often cited in these handouts, it may be more convenient while also saving paper!

Keep Records

Document the ways you have implemented the same book in a different manner for six weeks of preschool storytime sessions. The focus of your observations should be on *this one book*—not of each entire storytime—as well as on the responses of the children. You may want to add information about how much time you took to plan the presentations, what parents had to say, or anything else that would give useful data for planning your next series of repetitive preschool storytimes. Add a note at the end with other relevant information.

MANDATORY INFORMATION TO RECORD

Write one to five sentences for each week the book was used, in order to keep track of:

- The different ways the book was presented each week
- The responses of the children to each presentation

OPTIONAL INFORMATION TO RECORD

Write one to four sentences for each week the book was used, in order to keep track of:

- Time needed to plan
- Adult responses to the different presentations of the repetitive books
- Thoughts for additional presentation techniques or activities
- The skills targeted for development
- Anything you might want to follow up on for the next session
- Additional resources

These descriptions will be useful for:

- Choosing successful ways to present other repetitive books in upcoming pre-school storytimes
- Improving the already established plan, in order to recycle it in a year or two with a new group of children
- Explaining to adults who are confused by the repetition how the presentation differed each week
- Explaining to adults the skills being targeted and the value of the repetition
- Explaining to your supervisor why you are repeating a book six times, showing how each presentation varied in order to touch upon different senses
- Combining your observations with research findings to apply for funding for your programs

Example Record

Here is an example of good record keeping regarding repeated use of the book *Caps for Sale* by Esphyr Slobodkina.[4]

Week 1 Read the book and had the kids act like monkeys mimicking all the motions. (The kids loved this.) *—Encouraged creative expression.*

Week 2 Told the story using flannelboard characters. (Kids oohed and ahhed over the flannelboard characters.) Handed out monkey coloring sheets. *—Focused on the arts.*

Week 3 Pretended we were monkeys. Looked at photos of monkeys from nonfiction books. Asked the children who wanted to be the peddler to stand on one side of the room and those who wanted to be the monkeys to stand on the other side of the room. Read the book aloud and children acted out their parts. (Kids had fun with this.) *—Connected the book with life sciences; children followed directions.*

Week 4 Held up *Caps for Sale* and showed the cover without reading it. Asked: Who remembers what a peddler is? What did the peddler sell? Gave each child a construction paper coin (fifty cents). Acted like a peddler, called out the refrain, "sold" colored scarves to kids and pretended they were hats. Threw them up in the air. Read *Whose Hat?* by Margaret Miller.[5] (Kids liked "buying" the hats from the peddler and playing with the scarves. Didn't really get the connection with the book.) *—Memory, recall, sequences, colors.*

Week 5 Held up *Caps for Sale.* Asked kids if they remembered what the monkeys did? Talked about "imitation" and played Simon Says and Follow the Leader with different movements. Imitated monkey movements. Did fingerplay "Two Little Monkeys Jumping on the Bed." (Simon Says was okay, not great. Kids loved "Two Little Monkeys" fingerplay.) *—Experienced listening to directions and following instructions.*

Week 6 Repeated "Two Little Monkeys." Showed cover of *Caps for Sale* and told kids there was a similar book. Read *The Hatseller and the Monkeys: A West African Folktale.*[6] Gave each child a colored scarf and asked them to pretend it was a hat. Did what the monkeys did (pretend to throw them, wave them, drop them to the ground). Made hats out of paper plates. (*The Hatseller* was a little long, but kids loved the scarf activities afterward. They had fun making hats and proudly wore them.) *—Making comparisons: what's the same and what's different?*

Note: All five copies of *Caps for Sale* were on display at storytime and were checked out by the final session.

EVALUATION

A sample evaluation form can be found in the appendix to help with record keeping.

A Brief Explanation of Six Consecutive Sessions Utilizing Repetition with Variety

Chapters 3 and 4 present six-week programs involving specific books. The first set of scripts is for Paul Galdone's book *The Three Bears*. The second set is for *The Princess and the Pea*, adapted and illustrated by Janet Stevens. Each of these script sets includes fully written out storytime programs for six consecutive weeks. It provides all of the words for rhymes, songs, and fingerplays, directions, developmental tips, and titles of books. At the end of each week, a number of alternative books are listed that can easily be substituted for the nonessential books (anything other than the selected one that is being repeated).

Chapters 5 through 10 present ideas for six-week programs focusing on six different texts. Rather than spelling out everything that is happening during the storytime, these will focus on the book to be repeated and give suggestions for implementing it in different ways. Included are lists of complementary books to use, possible themes for storytimes, developmental tips, and a variety of activities to go along with the sessions.

Resources for Planning

There are many books and websites with terrific ideas that can assist with planning. Googling the title of a picture book, the author or illustrator's name, or "preschool storytime" with your theme will bring up a variety of websites with different implementation ideas. Classic older materials such as books by Carolyn Feller Bauer, or more recent sources, such as books written by Rob Reid, give a plethora of ways to use picture books in storytimes. It takes time to sift through the ideas. It is easiest to look in the index for the title of your selected picture book and see if there is related material. Or, browse through activities on a similar theme and see if there is something that will work. An older series of books called Story Stretchers lists a variety of book-related activities for the classroom. Many of these can easily be adapted for the preschool storytime environment. Other books present wonderful movement activities, food-related games, crafts, and other story suggestions that are just right for preschool storytimes. Books addressing programming for infants and toddlers often have rhymes, games, or activities that can work well with the preschool crowd.

Here is a list of books with great ideas for planning preschool storytimes:

Badegruber, Bernie. 2005. *101 Life Skills Games for Children: Learning, Growing, Getting Along (Ages 6 to 12)*. Alameda, CA: Hunter House.

Barlin, Ann Lief. 1979. *Teaching Your Wings to Fly: The Nonspecialist's Guide to Movement Activities for Young Children*. Santa Monica, CA: Goodyear.

Barlin, Ann Lief, and Paul Barlin. 1971. *The Art of Learning through Movement*. Santa Mercer Island, WA: Ward Ritchie.

Bauer, Caroline Feller. 1983. *This Way to Books*. New York: H. W. Wilson.

———.1985. *Celebrations: Read-Aloud Holiday and Theme Book Programs*. Chicago: American Library Association.

———.1993. *Carolyn Feller Bauer's New Handbook for Storytellers*. Chicago: American Library Association.

———.1995. *The Poetry Break: An Annotated Anthology with Ideas for Introducing Children to Poetry*. New York: H. W. Wilson.

———.1996. *Leading Kids to Books through Magic*. Chicago: American Library Association.

———.1997. *Leading Kids to Books through Puppets*. Chicago: American Library Association.

———.2000. *Leading Kids to Books through Crafts*. Chicago: American Library Association. Bauer, Caroline Feller, and Lynn G. Bredeson.

Bauer, Caroline Feller, and Lynne G. Bredeson. 1993. *Caroline Feller Bauer's New Handbook for Storytellers: With Stories, Poems, Magic, and More*. Chicago: American Library Association.

Blackwell, Wendy Camilla, et al. 2009. *Family Literacy Projects on a Budget*. Washington, DC: National Children's Museum.

Bromann, Jennifer. 2003. *Storytime Action!* New York: Neal-Schuman.

Brown, Marc. 1985. *Hand Rhymes*. New York: Dutton Children's Books.

Carlson, Ann, and Mary Carlson. 2005. *Flannelboard Stories for Infants and Toddlers*. Chicago: American Library Association Editions.

Cass-Beggs, Barbara. 1978. *Your Baby Needs Music*. North Vancouver, British Columbia: Douglas and McIntyre.

———.1986. *Your Child Needs Music*. Oakville, Ontario: Frederick Harris Music.

Castellano, Marie. 2003. *Simply Super Storytimes: Programming Ideas for Ages 3–6*. Fort Atkinson, WI: Upstart Books.

Charner, Kathy, and Maureen Murphy. 2004. *The Giant Encyclopedia of Preschool Activities for Four-Year-Olds*. Beltsville, MD: Gryphon House.

Church, Ellen Booth. 2003. *Best-Ever Circle Time Activities: Back to School: 50 Instant and Irresistible Meet-and-Greet Activities, Learning Games, and Language-Building Songs and Rhymes*. New York: Scholastic Professional Books.

Cobb, Jane. 1996. *I'm a Little Teapot! Presenting Preschool Storytime*. Vancouver, British Columbia: Black Sheep Press.

Codell, Esmé Raji. 2003. *How to Get Your Child to Love Reading*. Chapel Hill, NC: Algonquin Books of Chapel Hill.

Cullum, Carolyn N. 1990. *The Storytime Sourcebook*. New York: Neal-Schuman.

Davis, Robin Works. 1998. *Toddle On Over*. Fort Atkinson, WI: Alleyside Press.

DeSalvo, Nancy N. 1993. *Beginning with Books*. Hamden, CT: Library Professional Publications.

Diamant-Cohen, Betsy. 2006. *Mother Goose on the Loose*. New York: Neal-Schuman.

Diamant-Cohen, Betsy, and Selma Levi. 2009. *Booktalking Bonanza*. Chicago: American Library Association Editions.

Dunleavy, Deborah. 2001. *The Kids Can Press Jumbo Book of Music*. Tonowanda, NY: Kids Can Press.

Ernst, Linda L. 2001. *Lapsit Services for the Very Young II*. New York: Neal-Schuman.

Falk, John H., Robert L. Pruitt II, Kristi S. Rosenberg, and Tali A. Katz. 1996. *Bubble Monster and Other Science Fun*. Chicago: Chicago Review Press.

Feierabend, John M. 2000. *The Book of Bounces: Wonderful Songs and Rhymes Passed Down from Generation to Generation for Infants and Toddlers*. Chicago: GIA First Steps.

Fox, Mem. 2001. *Reading Magic: Why Reading Aloud to Our Children Will Change Their Lives Forever*. New York: Harcourt.

Freeman, Judy. 1984. *Books Kids Will Sit Still for: A Guide to Using Children's Literature for Librarians, Teachers, and Parents*. Hagerstown, MD: Alleyside.

———. 1990. *Books Kids Will Sit Still for: The Complete Read-Aloud Guide*. New York: Bowker.

———. 1997. *Hi Ho Librario! Songs, Chants, and Stories to Keep Kids Humming*. Bala Cynwyd, PA: Rock Hill Press.

———. 2007. *Once Upon a Time: Using Storytelling, Creative Drama, and Reader's Theater with Children in Grades PreK–6*. Westport, CT: Libraries Unlimited.

Garrity, Linda K. (author), and Jackie Moore (illustrator). 1991. *After the Story's Over: Your Enrichment Guide to 88 Read-Aloud Children's Classics*. Glenview, IL: Scott, Foresman and Company.

Ghoting, Saroj Nadkarni, and Pamela Martin-Díaz. 2006. *Early Literacy Storytimes @ your library*. Chicago: American Library Association.

Greenfield, Judith C. 1985. *Patterns for Preschoolers: Programs and Services for Young Children in Public Libraries*. New York: New York Library Association, Youth Services Section.

Irving, Jan, and Robin Currie. 1986. *Mudlicious: Stories and Activities Featuring Food for Preschool Children*. Littleton, CO: Libraries Unlimited.

Jay, M. Ellen, and Hilda L. Jay. 1998. *250+ Activities and Ideas for Developing Literacy Skills*. New York: Neal-Schuman.

Jeffrey, Debby Ann. 1995. *Literate Beginnings*. Chicago: American Library Association.

Johnson, Jeff A., and Tasha A. Johnson. 2006. *Do-It-Yourself Early Learning: Easy and Fun Activities and Toys from Everyday Home Center Materials*. St. Paul, MN: Red Leaf Press.

Jones, Taffy. 1989. *Library Programs for Children*. Jefferson, NC: McFarland.

Kaye, Peggy. 1991. *Games for Learning*. New York: Farrar Straus Giroux.

———. 2002. *Games with Books*. New York: Farrar Straus Giroux.

Korup, Daveed. 2002. *Tao Te Drum: Eastern Drumming for the Western Drummer*. Baltimore, MD: Drumfest!

Linder, Toni W. 1999. *Read, Play, and Learn! Storybook Activities for Young Children*. Teacher's guide. Baltimore: Paul H. Brookes.

Lipman, Doug. 1995. *Storytelling Games: Creative Activities for Language, Communication, and Composition across the Curriculum*. Phoenix, AZ: Oryx Press.

Lowe, Joy L., and Kathryn I. Matthew. 2008. *Puppet Magic*. New York: Neal-Schuman.

Lunsford, Susan. 2004. *Teaching with Favorite Read-Alouds in Kindergarten: 50 Must-Have Books with Lessons and Activities That Build Skills in Vocabulary, Comprehension, and More*. New York: Scholastic Professional Books.

MacDonald, Margaret Read. 1995. *Bookplay: 101 Creative Themes to Share with Young Children*. North Haven, CT: Library Professional Publications.

MacMillan, Kathy. 2006. *Try Your Hand at This: Easy Ways to Incorporate Sign Language into Your Programs*. Lanham, MD: Scarecrow Press.

MacMillan, Kathy and Christine Kirker. 2009. *Storytime Magic: 400 Fingerplays, Flannelboards, and Other Activities*. Chicago: American Library Association.

Maddigan, Beth, Roberta Thompson, and Stefanie Drennan. 2003. *The Big Book of Stories, Songs, and Sing-Alongs: Programs for Babies, Toddlers, and Families*. Westport, CT: Libraries Unlimited.

Marino, Jane. 1999. *What Works: Developmentally Appropriate Library Programs for Very Young Children*. Albany, New York: Youth Services Section, New York Library Association.

———. 2003. *Babies in the Library!* Lanham, MD: Scarecrow Press.

McKinnon, Elizabeth, and Barb Tourtillotte. 1992. *Learning and Caring about Our Town*. Everett, WA: Warren.

Meisenheimer, Sharon. 1988. *Special Ways with Ordinary Days*. Carthage, IL: Fearon Teacher Aids.

Murphy, Pat, Ellen Macaulay, Jason Gorski, and the staff of the Exploratorium. 2006. *Exploratopia*. New York: Little, Brown.

Nespeca, Sue McLeaf. 1994. *Library Programming for Families with Young Children*. New York: Neal-Schuman.

Nespeca, Sue McCleaf, and Joan B. Reeve. 2003. *Picture Books Plus: 100 Extension Activities in Art, Drama, Music, Math, and Science*. Chicago: American Library Association.

Nichols, Judy. 1998. *Storytimes for Two-Year-Olds*. Chicago: American Library Association.

Northwest Territories Literary Council. *TV Free from A to Z How-to-Kit: More than 26 Fun Activities to Keep Your Family Engaged and the TV Off!* Canada: NWTLC. www.nwt.literacy.ca/resources/famlit/howtokit/tvfree/tvfree.pdf.

Oberlander, June R. (author), and Barbara Oberlander Jansen (illustrator). 2002. *Slow and Steady, Get Me Ready: A Parents' Handbook for Children From Birth to Age 5*. Burke, VA: Bio-Alpha.

Oppenheim, Joanne and Stephanie. 2006. *Read It! Play It! with Babies and Toddlers*. New York: Oppenheim Toy Portfolio.

Pflomm, Phyllis Noe. 1986. *Chalk in Hand: The Draw and Tell Book*. Metuchen, NJ: Scarecrow.

Pica, Roe. 2001. *Wiggle, Giggle, and Shake*. Beltsville, MD: Gryphon House.

Potter, Jean. 1998. *Science in Seconds with Toys*. New York: John Wiley and Sons.

Poulsson, Emilie (author), L. J. Bridgman (illustrator), Cornelia C. Roeske (composer). 1971. *Finger Plays for Nursery and Kindergarten*. New York: Dover.

Raines, Shirley, and Robert J. Canady. 1989. *Story S-t-r-e-t-c-h-e-r-s: Activities to Expand Children's Favorite Books*. Beltsville, MD: Gryphon House.

———. 2002. *More Story S-t-r-e-t-c-h-e-r-s: More Activities to Expand Children's Favorite Books*. Beltsville, MD: Gryphon House.

Raines, Shirley, Karen Miller, and Leah Curry-Rood. 2002. *Story S-t-r-e-t-c-h-e-r-s for Infants, Toddlers, and Twos*. Beltsville, MD: Gryphon House.

Reid, Rob. 1999. *Family Storytime: Twenty-Four Creative Programs for All Ages*. Chicago: American Library Association.

———. 2003. *Something Funny Happened at the Library: How to Create Humorous Programs for Children and Young Adults*. Chicago: American Library Association.

———. 2007. *Children's Jukebox: The Select Subject Guide to Children's Musical Recordings*. Chicago: American Library Association.

———. 2009. *Children's Jukebox*. Chicago: American Library Association.

———. 2009. *Something Musical Happened at the Library: Adding Song and Dance to Children's Story Programs*. Chicago: American Library Association.

Reid, Rob (author) and Nadine Bernard Westcott (illustrator). 2009. *Comin' Down to Storytime*. Janesville, WI: Upstart Books.

Reitzes, Fretta, and Beth Teitelman, with Lois Alter Mark. 1985. *Wonderplay: Interactive and Developmental Games, Crafts, and Creative Activities for Infants, Toddlers, and Preschoolers*. Philadelphia: Running Press.

Roberts, Ken. 1987. *Pre-School Storytimes*. Ottawa: Canadian Library Association.

Robinson, Jeri (author) and Barbara Bruno (illustrator). 1983. *Activities for Anyone, Anytime, Anywhere*. Boston: Little, Brown.

Schiller, Pam. 1999. *Start Smart! Building Brain Power in the Early Years*. Beltsville, MD: Gryphon House.

Scott, Barbara A. 2010. *1,000 Fingerplays and Action Rhymes: A Sourcebook and DVD*. New York: Neal-Schuman.

Silberg, Jackie. 1998. *The I Can't Sing Book for Grownups Who Can't Carry a Tune in a Paper Bag . . . But Want to Do Music with Young Children*. Beltsville, MD: Gryphon House.

Stanson, Carolyn Booth. 1989. *Once Upon a Storytime: A Workbook for Planning and Presenting Creative Storytimes for Children Two-Six Years of Age*. Rochester, MN: Minnesota Association for Library Friends.

Trelease, Jim. 2006. *The Read-Aloud Handbook*. 6th ed. New York: Penguin.

Vardell, Sylvia M. 2008. *Children's Literature in Action: A Librarian's Guide*. Westport, CT: Libraries Unlimited.

———. 2008. *Poetry Aloud Here! Sharing Poetry with Children in the Library*. Chicago: American Library Association.

Wallace, Mary. 2002. *I Can Make That! Fantastic Crafts for Kids*. Toronto: Maple Leaf Press.

Washburn Child Guidance Center. 1997. *Every Day Matters: Activities for You and Your Child*. Circle Pines, MN: AGS.

White, Laurence B., Ray Broekel, and Meyer Seltzer. 1991. *Shazam! Simple Science Magic*. Morton Grove, IL: A. Whitman.

Wilmes, Liz and Dick (authors), and Donna Dane (illustrator). 1982. *The Circle Time Book*. Dundee, IL: Building Blocks.

Building One Session upon Another

"What is the best way to repeat books from week to week?" you may ask. "Won't it get boring?" The answer is a resounding no if you plan and execute your sessions carefully.

To start a year's worth of programming, select a core collection of eight books that you think are "absolutely fabulous." From this collection, choose one book to highlight/repeat in your next six preschool storytimes. Other books that you think are wonderful can be used to fill the quota of complementary books for each storytime. These should not be repeated week to week but used only once during the six-week period. (A recurring theme, then, can be "Books loved by the librarian presenting the preschool storytime!")

After refreshing your memory by rereading the selected book, make a list of different ways to present it. Then choose a fingerplay, song, or rhyme for the opening and closing sections to be included in each of the six consecutive preschool storytimes. But don't forget to always add new material each week!

Librarians should look for ways to enrich children's connection with the selected book that involves many of the senses; instead of just hearing the book and looking at the pictures, children can be given chances to act it out, watch others acting it out, create a related piece of art, dance to music that connects with a part of the book, taste, touch, or smell something that can be related to the story.

THINGS TO KEEP IN MIND WHEN PLANNING YOUR STORYTIMES

Plan for all types of learners. Try to use many of the multiple intelligences:

- Linguistic
- Logical-mathematical
- Spatial
- Musical
- Bodily-kinesthetic
- Intrapersonal
- Interpersonal
- Emotional
- Social

Create an environment where children can practice life skills:

- Focus and self-control
- Perspective taking
- Communication
- Making connections
- Critical thinking
- Taking on challenges
- Self-directed, engaged learning

Consider that children learn best when there is

- Repetition with variety
- Learning as part of a loving relationship and a comfortable environment
- Music
- Movement (small and large)
- Joy and playfulness
- Use of different senses

- Time to absorb what has been learned
- Rituals
- Personal meaning

Try to find ways to incorporate as many of the senses as possible:

- Seeing
- Hearing
- Touching
- Tasting
- Smelling

Additional Information

DEALING WITH PARENTS

Before the mid-1980s many preschool storytimes in public libraries took place without parents. Parents were asked to say goodbye to their children at the door of the story room; preschool storytime was a place just for the children with their librarian. Most librarians today believe that preschool children respond better to programs when their parents or caregivers are with them. Adults present in programs supposedly make sure that their children are behaving well; adults and children also share positive literacy experiences through attending storytimes together. When parents know what has happened during library storytime, they are able to more easily create activities that expand upon the storytime experience and engage in conversations about the stories at home. To get optimum benefit from the presence of adults, explain that children like to have their parents close by and encourage the parents to sit on the floor next to the children.

When parents become a distraction rather than a help, though, librarians sometimes wish that preschool children were still attending programs without their adults! One remedy for this is to assume that parents who have made the effort and taken the time to come to the program want their child to get the most out of it. Tell parents during the welcoming comments that children love to imitate their adults and will get the most out of the program if the adults participate fully and enthusiastically. This is true. If a parent sings along with the songs and does the fingerplays, the child is more likely to participate with gusto. This information given during your welcoming comments encourages parents to participate without mentioning rules or forbidding certain types of behavior (such as talking on cell phones during the program).

Below are some suggestions for handling other sticky storytime situations.

1. When there is a child in storytime who likes to monopolize the conversation, try to mostly ask yes-or-no questions.
2. When the children seem to have lost interest in a story, stop reading and start paraphrasing, then skip to the end!

3. Bring out puppets to redirect children's focus.
4. Giving children something to hold that has a connection to the story may help them to pay attention. (Caution: It may have the opposite effect on others.)
5. When children seem sleepy, insert a rousing stand-up activity before continuing on with your program.
6. If everyone seems inattentive, perhaps they can't hear you. Speak louder!
7. If an energetic child repeatedly cannot settle down, suggest to his caregiver that they visit a park right before storytime. Expending energy in an appropriate place before the program begins can work wonders.

STORYTIME FOR GROUPS

Storytime for child care centers and home day cares differs because of the small ratio of adults to children.

1. Suggest that child care providers stay with their children in storytime rather than leaving to use the computers. Explain that children benefit most when their caregiver is actively engaged in the activities with them.
2. Provide labels and permanent markers on a table near the door. Ask the child care providers to create a name tag for each child. Knowing the individual names of the children and using them often makes for a more cooperative audience and builds a personal connection between you and your audience.
3. Preschool storytime works best when parent/child groups have separate programs from child care groups—when both groups are together, the mass of child care children can overwhelm individuals with their parents. If a child care group shows up unexpectedly for your scheduled preschool storytime and mentions that they intend to come on a regular basis, offer to present a separate program just for them. Logistically this may not be possible, but the quality of the programs is higher if the storytimes are offered separately.

ADAPTING STORYTIME

- If a child seems hard of hearing, invite her to sit near you, where it will be easier for her to participate.
- Try to include at least one ASL sign in storytime that everyone can do with you.
- Try to supply tactile experiences for storytime children with low vision. Prepare a bag ahead of time filled with a few objects and a stuffed animal related to the story. Ask the child's caregiver to hand the appropriate objects to the child as they appear in the story.
- Include lots of singing and avoid loud noises when working with children on the autism spectrum. Don't worry that they are not paying attention if they find it difficult to sit still.
- If a large group of non-English speakers attends your storytimes, ask one of the parents to teach you a children's song in the most prevalent language. Including

that song in your programs will help the other non-English-speaking parents and children feel more at home. It also creates another bridge between all storytime participants.

OVERCOMING OBSTACLES

The following chapters that outline how to present a book in different ways over six weeks are meant to make it easy to implement this new storytime model and then do your own scaffolded learning by creating original repetition-with-variety programs, using the book and your experience with it as a guide. However, switching gears after years of theme-based programs is not simple. Some librarians will resist the initial time it takes to orient themselves and prepare for this new way of presenting storytime (especially those practicing librarians who have a repertoire of storytime materials and activities that they use year after year). So, why go through the bother of transforming storytime?

Trying the model portrayed in the scripts will encourage librarians to freshen up tried-and-true storytime sessions while also providing the added benefits of repetition with variety. This book-centered model should provide a higher-quality program than a random theme-based program. And, as demonstrated in the scripts, many of the popular songs and rhymes that librarians already use can be easily integrated into the revised storytime sessions.

Librarian Summer Rosswog offers a suggestion to help with the transformation of storytimes: Try initially introducing your "transformed storytime" as a separate program from regular preschool storytime. This can be similar to the way public libraries have a several-weeks science or art program for children that is announced in the library

35 Ways to Present a Book

1. Read it aloud directly from the text.
2. Show the illustrations but "tell" the story rather than reading it.
3. Use flannelboard characters and tell the story with them.
4. Tell the story without reading the book.
5. Use puppets to act out the story.
6. Use any of your special talents to add to the story (e.g., guitar or kazoo playing)
7. Choose one scene from the story (e.g., going up in an elevator) and act it out.
8. Ask the children to draw a scene from the story.
9. Ask the children to describe what something that happened in the story feels like.
10. Create a variation of the story.
11. Act out the story together with the children.
12. Have children act out the story while you are narrating or reading aloud. You may want to give them craft stick puppets, stuffed animals, or masks to help them identify with their character.
13. Have the children act out the story and make up the dialogue. (The best time for this is the last session when children already know the story thoroughly.)
14. Encourage children to talk by asking questions about the book that require more than a yes-or-no answer.
15. Ask children to anticipate what is going to happen next before you turn each page.
16. Sing the words of the story, especially if the book comes from a song (e.g., "There Was an Old Lady Who Swallowed a Fly," "Going to the Zoo").
17. Draw the elements of the story while telling it.
18. Create a simple craft related to the story for children to do during storytime.

calendar. Recruit regular attendees from the community or a day care class and start implementing the transformed storytimes with them. As both you and the library visitors become familiar and comfortable with the new format, the benefits of repetition with variety in storytime will become clear. At that point, it could be transitioned to replace the traditional preschool storytime. Then, perhaps, attendees would not feel that they were losing something they enjoy; rather, they would feel that they were experiencing an improvement over something that was already successful.

NOTES

1. Diamant-Cohen, Betsy, and Saroj Nadkarni Ghoting. 2010. *Early Literacy Kit: A Handbook and Tip Cards*. Chicago: American Library Association.

2. Ghoting, Saroj Nadkarni, and Pamela Martin-Díaz. 2006. *Early Literacy Storytimes @ your library: Partnering with Caregivers for Success*. Chicago: American Library Association.

3. MacMillan, Kathy. 2006. *Try Your Hand at This: Easy Ways to Incorporate Sign Language into Your Programs*. Lanham, MD: Scarecrow Press.

4. Slobodkina, Esphyr. 2009. *Caps for Sale: A Tale of a Peddler, Some Monkeys and Their Monkey Business*. New York: HarperCollins.

5. Miller, Margaret. 1988. *Whose Hat?* New York: Greenwillow Books.

6. Diakité, Baba Wagué. 1999. *The Hatseller and the Monkeys: A West African Folktale*. New York: Scholastic.

19. Some stories lend themselves to paper folding.
20. Some stories work well as cut-and-tell.
21. Create artwork in the same style as the illustrator of the story.
22. Make or taste a type of food mentioned in the story.
23. Do a science experiment similar to one that was mentioned in the story.
24. Do a magic trick similar to one that was mentioned in the story.
25. Share a nonfiction book that is highly relevant to the topic or characters in the story.
26. Ask questions about the story and create a visual (chart, graph, list) of the answers given by the children.
27. Provide props for dress-up as characters in the story.
28. Create an environment for the story (e.g., a hula hoop on the floor can be a pond; a towel spread out on the rug can be a garden patch).
29. Use musical instruments to sound out a repeated phrase in the story.
30. Use colored scarves to imagine different situations in the story.
31. Retell the story from a different character's point of view.
32. Read or show other books by the same author or illustrator.
33. Read versions of the same story by other authors or illustrators.
34. Read aloud fractured versions of the same story.
35. Scream the story at the top of your lungs (not really).

PART II

Scripts Using Eight Different Books

I n the following pages, you will find full scripts for six weeks of consecutive story-times for two books, *The Three Bears* written and illustrated by Paul Galdone and *The Princess and the Pea* adapted and illustrated by Janet Stevens. These scripts are very detailed in order to clearly show different ways that programming with repetition and variation can be done. At the beginning of each week's program in chapters 3 and 4, there is a complete outline of all the books and activities that will be presented in that particular script.

Paul Galdone's *The Three Bears* is the foundation for the first complete six-week program. Although it is repeated each week, because each session is a full thirty-minute preschool storytime, books written or illustrated by others are included. But in order to introduce children to the selected book and present it in a way that involves many different senses and intelligences, the scripts also involve creative dramatics, songs, food, and games that are somehow tied in with it.

In the first session for each series, the selected book is introduced. We recommend that you choose a beginning and ending activity—such as a fingerplay—that repeats for all six weeks. After the first session the book can be used in a variety of ways. Telling the story, performing a puppet show, using the flannelboard, reenacting the story, playing games with the plot, getting to know the characters, smelling and tasting the food, creating walls, playing musical instruments, doing art projects, and participating in creative drama activities are just some of the ways the book can be repeated that appeal to different intelligences and senses. Each time children renew their acquaintance with the book, another connection is being formed that strengthens their knowledge of it while also helping to build their early literacy skills through play.

Since many librarians prefer to base their storytimes around themes, each of the story-times in chapter 3 has a theme that relates to *The Three Bears*. However, remember that themes are tools that are often used to help librarians feel comfortable planning programs and that *it is not necessary to have a theme*. Simply choosing good books to share with your audience is fine.

Additionally, remember that the complementary books and activities are not carved in stone. They are simply suggestions that have worked in tried-and-true storytimes. It is absolutely fine to substitute both books and activities. These scripts are meant to serve as a guideline for making programming easier, not as step-by-step instructions that must be followed to the letter in order to be successful. The scripts can be used as templates; librarians are encouraged to create their own programs by substituting the materials they have on hand.

Chapters 5 through 10 are streamlined. Suggestions of books and activities are given, but the assumption is that by this point librarians will be both comfortable and eager to try out their own ideas for repetition with variation. Additional resources are included, but the absence of a completely scripted session ensures that librarians personalize their storytimes. It is almost impossible for one library to have all the materials mentioned for a full six-week program; the list of alternative titles and activities present substitute choices and drives home the message that all preschool storytime presenters should feel free to substitute any book or activity that they feel will work.

The implementation ideas presented in the following chapters for the selected books are just a small selection of the dozens of ways in which they can be presented. Some are easier and some are harder to implement. Always remember that the best learning takes place through play, so the book should presented only in a way that you feel comfortable with, that is fun for both you and the children. Underlying the desire to connect children with books in a playful way, however, should be the intention to help children develop a wide variety of skills that encompass the domains of school readiness, multiple intelligences, life skills, and Every Child Ready to Read @ your library.

Opening "Wiggle" Song

Here is a fun song that you may want to use in your opening ritual for this series of storytimes.

Before we begin we need to take care of our wiggles. Everyone has wiggles and we need to put them away until after storytime. Ready? Everyone find your wiggles and grab them!

Have all kids wiggle and "grab" their wiggles. Have some sort of bag that will be the wiggle bag. Sing the following song and go from child to child and have them put their wiggles in the bag.

PUT YOUR WIGGLES IN THE BAG (to the tune of "If You're Happy and You Know It")

**Put your wiggles in the bag, in the bag
Put your wiggles in the bag, in the bag
Put your wiggles in the bag,
Where they can zig and zag
Put your wiggles in the bag, in the bag.**

chapter 3

Series 1
The Three Bears

Focus Text: *The Three Bears*

by Paul Galdone
(New York: Houghton Mifflin Harcourt, 2011)

When family of bears returns from a walk to let their porridge cool off, they find their porridge has been eaten, their chairs sat in, and their beds lain in. To everyone's surprise, Goldilocks, the perpetrator, is still in Baby Bear's bed.

Ways to Present *The Three Bears* in Storytime Sessions

Week 1: Introduce "The Three Bears." (bears)

Week 2: Tell "The Three Bears" as a flannelboard story. (trees and woods)

Week 3: Narrate the story and have children act it out. (hiding and finding)

Week 4: Read other versions of the story by different authors and illustrators. (food)

Week 5: Read a fractured version of the story; find opposites in the book. (opposites)

Week 6: Give children props to play with while they retell the story themselves. (bear families)

Week 1: Introduce *The Three Bears*

Week 1 Outline

Theme: Bears

Beginning Ritual
- **Introduction**
- **Fingerplay:** "Alligator, Alligator"

Story/Activity 1
- **Book:** Focus text, *The Three Bears* by Paul Galdone
- **Activity:** "Going on a Bear Hunt"

Story/Activity 2
- **Book:** *Bear Snores On* by Karma Wilson, illustrated by Jane Chapman
- **Activity:** "The Bear Hokey Pokey"
- **Developmental Tip:** Recognizing patterns and shapes

Story/Activity 3
- **Book:** Ten in the Bed by David Ellwand
- **Activity:** "Ten in the Bed"

Story 4
- **Book:** *Brown Bear, Brown Bear, What Do You See?* by Bill Martin Jr., illustrated by Eric Carle

Closing Ritual
- **Vote**
- **Fingerplay:** "Alligator, Alligator" (repeated from Beginning Ritual)

BOOKS NEEDED

Ellwand, David. 2000. *Ten in the Bed: A Counting Book.* New York: Handprint.

Galdone, Paul. 2011. *The Three Bears.* Boston: Houghton Mifflin Harcourt.

Martin, Bill, Jr. (author), and Eric Carle (illustrator). 1992. *Brown Bear, Brown Bear, What Do You See?* New York: Henry Holt.

Wilson, Karma (author), and Jane Chapman (illustrator). 2002. *Bear Snores On.* New York: Margaret K. McElderry.

Script

BEGINNING RITUAL

Introduction
Hi, my name is Susie Librarian, and I am delighted to see you here today.

Fingerplay: "Alligator, Alligator"
Let's start with a fingerplay called "Alligator, Alligator."

"Alligator, Alligator"
Alligator, alligator, sitting on a log. (*Place palms together; open and close hands like an alligator's mouth.*)

Down in the water he sees a frog. (*Place one hand over eyes as if searching for something.*)

Down goes the alligator, (*Hold left hand flat, palm facing up. Hold right hand poised over right shoulder. Dive right hand down, palm down, slapping left hand on the way.*)

Around goes the log, (*Make rolling motion with both hands.*)

Away swims the frog. (*Make swimming motion with both hands.*)

Say it again, loudly! (*Recite again, loudly.*)

Now softly. (*Recite again, softly.*)

Now in a normal tone of voice. (*Recite again.*)

STORY/ACTIVITY 1

Book: Focus text, *The Three Bears* by Paul Galdone
This is the story of *The Three Bears* by Paul Galdone. (*Hold up book.*) You probably already know the story of the three bears, and this one might be a little bit different. But that's okay! Are you ready? Here we go! (*Read book aloud.*)

Activity: "Going on a Bear Hunt"
Instead of using the activity suggested below, you can substitute another activity with puppets, fingerplays, songs, or flannelboard rhymes.

Let's go on a bear hunt. Start by tapping your knees like this and repeat everything I say and do.

"Going on a Bear Hunt"
We're going on a bear hunt.

I'm not scared at all.

Bye-bye, Mom. *(Wave good-bye.)*

Leave the house and close the door. *(Close door.)*

We walk through the tall grass, swishy, swishy. *(Rub hands together.)*

Look! Mud. Can't go under it, can't go over it, can't go around it! Must go through it!

Squelchy, squelchy. *(Lift up feet like you are stuck in mud.)*

Look! A lake! Can't go under it, can't go over it, can't go around it! Must go through it!

Splish, splash, splish splash. *(Make splashing motions with hands.)*

Look! There's a boat! Let's cross the lake! *(Sing "Row, Row, Row Your Boat.")*

Now up a mountain. Climb, climb, climb. *(Feet and arms go up and down.)*

Here's a river. Swim, swim, swim. *(Make swimming motions.)*

Look, there's a cave. Shhhh . . .

Walk in very slowly. Tiptoe, tiptoe, tiptoe.

Look! Two eyes . . . A black nose . . . Furry ears . . . a BIG mouth . . .

IT'S A BEAR!!!!

ARRAUGH!!!!!

QUICK, OUT OF THE CAVE. *(Run.)*

Across the river. *(Swim quickly.)*

Down the mountain. *(Quickly move feet and arms up and down.)*

Into the boat. *(Sing "Row, Row, Row Your Boat" as quickly as possible.)*

Through the mud, squelchy, squelchy. *(Lift feet up high.)*

Through the tall grass, swishy, swishy. *(Rub hands quickly together,)*

Open the door and into the house. *(Slam the door behind you.)*

Oh, hi, Mom! *(Wave.)*

Guess what? I found a bear! And I wasn't scared at all. Not even one little bit!

STORY/ACTIVITY 2

Book: *Bear Snores On* by Karma Wilson, illustrated by Jane Chapman
Read aloud.

Activity: "The Bear Hokey Pokey"
Sing and act out the bear hokey pokey using bear parts and no "right" or "left," because preschoolers most likely will not be able to distinguish between right and left. You may decide to use a different stand up activity that involves dance, creative dramatics, or movement songs.

"The Bear Hokey Pokey"
You put your front paw in *(hand or arm)*, you take your front paw out.

You put your front paw in, and you shake it all about.

You growl the hokey pokey and you turn yourself around.

That's what it's all about! *Growl!*

You put your back paw in *(leg or foot)*, you take your back paw out.
You put your back paw in, and you shake it all about.
You growl the hokey pokey and you turn yourself around.
That's what it's all about! *Growl!*

You put your head in *(head)*, you take your head out.
You put your head in, and you shake it all about.
You growl the hokey pokey and you turn yourself around.
That's what it's all about! *Growl!*

You put your tail in *(bottom)*, you take your tail out.
You put your tail in, and you shake it all about.
You growl the hokey pokey and you turn yourself around.
That's what it's all about! *Growl!*

You put your furry self in *(whole body)*, you take your furry self out.
You put your furry self in, and you shake it all about.
You growl the hokey pokey and you turn yourself around.
That's what it's all about! *Growl!*

NOW LET'S ALL GIVE A BIG GROWL . . . GRRRRRRRRRR!
And show our front paws . . . GRRRRR.
And show our back paws . . . GRRRRR.
And shake our heads . . . GRRRRR.
And wiggle our tails . . . GRRRRRRR.
And sit back down . . . GRRRRRRRRRR!

▶▶ DEVELOPMENTAL TIP

Through simple dances, children become aware of patterns and shapes. When children are asked to form a circle or stand in a line, physically acting out these shapes increases their understanding of the related words. Since young children cannot distinguish between right and left, it is best to say, "Put your foot in" rather than specifying right or left foot.

STORY/ACTIVITY 3

Book: *Ten in the Bed* by David Ellwand

Sing/read aloud this traditional song with photos of teddy bears while encouraging everyone to join in.

Activity: "Ten in the Bed"

When planning your own programs, this activity can involve a puppet, fingerplay, song, flannelboard rhyme OR dance, creative dramatics, or movement songs. Below is a dramatization of the book that was just presented.

Begin by asking all the children to stand up in a line. If you have more than twelve children in your program, ask them to form two lines. Be sure to give each child a chance to "fall out of bed."

We are all going to sing "Ten in the Bed" together, and each time one of the bears rolls over, we are going to twirl around in a circle. The person at the end of the line will "fall down" (lie on the ground) while we continue the song:

"Ten in the Bed"

There were ten in the bed and the little one said, "Roll over, roll over."
So they all rolled over and one fell out.
There were nine in the bed . . .
Continue singing until the little one says, "I'm lonely!"

STORY 4

Book: *Brown Bear, Brown Bear, What Do You See?* by Bill Martin Jr., illustrated by Eric Carle

You may already know this story, *Brown Bear, Brown Bear, What Do You See?* by Bill Martin Jr., with pictures by Eric Carle. If you know it, recite it along with me! If not, it is very easy to pick up, so feel free to join in whenever you are ready. *(Read aloud.)* And that is the story of *Brown Bear, Brown Bear, What Do You See?*

CLOSING RITUAL

Vote

It's almost time to end our storytime, but I'd like to find out what books you liked the best. Everyone who liked the first book we read, *The Three Bears* by Paul Galdone, please raise your hand.

Anyone who liked second book we read, *Bear Snores On* by Karma Wilson with illustrations by Jane Chapman, please raise your hand.

Anyone who liked the third book we read, *Ten in the Bed* by David Ellwand, please raise your hand.

Anyone who liked the last book we read, *Brown Bear, Brown Bear, What Do You See?* by Bill Martin Jr. with illustrations by Eric Carle, please raise your hand.

And anyone who liked all the books we read today, please raise both hands, wave them around, and say, "WOO WOO WOO WOO WOO!" *(Do this with the children.)*

Fingerplay: "Alligator, Alligator"
Now it's time to end with "Alligator, Alligator." You probably remember it from the beginning of our storytime. Let's all recite it together. (Recite "Alligator, Alligator.")

"Alligator, Alligator"
Alligator, alligator, sitting on a log. *(Place palms together; open and close hands like an alligator's mouth.)*

Down in the water he sees a frog. *(Place one hand over eyes as if searching for something.)*

Down goes the alligator, *(Hold left hand flat, palm facing up. Hold right hand poised over right shoulder. Dive right hand down, palm down, slapping left hand on the way.)*

Around goes the log, *(Make rolling motion with both hands.)*

Away swims the frog. *(Make swimming motion with both hands.)*

Repeat a few times.

Thanks for coming, and I hope to see you next week.

BOOKS ABOUT BEARS

Arnosky, Jim. 1996. *Every Autumn Comes the Bear*. New York: Paper Star.

Blackstone, Stella (author), and Debbie Harter (illustrator). 2001. *Bear at Home*. New York: Barefoot Books.

Bodkin, Odds. 2002. *Doing, Doing, Doing*. Watertown, MA: Perkins School for the Blind. This book is part of the Perkins Panda Early Literacy Set. It has large print and high-contrast illustrations as well as braille.

Dann, Penny. 2001. *Teddy Bear, Teddy Bear, Turn Around*. Hauppauge, NY: Barron's Educational Series, Inc.

de Beer, Hans. 2010. *The Little Polar Bear*. New York: North-South Books.

Guiberson, Brenda Z. 2010. *Moon Bear*. New York: Henry Holt.

Haas, Robert B. 2008. *African Critters*. Washington, DC: National Geographic.

Meyers, Susan (author), and Amy June Bates (illustrator). 2010. *Bear in the Air*. New York: Abrams Books for Young Readers.

Parenteau, Shirley. 2009. *Bears on Chairs*. Cambridge, MA: Candlewick Press.

Schertle, Alice. 2007. *Very Hairy Bear*. Orlando: Harcourt Children's Books.

Waddell, Martin (author), and Jill Barton (illustrator). 1995. *Little Mo*. Cambridge, MA: Candlewick Press.

Wong, Herbert Yee. 1993. *Big Black Bear*. Boston: Houghton Mifflin.

Wright, Dare. 1999. *The Lonely Doll*. Boston: Houghton Mifflin.

Week 2: Tell *The Three Bears* as a Flannelboard Story

Week 2 Outline

Repetition with Variety: Use "The Three Bears" in a new way: retold as a flannelboard story.

Theme: Trees and woods

Beginning Ritual
- **Introduction**
- **Fingerplay:** "Alligator, Alligator" (repeated from week 1)

Story/Activity 1
- **Book:** Focus text retold as a flannelboard story, *The Three Bears* by Paul Galdone
- **Activity:** "Open Them, Shut Them"

Story/Activity 2
- **Book:** *Our Walk in the Woods* by Charity Nebbe, illustrated by Jeffrey Ebbeler
- **Developmental Tip:** Learning through repetition
- **Activity:** "Going on a Bear Hunt," modified (repeated from week 1)

Story/Activity 3
- **Book:** *The Busy Tree* by Jennifer Ward, illustrated by Lisa Falkenstern
- **Activity:** "Two Red Apples in the Apple Tree"

Story 4
- **Book:** *Ten Apples on Top* by Theo LeSieg, illustrated by Roy McKie

Closing Ritual
- **Vote**
- **Fingerplay:** "Alligator, Alligator" (repeated from week 1)

ITEMS NEEDED

- flannelboard
- flannel pieces
- Goldilocks (figure 3.1)
- Papa Bear (figure 3.2)
- Mama Bear (figure 3.3)
- Baby Bear (figure 3.4)
- big porridge bowl (figure 3.5 enlarged)
- medium-sized porridge bowl (figure 3.5)
- small porridge bowl (figure 3.5 reduced)
- big chair (figure 3.6 enlarged)
- medium-sized chair (figure 3.6)
- small chair (figure 3.6 reduced)
- big bed (figure 3.7 enlarged)
- medium-sized bed (figure 3.7)
- small bed (figure 3.7 reduced)
- door (figure 3.8)
- window (a square of felt)
- stove (a rectangle of felt)

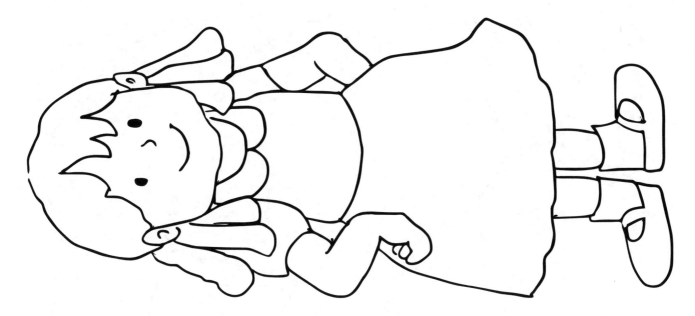

Figure 3.1 Goldilocks

Figure 3.2 Papa Bear

Figure 3.3 Mama Bear

Figure 3.4 Baby Bear

Figure 3.5 Bowl of porridge with spoon

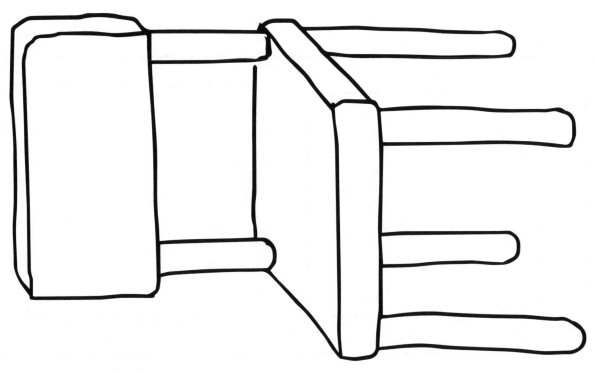

Figure 3.6 Chair

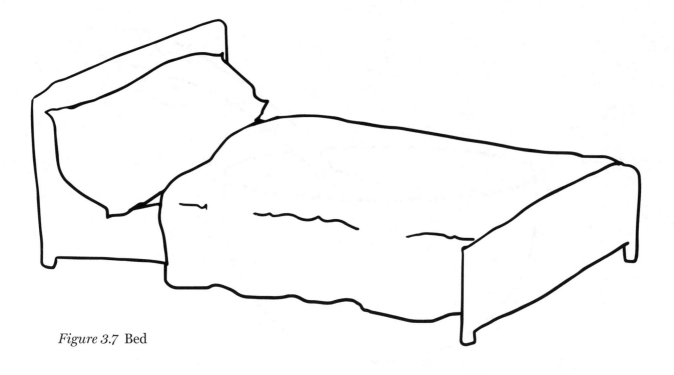

Figure 3.7 Bed

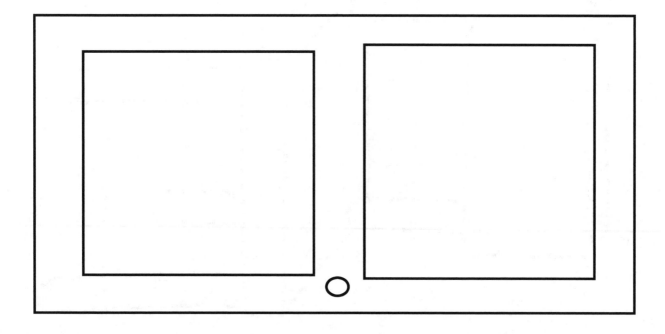

Figure 3.8 Door

BOOKS NEEDED

Galdone, Paul. 2011. *The Three Bears*. Boston: Houghton Mifflin Harcourt.

LeSieg, Theo (author), and Roy McKie (illustrator). 1961. *Ten Apples Up on Top!* New York: Beginner Books.

Nebbe, Charity (author), and Jeffrey Ebbeler (illustrator). 2008. *Our Walk in the Woods*. Ann Arbor, MI: Mitten Press.

Ward, Jennifer (author) and Lisa Falkenstern (illustrator). 2009. *The Busy Tree*. New York: Marshall Cavendish Children.

PREPARATION

Use a photocopy machine to reproduce figures 3.1 through 3.8. Use the enlarge function to make the bowl, chair, and bed in three different sizes. Color in the photocopies and use tacky glue to attach them to felt backings. Another option is to use online printable templates. Printable templates for the three bears and Goldilocks can be found at www.first-school.ws/t/craft/3bears_puppets.htm; a printable template for their cottage can be found at www.first-school.ws/t/craft/3bears_house.htm. The parent site, www.first-school.ws, has many more printable pages.

Script

BEGINNING RITUAL

Introduction
Introduce yourself and welcome everyone.

Fingerplay: "Alligator, Alligator"
Repeat from week 1.

STORY/ACTIVITY 1

Book: *The Three Bears* by Paul Galdone
Do you remember the story of *The Three Bears*? (Show everyone the cover of *The Three Bears* by Paul Galdone.) I read this story last week and it was lots of fun. This week, however, I'm not going to read the story again. Instead, I'm going to tell it using the flannelboard. Let's see what pieces I have. Can you name them? (Hold up a flannel piece and say its name. Ask the children to repeat the name of the object after you. Then tell the story using the flannel pieces.)

- Papa Bear
- Mama Bear
- Baby Bear
- stove
- big porridge bowl
- medium porridge bowl
- small porridge bowl
- table
- Goldilocks
- window
- door
- big chair
- medium chair
- small chair
- big bed
- medium bed
- small bed

Once upon a time there were three bears: a papa bear, a mama bear, and a baby bear. They lived in a house in the woods and they LOVED to eat porridge, which is like oatmeal.

One day, Papa Bear was making a big pot of porridge. He was standing in front of the stove stirring and stirring, and finally the porridge seemed ready. He poured it into the bowls, put the bowls on the kitchen table, and called his family in for breakfast.

Papa Bear, Mama Bear, and Baby Bear sat down at their chairs, picked up their spoons, and got ready for a yummy breakfast! But the porridge was too hot! OUCH! "I almost burnt my mouth!" said Baby Bear. "This porridge is TOO hot!" said Mama Bear. "It's a lovely day!" said Papa Bear. "Why don't we go for a walk in the forest? By the time we return home, our porridge will be cool enough to eat."

So the three bears went for a walk in the forest.

On the edge of the forest, there was a house, and inside the house lived a little girl named Goldilocks. Goldilocks had never been in the forest before, but it was such a beautiful day that she decided to explore. She went walking through the trees and flowers, singing "TRA-LA-LA-LA-LA," and suddenly she came across the bears' cottage.

She peeked through the window and saw three bowls sitting on the kitchen table. She knocked at the door, but no one answered. She was very, very curious, and so she tried the door handle, and it swung right open! Goldilocks walked into the cottage.

She looked at the porridge in the bowls on the table, and it looked yummy. She sat down in Papa Bear's chair, picked up his spoon, and scooped a bite of porridge out of his bowl.

"This porridge is too hot!" she said. So she moved on to Mama Bear's chair. She picked up Mama Bear's spoon and scooped a bite of porridge out of her bowl. "This porridge is too cold!" She exclaimed. She then moved on to Baby Bear's chair, picked up his spoon, and scooped a bite of porridge out of his bowl. "This porridge is just right!" she said, and she ate it all up.

When she finished breakfast, she wanted a quick rest, so she went into the living room. There was no television, but there were three very comfortable-looking chairs.

First, she sat down in Papa Bear's chair. "This chair is too hard!" she said.

Then she sat down in Mama Bear's chair. "This chair is too soft!" she said.

Then she sat down in Baby Bear's chair. "This chair is just right!" she said. And she liked it so much that she rocked back and forth, and back and forth, and back and forth, until the chair fell to pieces.

By now, Goldilocks was quite tired, so she decided to look for a place to have a nap. She went upstairs to the bedroom. There were three beds.

First she tried Papa Bear's bed, but it was too high.

Then she tried Mama Bear's bed, but it was too low.

Then she tried Baby Bear's bed, and it was just right.

She climbed into Baby Bear's bed, pulled the covers up tight, and fell asleep. ZZZZzzzz.

Meanwhile, the Bear family returned from their walk in the forest. They were hungry and wanted to eat breakfast. But when they walked into the kitchen, they found an unpleasant surprise.

"Someone's been eating my porridge!" said Papa Bear.

"Someone's been eating my porridge!" said Mama Bear.

"Someone's been eating my porridge, and ate it all up!" said Baby Bear, "Oh, dear!"

"Let's sit down and try to figure out who could have done this," said Mama Bear.

So the three bears went into the living room, but there was an unpleasant surprise there as well.

"Someone's been sitting in my chair," said Papa Bear.

"Someone's been sitting in my chair!" said Mama Bear.

"Someone's been sitting in my chair and broke it all to pieces!" said Baby Bear, "Oh, dear!"

"This is so distressing! I think we could use a nap," said Mama Bear.

So the three bears went upstairs to their bedroom. But there was another unpleasant surprise there.

"Someone's been sleeping in my bed," said Papa Bear.

"Someone's been sleeping in my bed!" said Mama Bear.

"Someone's been sleeping in my bed—and she's still here!" said Baby Bear. "Look!"

The three bears gathered around the bed and looked down on sleeping Goldilocks.

"Wake up," said Papa Bear.

"Wake up," said Mama Bear.

"Wake up and get out of my bed!" said Baby Bear.

Goldilocks opened her eyes and saw that she was surrounded by the three bears. She jumped out of bed and ran out of the house as quickly as she could. She ran all the way home and promised her mother that she would never go into the forest again.

And as for the three bears . . . well, they learned a lot.

While Papa Bear made a new batch of porridge on the stove, Mama Bear installed some locks on the front door, and Baby Bear called Grandma to tell her all about their exciting morning.

The end!

Activity: "Open Them, Shut Them"
Start with closed fists and follow the directions in the song.

Open them, shut them.
Open them, shut them.
Give a little clap.

Open them, shut them
Open them, shut them.
Put them in your lap.

Creep them, creep them,
Creep them, creep them.
Right up to your chin.

Open up your little mouth . . .
But do not let them in!

STORY/ACTIVITY 2

Book: *Our Walk in the Woods* by Charity Nebbe, illustrated by Jeffrey Ebbeler
Read aloud.

>> DEVELOPMENTAL TIP
Children (and adults!) learn best through repetition. It is unlikely to learn the words of a song that you have heard only once. Yet after hearing the song a few times it often becomes easy to join in without even thinking about the lyrics. Stories and songs are rich in vocabulary words. Children who hear a song or story just once may or may not absorb everything. If it is repeated again and again, their connection with that story or song—and all the different ways they can learn from it—greatly increases.

Activity: "Going on a Bear Hunt"
Repeat "Going on a Bear Hunt" from week 1, but add a new line, "Look! There's a bicycle. Let's ride it!" in sing-song voice, recite "Pedal, pedal, pedal."

STORY/ACTIVITY 3

Book: *The Busy Tree* by Jennifer Ward, illustrated by Lisa Falkenstern
Read aloud.

Activity: "Two Red Apples in the Apple Tree"

Two red apples in the apple tree. (Hold up two fingers.)
Two red apples smiled down at me. (Point to a your big smile.)
I shook that tree as hard as I could. (Make shaking motions with both hands.)
Down fell the apples . . . (Swoop hands from up to down.)
MMMmmm they were good! (Rub tummy.)
Repeat this rhyme twice.

STORY 4

Book: *Ten Apples on Top* by Theo LeSieg, illustrated by Roy McKie
Read aloud.

CLOSING RITUAL

Vote

It's almost time to end our storytime, but I'd like to find out what books you liked the best. Everyone who liked the first story we heard, *The Three Bears* as a flannelboard story, please raise your hand.

Anyone who liked the book *Our Walk in the Woods* by Charity Nebbe, illustrated by Jeffrey Ebbeler, please raise your hand.

Anyone who liked the book *The Busy Tree* by Jennifer Ward, illustrated by Lisa Falkenstern, please raise your hand.

Anyone who liked the last book *Ten Apples on Top* by Theo LeSieg, illustrated by Roy McKie, please raise your hand.

And anyone who liked all the books we read today, please raise both hands, wave them around, and say, "WOO WOO WOO WOO WOO." *(Do this with the children.)*

Fingerplay: "Alligator, Alligator"

Now it's time to end with "Alligator, Alligator." (Repeat from week 1.)

Thanks for coming, and I hope to see you next week.

HANDOUT FOR PARENTS

Print out the printable coloring sheet with Baby Bear discovering Goldilocks at www.first-school.ws/t/cp_fstories/3bears_goldie.htm.

Dear parents,

Here is a coloring sheet relating to the story of "The Three Bears." Although many 3-to-5-year-olds cannot color within the lines, they may enjoy decorating the page. You may also want to use it as a springboard for discussing the story of "The Three Bears" with your children.

1. Ask if they remember what Papa Bear said. Mama Bear? Baby Bear?
2. What did Goldilocks do first: sit in the chair, eat the porridge, or sleep in the bed?
3. Ask your children to tell you their own version of the story. There is no right or wrong; free-flow storytelling gives them a chance to combine memory with imagination and develop narrative skills (learning that stories have a beginning, a middle, and an end).

BOOKS ABOUT TREES AND WOODS

Alborough, Jez. 2001. *My Friend Bear.* Cambridge, MA: Candlewick Press.

Braun, Sebastien. 2009. *On Our Way Home.* London: Boxer Books.

Gackenback, Dick. 1984. *Poppy the Panda.* New York: Clarion Books.

Henkes, Kevin. 2008. *Old Bear.* New York: Greenwillow Books.

Hoff, Syd. 1984. *Grizzwold.* New York: HarperCollins.

Lacome, Julie. 1993. *Walking through the Jungle.* Cambridge, MA: Candlewick Press.

Rueda, Claudia (author), and Elisa Amado (translator). 2010. *No.* Toronto: Groundwood Books/House of Anansi Press.

Sams, Carl R., and Jean Stoick. 2010. *Stranger in the Woods: A Photographic Fantasy.* Milford, MI: C. R. Sams II Photography.

Wilson, Karma (author), and Jane Chapman (illustrator). 2008. *Bear Feels Scared.* New York: Margaret K. McElderry.

Week 3: Narrate the Story and Have Children Act It Out

Week 3 Outline

Repetition with Variety: Use "The Three Bears" in a new way by telling it while the children act it out

Theme: Hiding and Finding

Beginning Ritual
- **Introduction**
- **Fingerplay:** "Alligator, Alligator" (repeated from weeks 1 and 2)

Story/Activity 1
- **Book:** *Peace at Last* by Jill Murphy
- **Activity:** "Open Them, Shut Them" (repeated from week 2)

Story/Activity 2
- **Book:** Focus text retold while children act it out, *The Three Bears* by Paul Galdone
- **Developmental Tip:** The value of dramatic play
- **Activity:** "Going on a Bear Hunt," modified (repeated from weeks 1 and 2)

Story/Activity 3
- **Book:** *The Three Billy Goats Gruff* by Paul Galdone
- **Activity:** "Two Red Apples in the Apple Tree" (repeated from week 2)
- **Activity:** Fun with Scarves: "Peek-a-Boo," "This Is the Way We Wash," "Oh Where, Oh Where Has My Little Head Gone?" and "Scarves Away"

Story 4
- **Book:** *Peek-a-Moo* by Marie Torres Cimarusti, illustrated by Stephanie Peterson

Closing Ritual
- **Vote**
- **Fingerplay:** "Alligator, Alligator" (repeated from weeks 1 and 2)

BOOKS NEEDED

Cimarusti, Marie Torres (author), and Stephanie Peterson (illustrator). 1998.
    Peek-a-Moo. New York: Dutton's Children's Books.
Galdone, Paul. 2001. *The Three Billy Goats Gruff*. New York: Clarion.
———. 2011. *The Three Bears*. Boston: Houghton Mifflin Harcourt.
Murphy, Jill. 1980. *Peace at Last*. New York: Dial Press.

Script

BEGINNING RITUAL

Introduction
Introduce yourself and welcome everyone.

Fingerplay: "Alligator, Alligator"
Remember "Alligator, Alligator"? Let's do it together! (Repeat from weeks 1 and 2.)

STORY/ACTIVITY 1

Book: *Peace at Last* by Jill Murphy

Here's a story called *Peace at Last* by Jill Murphy about a bear family. Papa Bear is very tired and wants to sleep, but there is always a noise that keeps him awake. As I am reading the story aloud, please make the noises with me. *(Read aloud. Children make the noises with you.)*

Activity: "Open Them, Shut Them"

Repeat from week 2.

STORY/ACTIVITY 2

Book: *The Three Bears* by Paul Galdone

Do you remember the story of the *Three Bears?* (Hold up the book by Paul Galdone while asking the question.) We've heard the story for two weeks, now. And this week I would like to tell the story while you act it out.

Everyone who wants to be Goldilocks, stand over on this side! *(Point to where you want the children to stand.)*

Everyone who wants to be Papa Bear, stand over here. *(Point to where you want the children to stand.)*

Everyone who wants to be Mama Bear, stand over here. *(Point to where you want the children to stand.)*

Everyone who wants to be Baby Bear, stand over here. *(Point to where you want the children to stand.)*

As I tell the story, I would like you to act out your parts. Here we go! *(Tell the story.)*

Once upon a time there were three bears. A papa bear, a mama bear, and a baby bear. They lived in a house in the woods and they LOVED to eat porridge, which is like oatmeal.

One day, Papa Bear was making a big pot of porridge. He was standing in front of the stove stirring and stirring, and finally the porridge seemed ready. He poured it into the bowls, put the bowls on the kitchen table, and called his family in for breakfast.

Papa Bear, Mama Bear, and Baby Bear sat down at their chairs, picked up their spoons, and got ready for a yummy breakfast! But the porridge was too hot! OUCH! "I almost burnt my mouth!" said Baby Bear. "This porridge is TOO hot!" said Mama Bear. "It's a lovely day!" said Papa Bear. "Why don't we go for a walk in the forest? By the time we return home, our porridge will be cool enough to eat."

So the three bears went for a walk in the forest.

On the edge of the forest, there was a house, and inside the house lived a little girl named Goldilocks. Goldilocks had never been in the forest before, but it was such a beautiful day that she decided to explore. She went walking through the trees and flowers, singing "TRA-LA-LA-LA-LA," and suddenly she came across the bears' cottage.

She peeked through the window and saw three bowls sitting on the kitchen table. She knocked at the door—KNOCK, KNOCK, KNOCK—but no one answered. She was very, very curious, and so she tried the door handle, and it swung right open! Goldilocks walked into the cottage.

She looked at the porridge in the bowls on the table, and it looked yummy—YUM, YUM, YUM! She sat down in Papa Bear's chair, picked up his spoon, and scooped a bite of porridge out of his bowl.

"This porridge is too hot!" she said. So she moved on to Mama Bear's chair. She picked up Mama Bear's spoon and scooped a bite of porridge out of her bowl. "This porridge is too cold!" She exclaimed. She then moved on to Baby Bear's chair, picked up his spoon, and scooped a bite of porridge out of his bowl. "This porridge is just right!" she said, and she ate it all up—GOBBLE, GOBBLE, GOBBLE.

When she finished breakfast, she wanted a quick rest, so she went into the living room. There was no television, but there were three very comfortable-looking chairs.

First, she sat down in Papa Bear's chair. "This chair is too hard!" she said.

Then she sat down in Mama Bear's chair. "This chair is too soft," she said.

Then sat down in Baby Bear's chair. "This chair is just right!" she said. And she liked it so much that she rocked back and forth, and back and forth, and back and forth, until the chair fell to pieces.

By now, Goldilocks was quite tired, so she decided to look for a place to have a nap. She went upstairs to the bedroom. There were three beds.

First she tried Papa Bear's bed, but it was too high.

Then she tried Mama Bear's bed, but it was too low.

Then she tried Baby Bear's bed, and it was just right.

She climbed into Baby Bear's bed, pulled the covers up tight, and fell asleep. ZZZZZZZzzzzzz . . .

Meanwhile, the Bear family returned from their walk in the forest. They were hungry and wanted to eat breakfast. But when they walked into the kitchen, they found an unpleasant surprise.

"Someone's been eating my porridge!" said Papa Bear.

"Someone's been eating my porridge!" said Mama Bear.

"Someone's been eating my porridge, and ate it all up!" said Baby Bear, "Oh, dear!"

"Let's sit down and try to figure out who could have done this," said Mama Bear.

So the three bears went into the living room, but there was an unpleasant surprise there, as well.

"Someone's been sitting in my chair," said Papa Bear.

"Someone's been sitting in my chair!" said Mama Bear.

"Someone's been sitting in my chair and broke it all to pieces!" said Baby Bear, "Oh, dear!"

"This is so distressing! I think we could use a nap," said Mama Bear.

So the three bears went upstairs to their bedroom. But there was another unpleasant surprise there.

"Someone's been sleeping in my bed," said Papa Bear.

"Someone's been sleeping in my bed!" said Mama Bear.

"Someone's been sleeping in my bed—and she's still here!" said Baby Bear. "Look!"

The three bears gathered around the bed and looked down on sleeping Goldilocks.

"Wake up," said Papa Bear.

"Wake up," said Mama Bear.

"Wake up and get out of my bed!" said Baby Bear.

Goldilocks opened her eyes and saw that she was surrounded by the three bears. She jumped out of bed and ran out of the house as quickly as she could. She ran all the way home and promised her mother that she would never go into the forest again.

And as for the three bears . . . well, they learned a lot.

While Papa Bear made a new batch of porridge on the stove, Mama Bear installed some locks on the front door, and Baby Bear called Grandma to tell her all about their exciting morning.

The end!

>> DEVELOPMENTAL TIP

Acting out stories introduces children to the theater arts. Well-loved stories such as *The Three Bears* shows children that stories have a beginning, a middle, and an end. Because dramatic play incorporates a variety of senses, it allows children to experience a story in an immediate way and helps them internalize the structure as well as the content of the story.

Activity: "Going on a Bear Hunt"

Repeat "Going on a Bear Hunt" from weeks 1 and 2, including "Look! There's a bicycle. Let's ride it!" (in a sing-song voice, recite "Pedal, pedal, pedal"). Add another line: "Look! A tree. Can't go through it. Must climb up! Must climb back down." (make climbing motions).

STORY/ACTIVITY 3

Book: *The Three Billy Goats Gruff* by Paul Galdone

Here's another book written by Paul Galdone. This one is called *The Three Billy Goats Gruff*. As you can see, the illustrations seem a bit similar to the ones in *The Three Bears*. That's because Paul Galdone drew all the pictures in both books! And this story is similar to *The Three Bears* because there are also parts you can say with me. When the goats go over the bridge, it makes a noise: "Trip, trap, trip, trap."

Can you try that with me? (*Pause while the children say, "Trip, trap, trip, trap."*) Great! Now I'm going to read the story aloud and want to you help me with the bridge sounds wherever you can. (*Read aloud.*)

Activity: "Two Red Apples in the Apple Tree"

The three goats went to the other side of the bridge so they could get some grass to eat . . . Well, I am getting hungry too and I would LOVE to have one nice, red apple. Hmm, where do you think I can find one? (Repeat from week 2.)

Activity: Fun with Scarves

Hand out colored scarves to everyone. Walk around and briefly play peekaboo with each child.

Let's pretend these scarves are washcloths. *(Pretend the scarves are washcloths.)* Let's scrunch them up into balls and wash our necks.

"This Is the Way We Wash"

This is the way we wash our neck, wash our neck, wash our neck,
This is the way we wash our neck, so early in the morning.

What else can we wash? *(Take suggestions from the children, and using their suggestions, sing a few more verses.)*

Now put your scarves over your heads and let's sing this song.

"Oh Where, Oh Where Has My Little Head Gone?"
(to the tune of "Oh Where, Oh Where, Has My Little Dog Gone?")

Oh where, oh where has my little head gone?
Oh where, oh where can it be?
Oh where, oh where has my little head gone?
Oh where, oh where can it be?
1 . . . 2 . . . 3 . . . HERE IT IS! (Pull off scarf.)

Repeat with hand, knee, foot.

Now it's time to put our scarves away.

Collect scarves by walking around with an open tote bag. Encourage the children to drop their scarves in the bag by singing:

"Scarves Away" *(by Barbara Cass-Beggs)*

Scarves away, scarves away,
Put your scarves away today.

A recording of this song can be found at www.cdbaby.com/cd/bdcr/ on Listen, Like, Learn with Mother Goose on the Loose, *track 90.*

STORY 4

Book: *Peek-a-Moo* by Marie Torres Cimarusti, illustrated by Stephanie Peterson

We've had a chance to play peekaboo with our scarves; now let's see how some animals play peekaboo. Can you help me with the sounds the animals make in this book, *Peek-a-Moo* by Marie Torres Cimarusti, illustrated by Stephanie Peterson? *(Read the book aloud, encouraging the children to chime in.)*

CLOSING RITUAL

Vote

It's almost time to end our storytime, but I'd like to find out what books you liked the best. Everyone who liked the first story we heard, *Peace At Last* by Jill Murphy, please raise your hand.

Anyone who liked acting out the story of *The Three Bears*, please raise your hand.

Anyone who liked the book *The Three Billy Goats Gruff* by Paul Galdone, please raise your hand.

Anyone who liked the last book, *Peek-a-Moo* by Marie Torres Cimarusti, illustrated by Stephanie Peterson, please raise your hand.

And anyone who liked all the books we read today, please raise both hands, wave them around, and say, "WOO WOO WOO WOO WOO."

Fingerplay: "Alligator, Alligator"

Now it's time to end with "Alligator, Alligator." (Repeat from weeks 1 and 2.)

Thanks for coming, and I hope to see you next week.

BOOKS ABOUT HIDING AND FINDING

Cimarusti, Marie Torres (author), and Stephanie Peterson (illustrator). 1998. *Peek-a-Moo*. New York: Dutton Children's Books.

———. 2005 *Peek-a-Boooo!* New York: Dutton Children's Books.

Isadora, Rachel. 2008. *Peekaboo Morning*. New York: G. P. Putnam's Sons.

Klassen, Jon. 2011. *I Want My Hat Back*. Somerville, MA: Candlewick Press.

Meyer, Mercer. 2003, *A Boy, A Dog, and a Frog*. New York: Dial.

Rosen, Michael (author), and Helen Oxenbury (illustrator). 2009. *We're Going on a Bear Hunt*. New York: Margaret K. McElderry. (This book is available on Amazon.com in many languages, including Chinese, Vietnamese, English and Czech, Portuguese, Serbo-Croatian, Tamil, Turkish, and Farsi.)

Scarry, Patsy (author), and Richard Scarry (illustrator). 2001. *Good Night, Little Bear*. New York: Golden Books.

BOOKS ABOUT NOISES

Burleigh, Robert (author), and Beppe Giacobbe (illustrator). 2009. *Clang-Clang! Beep-Beep! Listen to the City.* New York: Simon & Schuster Books for Young Readers.

Hillenbrand, Will. 2011. *Spring Is Here!* New York: Holiday House.

Joosse, Barbara M. (author), and Jan Jutte (illustrator). 2009. *Roawr!* New York: Philomel Books.

Martin, Bill, Jr. (author), and Eric Carle (illustrator). 2011. *Polar Bear, Polar Bear, What Do You Hear?* New York: Henry Holt.

Underwood, Deborah. 2011. *The Loud Book.* Boston: Houghton Mifflin Books for Children.

Week 4: Read Other Versions of the Story by Different Authors and Illustrators

Week 4 Outline

Repetition with Variety: Read the same story by a different author and illustrator, make oatmeal and have a porridge party

Theme: Food

Beginning Ritual
- **Introduction**
- **Fingerplay:** "Alligator, Alligator" (repeated from weeks 1–3)

Story/Activity 1
- **Book:** *The Little Mouse, the Red Ripe Strawberry, and the Big Hungry Bear* by Don and Audrey Wood, illustrated by Don Wood
- **Activity:** "The Bear Hokey Pokey" (repeated from week 1)

Story/Activity 2
- **Book:** Same story as focus text, but by a different author and illustrator, *Goldilocks and the Three Bears* by Jan Brett
- **Activity:** "Porridge Party"
- **Developmental Tip:** Cooking with your children
- **Activity:** "Pease Porridge Hot"

Story/Activity 3
- **Book:** *No Mush Today* by Sally Derby, illustrated by Nicole Tadgell
- **Activity:** Fun with Bells: "We Ring Our Bells Together," "Pease Porridge Hot," "Frère Jacques," "Grandfather's Clock," "Bells Away" (adapted from "Scarves Away" from week 3)

Story 4
- **Book:** *Food: A Lift-the-Flap Shadow Book* by Roger Priddy

Closing Ritual
- **Vote**
- **Fingerplay:** "Alligator, Alligator" (repeated from weeks 1–3)

ITEMS NEEDED

- packages of instant oatmeal
- electric kettle, filled with water
- plastic spoons (enough for each participant)
- "hot cups" (enough for each participant)
- big bowl
- napkins
- trash can nearby

BOOKS NEEDED

Brett, Jan. 1987. *Goldilocks and the Three Bears*. New York: Dodd, Mead.

Derby, Sally, and Nicole Tadgell. 2008. *No Mush Today*. New York: Lee & Low.

Galdone, Paul. 2011. *The Three Bears*. Boston: Houghton Mifflin Harcourt.

Priddy, Roger. 2010. *Food: A Lift-the-Flap Shadow Book*. New York: Priddy Books.

Wood, Don and Audrey (authors), and Don Wood (illustrator). 2003. T*he Little Mouse, the Red Ripe Strawberry, and the Big Hungry Bear*. New York: Scholastic.

SETUP

Fill the kettle with water.

Script

BEGINNING RITUAL

Introduction
Introduce yourself and welcome everyone.

Today we are going to have a porridge party in storytime! But first, let's recite "Alligator, Alligator."

Fingerplay: "Alligator, Alligator"
Repeat from weeks 1–3.

STORY/ACTIVITY 1

Book: *The Little Mouse, the Red Ripe Strawberry, and the Big Hungry Bear* by Don and Audrey Wood, illustrated by Don Wood

Our first story is *The Little Mouse, the Red Ripe Strawberry, and the Big Hungry Bear* by Don and Audrey Wood. *(Hold up the book to show the cover.)* Look at the cover of this book and see if you can guess what it is about. *(Pause to listen for answers.)* Now I am going to read the story, and you will see if you read the clues on the cover correctly! *(Read the book aloud.)*

Activity: "The Bear Hokey Pokey"

Let's all stand up and do the bear hokey pokey! (Repeat from week 1.)

STORY/ACTIVITY 2

Book: *Goldilocks and the Three Bears* by Jan Brett

For the past couple of weeks, we've been reading or talking about Paul Galdone's version of "The Three Bears." Today, I have another version to read to you of the same story. Look carefully at the illustrations and tell me afterward what pictures looked the same and which ones looked different from the book we were using before. *(After reading the story aloud, ask the children what was the same and what was different.)*

Activity: "Porridge Party"

Do you remember that I said we were going to have a porridge party today? Well, here is our special treat! *(Hold up a packet of instant oatmeal.)* Have you ever seen this before? Do you know what it is?

It's instant oatmeal. And the type of hot cereal that we call *oatmeal,* in some places might be called *porridge.* That's right . . . the hot cereal that Papa Bear made for his family in the story of the Three Bears might have been oatmeal.

Everyone who has ever tasted oatmeal, please raise their hands. *(Count aloud the number of hands raised.)* Wow, that's a good amount. Well, I am going to make some oatmeal today, and anyone who wants to try some is welcome to have a bit. *(Follow each spoken description below with the corresponding action.)*

First I am going to open a package of instant oatmeal and put it in a bowl.

Then I am going to boil some water in this electric kettle and wait until it clicks, which means that the kettle is hot enough and the water has boiled.

Then I am going to pour the water into this bowl and stir it around.

I need to wait a few minutes for all the water to be absorbed.

Now I am going to dish a bit of oatmeal out into these small cups, so that I have enough for everyone.

Please take a spoon as I pass the cups around.

On the count of three, let's all take a taste of our oatmeal. 1, 2, 3 . . . Isn't it good?

I think this is just like the porridge that the Three Bears ate! Only ours isn't too hot, it isn't too cold . . . it is just right!

>> DEVELOPMENTAL TIP

When at home, cook with your children! Talk about what you are doing as you do it, to help them understand all the steps involved. These types of experiences help children understand the world around them and deepen their connection with you at the same time.

Activity: "Pease Porridge Hot"

Clap your hands and tap your legs to the beat as we recite this rhyme:

"Pease Porridge Hot"

Pease porridge hot.
Pease porridge cold.
Pease porridge in the pot,
Nine days old.

Some like it hot.
Some like it cold.
Some like it in the pot,
Nine days old.

Repeat.

STORY/ACTIVITY 3

Book: *No Mush Today* by Sally Derby, illustrated by Nicole Tadgell

Here's a book called *No Mush Today* by Sally Derby, illustrated by Nicole Tadgell. *(Read story aloud.)*

Activity: "Fun with Bells"

Hand out bells to everyone. Sing together.

"We Ring Our Bells Together"
(by Barbara Cass-Beggs; to the tune of "The Farmer in the Dell")

We ring our bells together. We ring our bells together.
We ring our bells together, because it's fun to do.
We ring our bells together. We ring our bells together.
We ring our bells together, because it's fun to do.

Ring them up high. *(Sing in a high voice while ringing the bell above your head.)*
Ring them down low. *(Sing in a low voice while ringing the bell way down low.)*
Ring them in the middle. *(Sing in your normal voice while ringing the bell in front of you.)*

A recording of this song can be found at www.cdbaby.com/cd/bdcr/ on Listen, Like,
Learn with Mother Goose on the Loose, *track 79.*

Let's ring our bells to the beat of "Pease Porridge Hot":

"Pease Porridge Hot"

Pease porridge hot.
Pease porridge cold.
Pease porridge in the pot,
Nine days old.

Some like it hot.
Some like it cold.
Some like it in the pot,
Nine days old.

Continue ringing your bells to this song.

"Frère Jacques"

Are you sleeping? Are you sleeping?
Brother John? Brother John?
Morning bells are ringing. Morning bells are ringing.
Ding, ding, dong. Ding, ding, dong.

Frère Jacques, frère Jacques,
Dormez vous? Dormez vous?
Sonnez les matines, sonnez les matines,
Ding ding dong. Ding, ding, dong.

One more song!

"Grandfather's Clock"

Grandfather's clock goes, "Tick, tock, tick tock." *(Ring bells slowly on the beat to "Tick, tock, tick tock.")*
Mother's kitchen clock goes, "Tick, tock, tick, tock, tick, tock, tick, tock." *(Ring bells to a quicker beat on each "Tick, tock.")*
Brother's little watch goes, "Tick, tick, tick, tick, tick, tick, tick, tick, tick, tick, tick, tick . . . STOP!" *(Ring bells very quickly to each "tick" and then STOP.)*

Now we'll put our bells away. *(Walk around collecting bells while singing.)*

"Bells Away"
(adapted from "Scarves Away" from week 3, by Barbara Cass-Beggs)
Bells away, bells away,
Put your bells away today.

A recording of this song can be found at www.cdbaby.com/cd/bdcr/ on Listen, Like, Learn with Mother Goose on the Loose, *track 86.*

STORY 4

Book: *Food: A Lift-the-Flap Shadow Book* by Roger Priddy
Can you name the different foods in this book, *Food* by Roger Priddy? *(Read aloud, pausing to allow children to call out the answers.)*

CLOSING RITUAL

Vote
It's almost time to end our storytime, but I'd like to find out which parts of storytime you liked. Everyone who liked the first story we heard, *The Little Mouse, the Red Ripe Strawberry, and the Big Hungry Bear* by Don and Audrey Wood, please raise your hand.

Anyone who liked Jan Brett's version of *Goldilocks and The Three Bears*, please raise your hand.

Anyone who liked the porridge party, please raise your hand.

Anyone who liked the book *No Mush Today* by Sally Derby with illustrations by Nicole Tadgell, please raise your hand.

Anyone who liked our final book, *Food* by Roger Priddy, raise your hand.

And anyone who liked all of the books we read today, please raise both hands, wave them around, and say, "WOO WOO WOO WOO WOO."

Fingerplay: "Alligator, Alligator"
Now it's time to end with "Alligator, Alligator." (Repeat from weeks 1–3.)

Thanks for coming, and I hope to see you next week.

HANDOUT FOR PARENTS

(For a giveaway for children and their parents, go to this website: www.firstpalette.com/ Craft_themes/Animals/circlesbear/circlesbear.html. Prepare the pieces for a bear and put

it in a zip-close sandwich bag for the children to do at home with their parents. Or, simply give the parents the web address and encourage them to work together with their children on the project.)

BOOKS ABOUT FOOD

Berkner, Laurie. 2007. *Victor Vito and Freddie Vasco*. New York: Cartwheel Books.
This book comes with an entertaining CD; children will enjoy singing along.

Blackall, Sophie, and Meg Rosoff. 2008. *Wild Boars Cook*. New York: Henry Holt.

Degen, Bruce. 2008. *Jamberry*. New York: HarperCollins.

Denise, Anika (author), and Christopher Denise (illustrator). 2007. *Pigs Love Potatoes*. New York: Philomel Books.

Derby, Sally. 2008. *No Mush Today*. New York: Lee & Low.
Fed up with the new baby in the house, an African American girl refuses to eat her mushy porridge.

Goldstone, Bruce (author), and Blair Lent (illustrator). 2001. *The Beastly Feast*. New York: Henry Holt.

Grey, Mini. 2007. *Ginger Bear*. New York: Knopf Books for Young Readers.

McCloskey, Robert. 2010. *Blueberries for Sal*. New York: Puffin Books.

Page, Robin, and Steve Jenkins. 2011. *Time to Eat*. Boston: Houghton Mifflin Books for Children.

Pierce, Terry. 2008. *Blackberry Banquet*. Mount Pleasant, SC: Sylvan Dell.

Rayner, Catherine. 2011. *The Bear Who Shared*. New York: Dial Books for Young Readers.

Watanabe, Shigeo (author), and Yasuo Ohtomo (illustrator). 1982. *How Do I Eat It?* Harmondsworth: Puffin.

Wheeler, Lisa. 2010. *Ugly Pie*. Boston: Harcourt Children's Books.

Wilson, Karma (author), and Jane Chapman (illustrator). 2003. *Bear Wants More*. New York: Margaret K. McElderry.

Week 5: Read a Fractured Version; Find Opposites in the Book

Week 5 Outline

Repetition with Variety: Read a fractured version of the story; find opposites in the book

Theme: Opposites

Beginning Ritual
- **Introduction**
- **Fingerplay:** "Alligator, Alligator" (repeated from weeks 1–4)

Story/Activity 1
- **Book:** *Fortunately* by Remy Charlip
- **Developmental Tip:** Explaining the meaning of words
- **Activity:** "Open Them, Shut Them" (repeated from weeks 2 and 3)

Story/Activity 2
- **Book:** Fractured version of focus text, *The Three Bears and Goldilocks* by Margaret Willey, illustrated by Heather Solomon
- **Activity:** "What Is the Same or Different?"
- **Activity:** "The Bear Hokey Pokey" (repeated from weeks 1 and 4)
- **Activity:** "Bear Creative Dramatics"

Story/Activity 3
- **Book:** *Fast Slow / Rápido lento* by Sharon Gordon
- **Activity:** "Two Little Brown Bears Playing in the Snow"

Story/Activity 4
- **Book:** *A Garden of Opposites* by Nancy Davis
- **Activity:** "Finding Opposites in *The Three Bears*"

Story 5 (if there is time)
- **Book:** *Opposites* by Eric Carle

Closing Ritual
- **Vote**
- **Fingerplay:** "Alligator, Alligator" (repeated from weeks 1–4)

ITEMS NEEDED

- flannelboard with white board or blackboard on the other side
- erasable markers or chalk
- possibly poster tape and masking tape

BOOKS NEEDED

Charlip, Remy. 1986. *Fortunately*. New York: Four Winds Press.

Davis, Nancy. 2009. *A Garden of Opposites*. New York: Schwartz & Wade.

Galdone, Paul. 2011. *The Three Bears*. Boston: Houghton Mifflin Harcourt.

Gordon, Sharon. 2007. *Fast Slow / Rápido lento*. New York: Marshall Cavendish Benchmark

Willey, Margaret (author), and Heather Solomon (illustrator). 2008. *The Three Bears and Goldilocks*. New York: Atheneum Books for Young Readers.

Script

BEGINNING RITUAL

Introduction
Introduce yourself and welcome everyone.

Today we are going to talk about opposites in storytime! But first, let's do "Alligator Alligator."

Fingerplay: "Alligator, Alligator"
Repeat from weeks 1–4.

STORY/ACTIVITY 1

Book: *Fortunately* by Remy Charlip
Raise your hand if you know what *fortunately* means. It means "luckily." When something good happens to you by chance, it is *fortunate*. But if something bad happens just by chance, it is *unfortunate*. Here is a story called *Fortunately* by Remy Charlip. *(Read aloud.)*

>> DEVELOPMENTAL TIP
Having a large vocabulary helps children understand what they hear and what they will later read. When reading a story aloud to your child, instead of replacing unfamiliar words, explain them.

Activity: "Open Them, Shut Them"
Repeat from weeks 2 and 3.

STORY/ACTIVITY 2

Book: *The Three Bears and Goldilocks* by Margaret Willey, illustrated by Heather Solomon
Do you remember this book? *(Hold up a copy of Paul Galdone's* The Three Bears.*)* Here is a different version of the story, told by someone else in a totally different way! It is called *The Three Bears and Goldilocks,* and it was written by Margaret Willey and illustrated by Heather Solomon. *(Hold up a copy of this book.)* This is called a fractured fairy tale because it does not tell the story the way you or I tell it. It has a lot of new developments. Let me know at the end if you've noticed anything different about this story from the one we read before. *(Read aloud.)*

Activity: "What is the same or different?"

Raise your hand if you noticed anything different in this book *(hold up a copy of Willey's book)* from this book *(hold up a copy of Galdone's book).* *(You may or may not choose to ask the children what they noticed, depending on time considerations and the nature of your group.)*

Time to stand up!

Activity: "The Bear Hokey Pokey"

Stand up and do the bear hokey pokey (repeat from weeks 1 and 4). At the end, ask the children to remain standing.

Let's all give a big growl: GRRRRRRR! But don't sit down yet . . .

Activity: "Bear Creative Dramatics"

Did you know that bears like to sleep in their caves in the wintertime? That's called *hibernation.* Can you pretend to be a bear hibernating? *(Lie down.)*

Winter is over! Time to wake up! The bears are stretching *(stretch)* and yawning *(yawn)* and getting up to look for something to eat. *(Get up.)*

What do bears like to eat?

Right! They love to eat honey! So the bears start walking around looking for honey. *(Walk around.)*

Is there honey on the ground? No! The honey is in a beehive that is up in a tree. So look up high and see if you can spot a beehive. *(Pretend to be looking up high.)*

There's a beehive. It's too high to reach, so we'll have to climb up the tree. *(Pretend to climb.)*

Boy, this is very high. Paw over paw, paw over paw, we're going up, up, up.

There's the beehive, out on that branch! We'll have to crawl very carefully so we don't fall off.

Slowly, slowly, paw over paw, paw over paw, slowly, slowly, almost there . . . *(Mimic these motions.)*

The branch is bending, the branch is breaking . . . oh no, the branch is shaking!

Here's the beehive I just found . . . but now I'm falling to the ground . . . *(Pretend to fall.)*

Kerplop! *(Pretend to rub sore bottom.)*

That's wasn't funny. I wanted some honey. *(Pretend to cry.)*

It wasn't a joke, a branch simply broke!

But look, on the ground . . . it's a beehive I've found. *(Pretend to hold up a beehive.)*

Fortunately, it fell out of the tree.

Lucky, lucky, lucky me!

STORY/ACTIVITY 3

Book: *Fast Slow / Rápido lento* by Sharon Gordon

This is a book about opposites, two things that are totally different from each other. Can you help me with it? It's called *Fast Slow / Rápido lento* by Sharon Gordon. *(Read the book aloud. Encourage the children to call out the names of the opposites if they know them.)*

Activity: "Two Little Brown Bears Playing in the Snow"

Make your fingers into two little brown bears like this. *(Make hands into fists and hold them in front of you. Stick up the index finger on each hand.)*

"Two Little Brown Bears Playing in the Snow"

Two little brown bears playing in the snow. *(Gently bounce two fists up and down.)*
One named "Fast." *(Say quickly in a high voice while quickly extending one arm in front.)*
The other named "Slow." *(Say slowly in a deep voice while slowly extending the other arm.)*
Run away, Fast. *(Say this as quickly as possible while quickly moving one arm behind you.)*
Run away, Slow. *(Say this as slowly as possible in a deep voice while very slowly moving the other arm behind you.)*
Come back, Fast. *(Say this as quickly as possible while quickly bringing arm back.)*
Come back, Slow. *(Say this as slowly as possible in a deep voice while slowly bringing other arm back.)*

Repeat.

STORY/ACTIVITY 4

Book: *A Garden of Opposites* by Nancy Davis

Here's a book called *A Garden of Opposites* by Nancy Davis. Can you help me with this? *(Read aloud. Encourage the children to call out answers.)*

Activity: "Finding opposites in *The Three Bears*"

We've been talking about opposites today, and there are lots of opposites in this book. *(Hold up Paul Galdone's* The Three Bears.*)* You all know the story very well by now. I'm going to show you the illustrations and describe what is happening on the page. If I use words that are opposites, raise your hands. I'm going to turn the flannelboard around and if you can name the opposites mentioned, I will write your answers down. Let's see how many opposites we can find in this book! *(Turn the flannelboard/easel around. Use chalk or erasable marker—depending on the type of easel you have—to record the children's answers. If your easel does not have a place for writing on the nonflannel side, tape a sheet of poster paper over the flannelboard and write on that.)*

STORY 5 (IF THERE IS TIME)

Book: *Opposites* by Eric Carle

Please help me with this book, *Opposites* by Eric Carle, by calling out the names of objects and their opposites. *(Read aloud if there is time. Encourage the children to call out answers.)*

CLOSING RITUAL

Vote

It's almost time to end our storytime, but I'd like to find out what books you liked. Everyone who liked the first story we heard, *Fortunately* by Remy Charlip, please raise your hand.

Anyone who liked *The Three Bears and Goldilocks* by Margaret Willey with illustrations by Heather Solomon, please raise your hand.

Anyone who liked *Fast Slow / Rápido lento* by Sharon Gordon, please raise your hand.

Anyone who liked the book *A Garden of Opposites* by Nancy Davis, please raise your hand.

Anyone who liked the last book *Opposites* by Eric Carle, please raise your hand.

And everyone who liked all of the books we read today, please raise both hands, wave them around, and say, "WOO WOO WOO WOO WOO."

Fingerplay: "Alligator, Alligator"

Now it's time to end with "Alligator, Alligator." (Repeated from weeks 1–4.)

Thanks for coming, and I hope to see you next week. Here is a handout with the web address for an exciting British version of "Goldilocks and the Three Bears." Listen to it at home or at the library during the week and see if you hear the opposites in the story. *(Distribute handouts.)*

HANDOUTS FOR PARENTS

Computer Fun

Here is the web address from the BBC for an exciting British version of Goldilocks and the Three Bears. Listen to it at home or at the library during the week and see if you hear the opposites in the story: www.bbc.co.uk/cbeebies/fimbles/stories/threebears/.

Games to Play

A simple game to play with your child that can help build vocabulary, interest, and delight in language is the opposite game. Say a word (such as *go*) and ask your child "What's the opposite word?" *(stop)* Ask your child to name a word and you will guess the opposite.

BOOKS ABOUT OPPOSITES

Berenstain, Stan, and Jan Berenstain. 1998. *Old Hat, New Hat*. New York: Random House.

———. 1998. *The Berenstain Bears Big Bear, Small Bear*. New York: Random House.

Boyer, Robin. 2000. *Pumpkins! A Book of Opposites*. Grand Haven, MI: School Zone.

Brooks, Erik. 2010. *Polar Opposites*. Tarrytown, NY: Marshall Cavendish.

Crowther, Robert. 2005. *Opposites*. Cambridge, MA: Candlewick Press.

Dunbar, Joyce. 2000. *The Very Small*. Boston: Harcourt Children's Books.

Lamb, Albert. 2011. *Tell Me the Day Backwards*. Cambridge, MA: Candlewick Press.

Mayhew, James. 2008. *Can You See a Little Bear?* London: Frances Lincoln Children's Books.

Weill, Cynthia, Quirino Santiago, and Martin Santiago. 2009. *Opuestos: Mexican Folk Art Opposites in English and Spanish*. El Paso, TX: Cinco Puntos Press.

Week 6: Give Children Props to Play with While They Retell the Story Themselves

Week 6 Outline

Repetition with Variety: Invite the children to choose props and retell the story themselves

Theme: Bear Families

Beginning Ritual
- **Introduction**
- **Fingerplay:** "Alligator, Alligator" (repeated from weeks 1–5)

Story/Activity 1
- **Book:** *Bears for Kids* or *The Great American Bear* by Jeff Fair, with photographs by Lynn Rogers
- **Activity:** "Bear Creative Dramatics" (repeated from week 5)

Story/Activity 2
- **Book:** Brief retelling of focus text, *The Three Bears* by Paul Galdone
- **Activity:** Children use props to act out and help retell the story
- **Activity:** "Papa Bear and Baby Bear Playing with a Ball"
- **Activity:** Matching Sizes game using flannelboard pieces
- **Developmental Tip:** Appreciating others

Story 3 (if there is time)
- **Book:** *Just Like Daddy* by Frank Asch

Closing Ritual
- **Vote**
- **Fingerplay:** "Alligator, Alligator" (repeated from weeks 1–5)

ITEMS NEEDED

- 3 towels of different sizes
- stick puppets for each participant (made with craft sticks, glue sticks, and photocopied pictures)
- flannelboard
- 2 strips of felt
- felt bears (enough to give one to each participant)
- plastic sandwich bags

BOOKS NEEDED

Asch, Frank. 1996. *Just Like Daddy*. Boston: Houghton Mifflin.

Fair, Jeff (author), and Lynn L. Rogers (photographer). 1990. *The Great American Bear*. Minocqua, WI: NorthWord Press.

———. 1991. *Bears for Kids*. Minocqua, WI: NorthWord Press

Galdone, Paul. 2011. *The Three Bears*. Boston: Houghton Mifflin Harcourt.

PREPARATION

Stick puppets: Photocopy the templates for figures 3.1 through 3.8. Cut them out and glue them onto craft sticks to make enough stick puppets to give one of each character to each child.

Felt bears: Photocopy templates for Papa Bear, Mama Bear, and Baby Bear. Cut them out and use tacky glue to paste them onto pieces of felt. There should be one bear for each child.

Script

BEGINNING RITUAL

Introduction
Introduce yourself and welcome everyone.

Fingerplay: "Alligator, Alligator"
Today there is a VERY BIG alligator in the library, so let's do "Alligator, Alligator" with our big hand movements and deep voices. (Repeat "Alligator, Alligator" from weeks 1–5.)

Now let's try it for all the baby alligators, using very small hand movements and soft voices. *(Recite with appropriate hand movements and soft voices.)*

Let's do "Alligator, Alligator" one more time, using our regular hand movements and our normal voices. *(Recite with the appropriate hand movements and normal voices.)*

STORY/ACTIVITY 1

Book: *Bears for Kids* or *The Great American Bear* by Jeff Fair, with photographs by Lynn Rogers

Have you ever seen a real bear? Here are some photographs taken by Lynn Rogers of some real bears, published in this book written by Jeff Fair. *(Show pictures from a non-fiction book about bears.)*

Activity: "Bear Creative Dramatics"

Now that we have seen some real bears, let's practice our bear movements. *(Do some creative dramatics as in week 5—walk like a bear, eat like a bear, climb like a bear, hibernate like a bear.)*

Some bears are very, very big. Try walking like a big bear.

And some bears are very, very small. Show me how a small bear walks differently than a big bear.

STORY/ACTIVITY 2

Book: *The Three Bears* by Paul Galdone

This is the last week we are going to be using this book in storytime. *(Hold up a copy of Paul Galdone's* The Three Bears.*)* You probably all know the story by now. Let's run through it quickly. *(Show pictures as you recap the story.)*

Papa Bear was making porridge for the Bear Family, but it was too hot, so they went out for a walk. Goldilocks came to their house and since no one was home, she walked in and ate some of Papa Bear's porridge, but it was *(pause while the children answer)* "Too hot."

She ate some of Mama Bear's porridge, but it was *(pause while the children answer)* "Too cold."

She ate some of Baby Bear's porridge, and it was *(pause while the children answer)* "Just right," so she ate it all.

Then she wanted to sit down, so she went to Papa Bear's chair, but it was *(pause while the children answer)* "Too hard."

She went to Mama Bear's chair, but it was *(pause while the children answer)* "Too soft."

She went to Baby Bear's chair, and it was *(pause while the children answer)* "Just right," so she rocked and rocked in it until it broke.

Then Goldilocks was tired and wanted to lie down. She went to Papa Bear's bed, but it was *(pause while the children answer)* "Too high."

She went to Mama Bear's bed, but it was *(pause while the children answer)* "Too low."

She went to Baby Bear's bed, and it was *(pause while the children answer)* "Just right," so she fell asleep there.

When the Bears came home they saw a mess in their kitchen. Papa Bear said . . . *(Pause while the children answer.)*

Mama Bear said … *(Pause while the children answer.)*

Baby Bear said … *(Pause while the children answer.)*

The Bear family was so upset, they wanted to sit down. But Papa Bear looked at his chair and said … *(Pause while the children answer.)*

Mama Bear looked at her chair and said … *(Pause while the children answer.)*

Baby Bear looked at his chair and said … *(Pause while the children answer.)*

The Bears were so upset they wanted to go to sleep. But when they got to their bedroom, Papa Bear looked at his bed and said … *(Pause while the children answer.)*

Mama Bear looked at her bed and said … *(Pause while the children answer.)*

Baby Bear looked at his bed and said … *(Pause while the children answer.)*

Just then Goldilocks woke up and saw the bears looking at her. She was so scared, she jumped up and ran away.

And that is the story of the Three Bears.

Activity: Children use props to act out and help retell the story

Since you know the story so well, I think it is time for us to act it out. First, we need to decide where the story will take place. *(Designate areas in the room to be woods, a kitchen, a living room, and a bedroom.)*

This area is going to be the forest. *(Choose a corner of the room.)*

This area is going to be inside the house. Here is the kitchen. *(Point to an area in the room.)*

Here is the room with the chairs. *(Point to an area in the room.)*

Here is the bedroom. *(Point to an area in the room. Lay three towels of different sizes in the bedroom and ask the children to pretend that they are beds.)*

I have some things to give you, to help act out the story. *(Distribute masks or craft stick puppets and ask children to choose roles.)*

Everyone who wants to be Goldilocks, stand over on this side. *(Point to where you want the children to stand and hand each child a Goldilocks stick puppet, or a piece of yellow yarn to represent her hair.)*

Everyone who wants to be Papa Bear, stand over here. *(Point to where you want the children to stand and hand each child a Papa Bear stick puppet.)*

Everyone who wants to be Mama Bear, stand over here. *(Point to where you want the children to stand and hand each child a Mama Bear stick puppet.)*

Everyone who wants to be Baby Bear, stand over here. *(Point to where you want the children to stand and hand each child a Baby Bear stick puppet.)*

I am going to be your audience, and now I would like you to tell me the story of "The Three Bears."

One day … *(Pause while the children answer. If they need help, continue telling the story from session three, pausing wherever you can to give the children the opportunity to fill in the words and act it out.)*

And that is the story of "The Three Bears." *(Clap.)* What a great job you did!

Activity: "Papa Bear and Baby Bear Playing with a Ball"

Make your fingers into bears like this. (Make hands into fists and hold them in front of you. Stick up the index finger on each hand.)

"Papa Bear and Baby Bear Playing with a Ball"

Papa Bear and Baby Bear were playing with a ball.

Papa was BIG, *(Gently bounce one fist up and down while saying this with a loud voice.)*

And Baby was small. *(Gently bounce the other fist and speak in a soft voice.)*

Run away, BIG. *(Use a deep, loud voice; extend one arm behind you.)*

Run away, Small. *(Say as softly as possible; extend the other arm behind you.)*

Come back, BIG. *(Use a deep, loud voice; bring arm back.)*

Come back, Small. *(Say this as softly as possible; bring other arm back.)*

Repeat.

Activity: Matching sizes game using flannelboard pieces

I have a bunch of felt bears, and I am going to give one to each child. Some are big, some are medium sized, and some are little. *(Give each child one felt bear.)*

Now I am putting two lines on the flannelboard so it is divided into three sections. *(Divide up the flannelboard with two felt strips.)*

Here on top is Papa Bear *(put a big bear in the top section)*, in the middle is Mama Bear *(put a medium-sized bear in the middle section)*, and at the bottom is Baby Bear *(put a baby bear in the bottom section)*.

One at a time, please come up to the flannelboard and put your bear in the right place. We're going to give a round of applause as each child finishes, to show appreciation for a job well done. *(Ask the children to come up one at a time and put their bear in the correct section. Use encouraging words and applaud for a job well done.)*

That was terrific! When storytime is over, each child can choose one of the bears to take home and keep!

>> DEVELOPMENTAL TIP

Joyfully watching other children follow directions and applauding their success teaches children an important social skill: how to appreciate other people. Being successful in school requires more than being able to do the academic work; it also involves knowing how to get along with other children, how to wait your turn, and how to be part of a classroom community. This fun activity helps your child practice all those skills.

STORY 3

Book: *Just Like Daddy* by Frank Asch

Here's one last book about a young bear and his father, called *Just Like Daddy* by Frank Asch. Repeat this part with me, "Just like Daddy." *(Read aloud.)*

CLOSING RITUAL

Vote

It's almost time to end our storytime, but I'd like to find out what books you liked. Everyone who liked looking at the bear photographs from the first book we saw—*The Great American Bear* by Jeff Fair, with photographs by Lynn Rogers—please raise your hand.

Anyone who liked acting out *The Three Bears* by Paul Galdone, please raise your hand and wave it in a big motion.

Anyone who liked *Just Like Daddy* by Frank Asch, please raise your hand and wave it in a small motion.

And anyone who liked all the books we read today and all the things we did today, please raise both hands, wave them around with very big motions, and say, "WOO WOO WOO WOO WOO."

Fingerplay: "Alligator, Alligator"

Now it's time to end with "Alligator, Alligator." (Repeat from weeks 1–5.)

Thanks for coming! We've finished with *The Three Bears* in preschool storytime. I hope to see you next week and introduce you to some new books! Don't forget to come up to the flannelboard and choose a bear to take home with you!

ADDITIO

NAL RESOURCES

Below are different activities and books that you may choose to incorporate into your storytimes or to substitute for something written in the preceding "Three Bears" scripts.

SIGN LANGUAGE

The ASL (American Sign Language) sign for BEAR is made by crossing your arms over your chest with hands on shoulders and scratching twice.

OTHER BEAR SONGS

"The Bear Went over the Mountain" song with actions can replace "Going on a Bear Hunt" or creative drama activities. Another song could be "The Other Day I Met a Bear" (a call-and-response song).

"The Other Day I Met a Bear"

The other day *(Response: "The other day")*
I met a bear. *(Response: "I met a bear.")*
A great big bear . . . *(Response: "A great big bear . . .")*
A-way up there. *(Response: "A-way up there.")*
The other day I met a bear. A great big bear a-way up there. *(Sing all lines together)*

Continue call and response:
He looked at me.
I looked at him.
He sized me up.
I sized up him.
He looked at me, I looked at him. He sized up me, I sized up him. *(Sing all lines together)*

He said to me,
"You'd better run."
"I see you ain't . . ."
"Got any gun."
He said to me, "You'd better run. I see you ain't got any gun." *(Sing all lines together)*

And so I ran
Away from there.
But right behind
me was that bear.
And so I ran away from there, but right behind me was that bear. *(Sing all lines together)*

Ahead of me
I saw a tree.
A great big tree,
Oh, golly gee!
Ahead of me I saw a tree. A great big tree, oh, golly gee! *(Sing all lines together)*

The lowest branch
Was ten feet up.
I had to jump
And trust my luck.
The lowest branch was ten feet up. I had to jump and trust my luck. *(Sing all lines together)*

And so I jumped
Into the air.
But I missed that branch
A-way up there.
And so I jumped into the air, but I missed that branch a-way up there. *(Sing all lines together)*

Now don't you fret,
And don't you frown.
I caught that branch
On the way back down!
Now don't you fret, and don't you frown. I caught that branch on the way back down! *(Sing all lines together)*

BOOKS ABOUT BEAR FAMILIES

Bright, Paul (author), and Jane Chapman (illustrator). 2008. *The Bears in the Bed and the Great Big Storm.* Intercourse, PA: Good Books.

Brown, Peter. 2010. *Children Make Terrible Pets.* New York: Little, Brown.

Carlstrom, Nancy White (author), and Bruce Degan (illustrator). 2002. *Guess Who's Coming, Jesse Bear?* New York: Aladdin.

Carlstrom, Nancy White (author), and Bruce Degan (illustrator). 2002. *Jesse Bear, What Will You Wear?* New York: Aladdin.

Dunrea, Olivier. 2010. *Old Bear and His Cub.* Philomel Books.

Harrison, Joanna. 2008. *Grizzly Dad.* New York: David Fickling Books.

Kornell, Max. 2011. *Bear with Me.* New York: G. P. Putnam's Sons.

Rodman, Mary Ann (author), and G. Brian Karas (illustrator). 2009. *Surprise Soup.* New York: Viking.

Wilson, Karma (author), and Simon Mendez (illustrator). 2011. *Mama, Why?* New York: Margaret K. McElderry.

ADDITIONAL VERSIONS OF "THE THREE BEARS"

Aylesworth, Jim (reteller), and Barbara McClintock (illustrator). 2003. *Goldilocks and the Three Bears.* New York: Scholastic Press.

Barton, Bryon. 1997. *The Three Bears.* New York: HarperCollins.

Brett, Jan (reteller). 1987. *Goldilocks and the Three Bears.* Mount Joy, PA: Big Book Childcraft.

Chichester Clark, Emma. 2010. *Goldilocks and the Three Bears.* Somerville, MA: Candlewick Press.

Child, Lauren. 2009. *Goldilocks and the Three Bears.* New York: Disney/Hyperion Books.

Eisen, Armand (reteller), and Lynn Bywaters Ferris (illustrator). 1987. *Goldilocks and the Three Bears.* New York: Ariel Books.

Elya, Susan Middleton (author), and Melissa Sweet (illustrator). 2010. *Rubia and the Three Osos.* New York: Disney/Hyperion Books.

Guarnaccia, Steven. 2000. *Goldilocks and the Three Bears: A Tale Moderne*. New York: Abrams Books for Young Readers.
> These illustrations feature the modernist movement in art and include objects and their designers, such as a sofa by Alessandro Becchi, a table by Ismu Noguchi, and a clock by George Nelson.

Kurtz, John. 2005. *Goldilocks and the Three Bears*. New York: Jump at the Sun.

Marshall, James. 1988. *Goldilocks and Three Bears*. New York: Dial Books for Young Readers.

Rosales, Melodye. 2000. *Leola and the Honeybears: An African-American Retelling of Goldilocks and the Three Bears*. New York: Scholastic.

Sanderson, Ruth. 2009. *Goldilocks*. New York: Little, Brown.

Spirin, Gennadii. 2009. *Goldilocks and the Three Bears*. Tarrytown, NY: Marshall Cavendish Children.

Stevens, Janet. 1986. *Goldilocks and the Three Bears*. New York: Holiday House.

FRACTURED VERSIONS OF "THE THREE BEARS"

Browne, Anthony. 2010. *Me and You*. New York: Farrar Straus Giroux.
> A golden-haired girl is lost in the big city when she stumbles on a house with an open door. In the kitchen, three bowls of porridge have been left to cool . . .

Ernst, Lisa Campbell. 2000. *Goldilocks Returns*. New York: Simon & Schuster Books for Young Readers.
> After fifty years of feeling guilty, Goldilocks returns to fix up the three bears' cottage.

Maccarone, Grace (author), and Anne Kennedy (illustrator). 1996. *The Silly Story of Goldilocks and the Three Squares*. New York: Scholastic.
> One of Goldilocks's descendants visits a similar house but finds a geometric twist. Includes related activities.

Palatini, Margie (author), and Jack E. Davis (illustrator). 2011. *Goldie and the Three Hares*. New York: Katherine Tegen Books.
> A family of hares tries to help Goldilocks, but she is a very difficult guest.

Petach, Heidi. 1995. *Goldilocks and the Three Hares*. New York: Putnam & Grosset.
> A riotous retelling of the familiar folktale.

Stanley, Diane. 2003. *Goldie and the Three Bears*. New York: HarperCollins.
> Goldie is a strong-willed young woman who knows what she wants and doesn't want, as well as who she likes and doesn't like.

Tolhurst, Marilyn (author), and Simone Abel (illustrator). 1991. *Somebody and the Three Blairs*. New York: Orchard Books.
> In this entertaining twist, the three Blairs are people, and the somebody is actually a big furry animal!

Willems, Mo (reteller). 2012. *Goldilocks and the Three Dinosaurs*. New York: HarperCollins.

WEBSITES TO SUPPLEMENT "THE THREE BEARS"

Clarke, Darlene. "Goldilocks and the Three Bears." SignWriting for Sign Languages. www.signwriting.org/library/children/goldilocks/goldilocks.html.
> A storybook written in American Sign Language.

"Goldilocks and the Three Bears: Crafts: Coloring Pages: Fairy Tales: Preschool Lesson Plan Printable Activities." First-School Preschool Activities and Crafts. www.first-school.ws/activities/fairytales/3bears.htm.

Kizclub.com. "Stories and Props: Goldilocks and the Three Bears." Kizclub: Learning Resources for Kids. www.kizclub.com/storypatterns/folktales/goldilocks.pdf. Downloadable coloring sheets with all the characters and props needed for retelling the story.

Martin, Phillip. "Free Language Arts Clip Art by Phillip Martin." http://languagearts .phillipmartin.info/index.htm.
Free downloadable clip art that is quite nice.

Renouf, Helen. "Under5s—Goldilocks and the Three Bears—Mini Theme." Under5s—Early Years Education. www.underfives.co.uk/Golidilocks.htm.
Assorted activities explained and categorized by school readiness skills.

SONGS ABOUT BEARS

Fink, Cathy. 1987. "Jazzy Three Bears." *Grandma Slid down the Mountain.* Cambridge: Rounder.

Garcia, Jerry, and David Grisman. 1993. "Teddy Bear's Picnic." *Not for Kids Only.* San Rafael, CA: Acoustic Disc.

Haines, B., Joan E., and Linda L. Gerber. 1980. "Songs for Singing: The Three Bears." *Leading Young Children to Music, 147.* Upper Saddle River, NJ: Columbus.

Rahel (Ann Rachel), and Betsy Rosenberg. 2009. "The Three Bears." *Alice, Where Are You Going?* B&H Records/CD Baby.

POEMS ABOUT BEARS

McNaughton, Colin. 1990. "Who's Been Sleeping in My Porridge." In *Who's Been Sleeping in My Porridge: A Book of Wacky Poems and Rhymes*, 21. Cambridge, MA: Candlewick Press.

Newcome, Zita. 2002. "The Three Bears." In *Head, Shoulders, Knees, and Toes: And Other Action Rhymes*, 28–29.Cambridge, MA: Candlewick Press.

Silverstein, Shel. 2011. "Been in There." In *A Light in the Attic.* New York: Gardners Books.

A CD, A DVD, AND A VIDEO

Marshall, James. 2000. *Goldilocks and the Three Bears.* [Weston, Conn.]: Weston Woods. (8 minutes)

O'Neal, Tatum, Hoyt Axton, Alex Karras, Carole King, John Lithgow, and Gilbert Cates. 2004. *Goldilocks and the Three Bears.* Scottsdale, Ariz: Starmaker II, LCC.

Scelsa, Greg, and Steve Millang. 2000. "Goin' on a Bear Hunt." In *Kids in Action.* Los Angeles: Youngheart Records.

HELPFUL PROPS

ChildWood Magnets sells a "Three Bears" storytelling magnet collection that includes thirteen magnets, a reproducible mini-book, and other story activities. www.childwoodmagnets.com.

North American Bear Company sells nesting puppets with three sizes of bears and a small Goldilocks that fits into Papa Bear's pocket as well as a reversible Topsy Turvy Doll with Goldilocks on one side and the three bears on the other. www.nabear.com.

The Original Toy Company sells a set of four puppets called "Goldie Locks & 3 Bear Hand Puppet." www.theoriginaltoycompany.com.

Scott-Waters, Marilyn. The Toymaker. "Goldilocks and the Three Bears." Beautifully illustrated, downloadable finger puppets (in color!) can be found at www.thetoymaker.com/Toypages/51Goldilocks/51ThreeBears.html.

chapter 4

Series 2
The Princess and the Pea

Focus Text: *The Princess and the Pea*

by H. C. Andersen, adapted and illustrated by
Janet Stevens (Pine Plains, NY: Live Oak Media, 1996)

An overbearing mother hinders the prince's search
for a suitable princess until a soggy girl shows up on
the doorstep. Sleeping on forty mattresses with a pea
underneath leaves the girl battered and bruised, but
proves that she is a true princess.

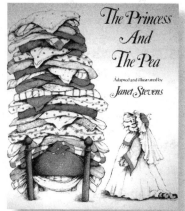

Ways to Present *The Princess and the Pea* in Storytime Sessions

Week 1: Introduce "The Princess and the Pea." (royalty)

Week 2: Tell "The Princess and the Pea" as a flannelboard story. (bedtime)

Week 3: Use dialectic reading, illustrations, and questions about the story. (peas)

Week 4: Read the same story by a different adapter; show different illustrations. (no theme)

Week 5: Read more versions of the story; dance with peas. (marriage and counting)

Week 6: Invite the children to retell the story in their own words. (rain and climbing)

Week 1: Introduce *The Princess and the Pea*

Week 1 Outline

Theme: Royalty

Beginning Ritual
- **Introduction**
- **Fingerplay:** "Five Fat Peas in a Peapod Pressed"

Story/Activity 1
- **Book:** *Prince Cinders* by Babette Cole
- **Activity:** Rain Songs: "Pitter Patter, Listen to the Rain," "Rain, Rain Go Away," "It's Raining, It's Pouring"

Story/Activity 2
- **Book:** Focus text, *The Princess and the Pea* adapted and illustrated by Janet Stevens
- **Activity:** "Head, Shoulders, Peas, and Toes"
- **Developmental Tip:** Singing about body parts
- **Activity:** "Peas Up High and Peas Down Low"

Story/Activity 3
- **Book:** *The Paper Bag Princess* by Robert Munsch, illustrated by Michael Martchenko
- **Activity:** "I Sat Next to the Princess at Tea"

Story 4
- **Book:** *Princess Baby* by Karen Katz

Closing Ritual
- **Vote**
- **Fingerplay:** "Five Fat Peas in a Peapod Pressed" *(repeated from Beginning Ritual)*

ITEMS NEEDED

- storytelling chair covered in fabric (optional)
- crown (optional)
- pile of laminated green circles (enough for each person in the room)

BOOKS NEEDED

Cole, Babette. 1997. *Prince Cinders*. New York: Putnam.

Katz, Karen. 2008. *Princess Baby*. New York: Schwartz & Wade.

Munsch, Robert N. (author), and Michael Martchenko (illustrator). 2009. *The Paper Bag Princess*. Toronto: Annick Press.

Stevens, Janet, and H. C. Andersen. 1982. *The Princess and the Pea*. New York: Holiday House.

PREPARATION

Cut 4-inch green circles out of construction paper (enough for each child and adult). Laminate the circles.

Make a crown out of aluminum foil or wear a premade crown when you are reading *The Princess and the Pea*.

If you would like to follow the storytime with a "make and take" decorate-your-own-crown activity, prism crowns or goldstone crowns can be purchased at a reasonable price from Oriental Trading (www.orientaltrading.com). Children can decorate them with stickers, fake gems, crayons, and markers on the non-shiny side. If you prefer to print out a template and create your own crowns, a simple pattern can be found at k2 Printables, at http://k2printables.com/documents/Julius/sample_crown.pdf. A fancy crown is available from Powerhouse Museum in Australia at http://play.powerhousemuseum.com/makedo/pdfs/kings_crown.pdf.

SETUP

You can turn your chair into a throne by covering it with red, purple, or gold fabric.

Script

BEGINNING RITUAL

Introduction

Hi, everyone, and welcome to preschool storytime. My name is Susie Librarian, and I am delighted to have you here today. We are going to start off with a fingerplay called "Five Fat Peas in a Peapod Pressed."

Fingerplay: "Five Fat Peas in a Peapod Pressed"

Five fat peas in a peapod pressed. *(Make a fist.)*

One grew, two grew, and so did all the rest. *(Lift up thumb and rest of fingers one by one.)*

They grew and they grew and they did not stop. *(Raise hand slowly into the air.)*

They got so big, *(Spread both hands out as wide as possible.)*
That the pod went "POP!" *(Clap hands together on "POP!")*

STORY/ACTIVITY 1

Book: *Prince Cinders* by Babette Cole

Anyone who knows the story of Cinderella, please raise your hands. *(Pause while hands are raised.)* Hands down! Here's a story that is a bit like Cinderella, except it is about a prince. His name is Prince Cinders, and this book was written and illustrated by Babette Cole. *(Read aloud.)*

Our next story is about a princess, or maybe someone who is not a princess. It's actually about a prince who is looking for a princess to marry and he can't find the right one until one day when it is raining . . . Let's sing some rain songs!

Activity: Rain Songs

A recording of the first song can be found at www.cdbaby.com/cd/bdcr/ from "Listen, Like, Learn with Mother Goose on the Loose," track 12.

"Pitter Patter, Listen to the Rain"

Pitter patter, pitter patter, listen to the rain. *(Lift both hands. Wiggle fingers while slowly lowering hands.)*
Pitter patter, pitter patter, on my window pane. *(Lift both hands. Wiggle fingers while slowly lowering hands.)*
Dropping, dropping, dropping, dropping, dropping to the ground. *(Lift both hands. Bend wrists so fingers are parallel with the floor. Drop hands bit by bit until they reach the ground.)*
Dropping, dropping, dropping, dropping, listen to the sound. *(Lift both hands. Bend wrists so fingers are parallel with the floor. Drop hands bit by bit until they reach the ground.)*

"Rain, Rain Go Away"

Rain, rain, go away. Come again another day.
Little Johnny wants to play, so rain, rain, go away.

"It's Raining, It's Pouring"

It's raining, it's pouring, the old man is snoring.
He bumped his head on the top of the bed, and he couldn't get up till the morning!

Now that we've had lots of rain, it's time for our story, *The Princess and the Pea* by Janet Stevens.

STORY/ACTIVITY 2

Book: Focus text, *The Princess and the Pea* adapted and illustrated by Janet Stevens

Read aloud.

And that is the story of *The Princess and the Pea* by Janet Stevens.

Activity: "Head, Shoulders, Peas, and Toes"

The pea in that story ended up in a museum; but I have some peas right here in the library. In fact, I have enough to give one to everyone here. *(Hand out construction-paper peas; give one to each person.)*

Everyone stand up with your peas! We are going to start out with a song you might already know, but we are going to sing it a bit differently. You may know it as "Head, Shoulders, Knees, and Toes," but we are going to sing, "Head, Shoulders, Peas, and Toes." We'll start by putting the pea on our head, then on our shoulders, but when we sing "Peas" stretch your arm out straight in front of you and hold your pea out for everyone to see. Then put the pea on your toes. Let's start by singing slowly until everyone gets the hang of it.

"Head, Shoulders, Peas, and Toes"

Head, shoulders, peas, and toes, peas and toes.
Head, shoulders, peas, and toes, peas and toes.
And eyes and ears and mouth and nose.
Head, shoulders, peas, and toes, peas and toes.

Once the children are able to match the movements with the song, try singing it faster and faster and faster.

›› DEVELOPMENTAL TIP

Songs that focus on body parts and the actions they perform are great learning tools. These songs increase children's awareness of how different parts of the body can start specific movements. At the same time, by using their muscles to make the motions in a song, children develop motor skills and positive self-awareness of their bodies.

Activity: "Peas Up High and Peas Down Low"

Lift your peas high up in the air, as high, as high, as you can. *(Say in a high voice.)*
Bring your peas down low, down low, down, low. *(Say in a low voice.)*
Up high, up high, up high. *(high voice)*
Down low, down low, down low. *(low voice)*
Up high. *(high voice)*
Down low. *(low voice)*

Turn around. *(normal voice)*

Put your pea on the ground, now sit on your pea!

STORY/ACTIVITY 3

Book: *The Paper Bag Princess* by Robert Munsch, illustrated by Michael Martchenko

Here's another story about an unusual princess. It is called *The Paper Bag Princess* by Robert Munsch, illustrated by Michael Martchenko. *(Read aloud.)*

Activity: "I Sat Next to the Princess at Tea"

Here's a silly song. Can you imagine what would happen if a princess invited you to come to her castle and join her for a cup of tea? You would probably get all dressed up and use your very best manners. And then, what would you do if some very strange and loud rumbling noises starting coming right from her abdomen (her stomach area)? *(Point to abdomen and pause for answers.)* How would you feel if you were trying to be on your best behavior? *(Pause for answers.)* And, how would you feel if no one wanted to embarrass the princess, so everyone looked at you instead of the princess? *(Pause for answers.)*

Everyone stand up. First, I'll say a line with movements and you can say it back to me.

Sing an adapted version of "I Sat Down with the Duchess to Tea." The original version of this song can be found in Peter Blood and Annie Patterson (eds.), Rise Up Singing, Sing Out, Sing Out Publications (1992/1989), p. 189. A version of this with children singing and using movements can be found on YouTube at www.youtube.com/watch?v= EjAzZh5_45g.

"I Sat Next to the Princess at Tea"

I sat next to the princess at tea. *(Pat your rear end.)*

It was just as I feared it would be. *(Clap face between both hands.)*

Her rum-bl-ings abdominal *(Hold belly with both hands, sway back and forth, and explain, "Those are the rumbling sounds coming from her abdomen.")*

Were simply phenomenal . . . *(Open arms wide and explain that in this case, phenomenal means "really extraordinary, unusual, and loud!")*

And everyone thought it was me! *(Point to self.)*

Let's try it again where I say a line and you say it back to me. *(Do this.)*

Now I'm going to sing a line, and you sing it back to me. *(Do this singing one line at time. Sing the song a number of times until you think the children are ready to sing it without repeating after you.)*

I sat next to the princess at tea. *(Pat your rear end.)*
It was just as I feared it would be. *("Clap" face between both hands.)*
Her rum-bl-ings abdominal *(Hold belly with both hands and sway.)*
Were simply phenomenal . . . *(Open arms WIDE.)*
And everyone thought it was me! *(Point to self.)*

That was great. Now sit back down on your peas and get ready for our final story, *Princess Baby* by Karen Katz.

STORY 4

Book: *Princess Baby* by Karen Katz
Read aloud.

CLOSING RITUAL

Vote

Fingerplay: "Five Fat Peas in a Peapod Pressed"
Five fat peas in a peapod pressed. *(Make a fist.)*
One grew, two grew, and so did all the rest. *(Lift up thumb and rest of fingers one by one.)*
They grew and they grew and they did not stop. *(Raise hand slowly into the air.)*
They got so big, *(Spread both hands out as wide as possible.)*
That the pod went "POP!" *(Clap hands together on "POP!")*

Bye, everyone! Thanks for coming and I'll see you next week.

HANDOUTS FOR PARENTS

Working on projects together with your children in a relaxed atmosphere gives them a positive experience with team work and collaboration. Visit www.nald.ca/library/learning/howtokit/tvfree/tvfree.pdf to get instructions on making a crown on pages 46–47 and a castle on page 48–49. Have fun building your creation together!

Source: Northwest Territories Literary Council. TV Free from A to Z How-to-Kit: More Than 26 Fun Activities to Keep Your Family Engaged and the TV Off! Canada: NWTLC.

MORE BOOKS ABOUT PRINCES AND PRINCESSES

Atwood, Margaret (author), and Aryann Kovalski (illustrator). 1995. *Princess Prunella and the Purple Peanut.* New York: Workman Publishing.
Lots of P words in this funny book for the more mature preschool audience.

Coyle, Carmela LaVigna, Mike Gordon, and Carl Gordon. 2003. *Do Princesses Wear Hiking Boots?* Flagstaff, AZ: Rising Moon.

Lobel, Arnold. 1979. *Prince Bertram the Bad.* New York: Random House Student Book Edition.

Numeroff, Laura Joffe, Nate Evans, and Lynn Munsinger (illustrator). 2011. *Ponyella.* New York: Disney/Hyperion Books.

Saxon, Victoria (author), and Lorelay Bove (illustrator). 2009. *The Princess and the Frog.* New York: Golden Books.

Week 2: Tell *The Princess and the Pea* as a Flannelboard Story

Week 2 Outline

Repetition with Variety: Tell "The Princess and the Pea" using a flannelboard and creative dramatics.

Theme: Bedtime
- **Beginning Ritual**
- **Introduction**
- **Fingerplay:** "Five Fat Peas in a Peapod Pressed" (repeated from week 1)

Story/Activity 1
- **Book:** Focus text retold as a flannelboard story, *The Princess and the Pea* adapted and illustrated by Janet Stevens
- **Activity:** "Creative Dramatics"
- **Activity:** "I Sat Next to the Princess at Tea" (repeated from week 1)

Story/Activity 2
- **Book:** *Peace at Last* by Jill Murphy (repeated from week 3 of "The Three Bears")
- **Activity:** "Two Little Monkeys Jumping on the Bed"

Story/Activity 3
- **Book:** *There's a Nightmare in My Closet* by Mercer Mayer
- **Activity:** "Ten in the Bed" (repeated from week 1 of "The Three Bears")

Story/Activity 4
- **Book:** *Maisy Goes to Bed* by Lucy Cousins
- **Activity:** "Twinkle, Twinkle, Little Star"
- **Developmental Tip:** The value of lullabies

Closing Ritual
- **Vote**
- **Fingerplay:** "Five Fat Peas in a Peapod Pressed" (repeated from week 1)

ITEMS NEEDED

- flannelboard
- flannel pieces
- wet princess (figure 4.1)
- dry princess (figure 4.2)
- queen (figure 4.3)
- prince (figure 4.4)
- king (figure 4.5)
- pea (figure 4.6)
- mattresses (figure 4.7) in many colors—enough to give one to each child (or you can substitute 2-inch felt squares)
- display stand (figure 4.8)
- princess with rumblings abdominal (figure 4.9) (optional)

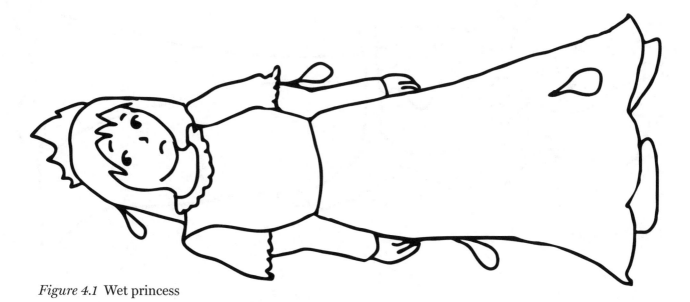

Figure 4.1 Wet princess

Figure 4.2 Dry princess

Figure 4.3 Queen

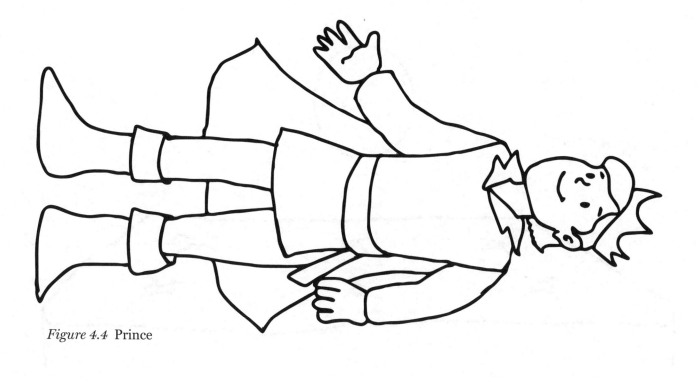

Figure 4.4 Prince

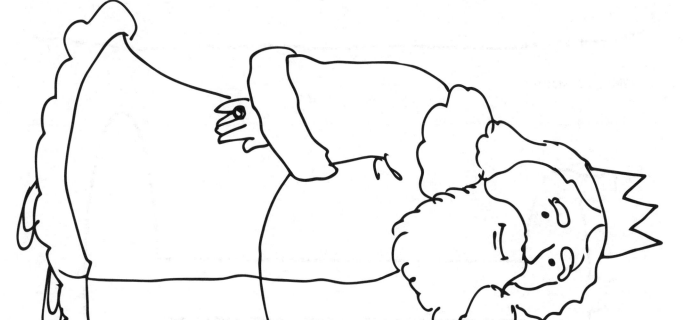

Figure 4.5 King

Figure 4.6 Pea

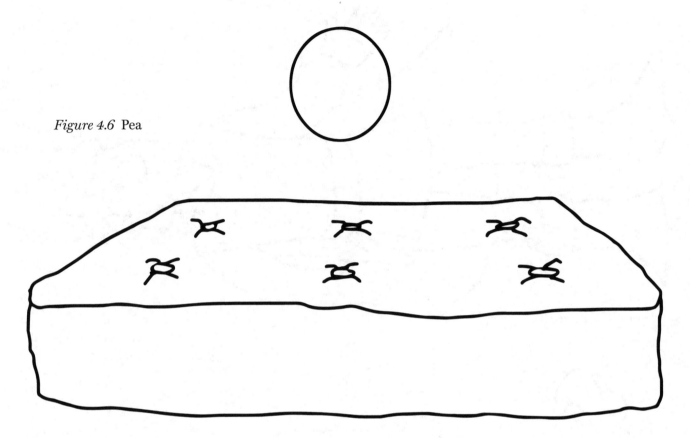

Figure 4.7 Mattress

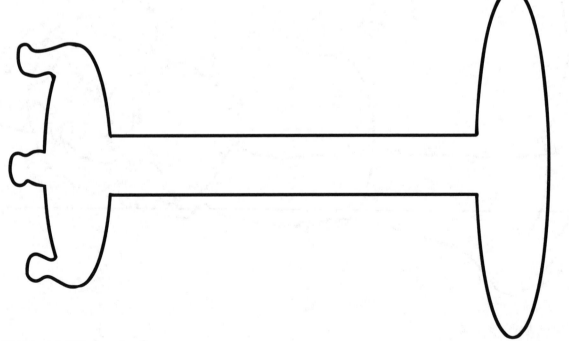

Figure 4.8 Display stand

Figure 4.9
Rumblings abdominal
(for "I Sat Next to the
Princess at Tea")

BOOKS NEEDED

Cousins, Lucy. 2010. *Maisy Goes to Bed.* Cambridge, MA: Candlewick Press.

Mayer, Mercer. 1994. *There's a Nightmare in My Closet.* New York: Dial.

Murphy, Jill. 2010. *Peace at Last.* London: Macmillan.

Stevens, Janet, and H. C. Andersen. 1982. *The Princess and the Pea.* New York: Holiday House.

Script

BEGINNING RITUAL

Introduction
Introduce yourself and welcome everyone enthusiastically.

Fingerplay: "Five Fat Peas in a Peapod Pressed"
Repeat from week 1.

STORY/ACTIVITY 1

Book: *The Princess and the Pea* adapted and illustrated by Janet Stevens

Do you remember the story we heard last week about the princess and the pea? *(Hold up book and show the cover, but do not open the book.)* Well, this week I'm going to tell it as a flannelboard story, but I am going to need your help. Each child will get a felt mattress, and when it is time for the queen to get the bed ready, I'd like you to come up to the flannelboard one at a time and add your mattress to the stack of mattresses on top of the pea.

Here's the story.

One day there was a queen who had a son, the prince. *(Put queen on flannelboard.)* She wanted the prince to marry a princess, but he could not find a princess that he liked. She took him to kingdom after kingdom, but he thought the princesses he met were too boring, too silly, too busy, or too serious for him. The queen was afraid that her son would never get married, and, since he was a prince, she wanted him to only marry a true princess.

One rainy day, when the sun was barely shining and there was not a patch of dry earth to be found, someone knocked at the castle door. The queen opened the door and saw a very wet young lady standing in front of her. *(Put wet princess on flannelboard.)*

"May I come in?" the young lady asked. "I am a princess, and it is very wet out here."

The queen immediately invited the princess in, brought her into the kitchen, and made her a hot cup of tea. She loaned the princess some clothing to wear while her wet clothes dried. *(Exchange wet princess for dry princess.)* The princess changed her clothes, brushed her hair, and was just taking a sip of tea when the prince entered the kitchen. *(Put prince on the flannelboard next to the princess.)* The prince sat down at the table, and he and princess started talking together. They talked about the weather, and their families, and the things they liked, and even their favorite books. They laughed together. The prince didn't think she was boring at all! She was not silly, she was not too busy for him, and she certainly was not too serious for him. By the end of the evening, the prince and the princess had fallen in love with each other and the prince wanted to ask the princess to marry him. *(Take princess off flannelboard.)*

But, when he told his mother, she was not sure. "You can only marry a princess," said the Queen. "Even though she says she's a princess, I have to find out for sure." *(Take the prince off the flannelboard.)*

So the queen invited the princess to stay overnight in the castle (it was still raining very heavily outside), and she went into the guest bedroom to prepare the bed.

Out of her pocket, she took a round, green pea. *(Hold up green felt circle and put in on the bottom of the flannelboard.)*

Then she put a mattress on top of the pea. *(Put a felt square on top of the pea.)* And she added another mattress *(Put this mattress just above the other mattress rather than on top of it.)* Then she added another *(invite a child to come up to the flannelboard and place his mattress over yours)*, and another *(invite another child)*, and another *(continue inviting the children to add their mattresses until each child has had a turn).*

When all the mattresses were in place, the queen told the princess that her bed was ready and she could finally go to sleep. *(Enter princess, exit queen.)*

The princess entered the guest room and began climbing up all the mattresses. The stack of mattresses was so high that she had to climb and climb and climb, but finally the princess got to the top. She was sure she would have a good sleep, since all those mattresses would make the bed very soft, but when she lay down, it felt as if something hard was poking into her back. *(Twist princess around.)*

She twisted and turned, and turned and twisted all night long, but she could not get comfortable. But what could possibly be annoying her through all those mattresses?

In the morning, the princess climbed down from all the mattresses *(climb down)* and joined the queen and the prince for another cup of tea. *(Enter queen and prince.)*

"How did you sleep?" asked the queen.

"I thank you for preparing such a nice bed," said the princess, "but I just couldn't sleep at all. It felt as if there was a rock underneath all the mattresses, and I just tossed and turned all night long."

"You ARE a real princess," shouted out the queen gleefully. "Princesses have very delicate skin, and only a princess would have felt the pea underneath the bottom mattress."

"Of course I am a princess," said the princess, "I told you so yesterday."

"Princess, will you marry me?" asked the prince, "I love you."

"I love you too," said the princess.

So the prince and princess were married in a big wedding at the castle. *(Hold up the pea.)*

And as for the pea, it is now on exhibit in a museum where anyone who wants can go to see the famous pea. *(Put pedestal on the flannelboard with the pea on top of it.)*

And that is the story of "The Princess and the Pea."

Activity: "Creative Dramatics"

Ask the children if they recall the routine of the princess. Did she brush her teeth? Brush her hair? Change into pajamas? Act it out. You may want to sing "Brush Your Teeth" by Rafi on Singable Songs for the Very Young *(1976).*

Let's act out all of the things the princess did.

First she walked around in the rain. *(Walk.)*

Then she knocked on the castle door. *(Knock.)*

Then she changed her clothes, brushed her hair and drank a cup of tea. *(Drink.)*

The she probably washed her face *(wash face)* and brushed her teeth *(brush teeth)* before bedtime, and climbed up all of those mattresses. *(Act out climbing up onto the top mattress.)*

Keep climbing. A little higher. A little higher. Just a few more mattresses to go . . . Don't lose your balance.

Whew! Made it to the top. *(Lean back.)*

Then she tried to sleep, but she kept tossing and turning and tossing and turning all night long. *(Sway.)*

In the morning, the princess climbed down from the top of that very high bed, one step at a time . . . (*Pretend to climb down.*)

And when she reached the bottom, she sat back at the kitchen table and then had another cup of tea. (*Drink tea.*)

Activity: "I Sat Next to the Princess at Tea"

Who remembers the song about the princess and the cup of tea that we sang last week? Let's try it again.

Repeat from week 1.

STORY/ACTIVITY 2

Book: *Peace at Last* by Jill Murphy

Read aloud. Children join along making all the noises that Mr. Bear hears.

Activity: "Two Little Monkeys Jumping on the Bed"

First recite this rhyme using two fists while everyone recites it with you. Then take out two monkey puppets (one on each hand) and ask everyone to do it again, pretending that they have monkey puppets on their hands too. When the rhyme is finished, have one monkey say to the other, "These children did such a good job reciting our rhyme, let's give them all a monkey kiss!" Walk around and give each child a "monkey kiss" by putting a monkey on each side of the child's cheek while making a kissing sound. Be sure that everyone who wants a monkey kiss gets one. You too!

"Two Little Monkeys Jumping on the Bed"

Two little monkeys jumping on the bed.
One fell off and bumped his head.
The other called the doctor and the doctor said,
"That's what you get for jumping on the bed!"

STORY/ACTIVITY 3

Book: *There's a Nightmare in my Closet* by Mercer Mayer

Read aloud.

Activity: "Ten in the Bed"

Act this song out. Ask everyone to stand in line while you sing, and when each one "rolls" off the bed, have them turn around in a way that rolls them out of the line and then sit down.

"Ten in the Bed"
There were ten in the bed and the little one said, "Roll over, roll over"
So they all rolled over and one fell out.
There were nine in the bed . . .

Continue counting down until the final verse.

There was one in the bed and the little one said, "Good night."

STORY/ACTIVITY 4

Book: *Maisy Goes to Bed* by Lucy Cousins
Read aloud.

Activity: "Twinkle, Twinkle, Little Star"
Has anyone ever sung a lullaby to you to help you fall asleep? Close your eyes, hug yourself, and gently rock while singing "Twinkle, Twinkle, Little Star" very slowly. It can be just like a lullaby! *(Close eyes and rock yourself while singing. Be sure to keep a slow pace.)*

>> DEVELOPMENTAL TIP
Singing lullabies to children of all ages often transports them to a safe, calm, soft place where they find it easier than usual to settle down. So, continue singing lullabies to your children, even when they are no longer babies.

CLOSING RITUAL

Vote

Fingerplay: "Five Fat Peas in a Peapod Pressed"
Repeat from week 1.

BOOKS ABOUT BEDTIME

Arnold, Tedd. 2012. *No Jumping on the Bed.* New York: Dial Anniversary Edition.

Cabera, Jane. 20026. *Ten in the Bed.* New York: Holiday House.

Calitri, Susan Chapman. 2010. *Ten in the Bed.* New York: Scholastic. Big book.

Christelow, Eileen. 2006. *Five Little Monkeys Jumping on the Bed.* San Anselmo, CA: Sandpiper. Big book.

Ellwand, David. 2002. *Ten in the Bed.* San Francisco: Chronicle Books.

Mayer, Mercer. 1987. *There's an Alligator under My Bed.* New York: Dial.

Week 3: Use Dialectic Reading, Illustrations, and Questions about the Story

Week 3 Outline

Repetition with Variety: Use dialectic reading, show illustrations, and ask questions about the story

Theme: Peas

Beginning Ritual
- **Introduction**
- **Fingerplay:** "Five Fat Peas in a Peapod Pressed" (repeated from weeks 1 and 2)

Story/Activity 1
- **Book:** Focus text read dialectically, *The Princess and the Pea* adapted and illustrated by Janet Stevens
- **Activity:** "Making Pea Soup"
- **Activity:** "The Hokey Pea-okey" (adapted from week 1 of "The Three Bears")
- **Activity:** "Head, Shoulders, Peas, and Toes" (repeated from week 1)

Story/Activity 2
- **Book:** *LMNO Peas* by Keith Baker
- **Activity:** "I Sat Next to the Princess at Tea" (repeated from weeks 1 and 2)

Story/Activity 3
- **Book:** *Eat Your Peas, Louise!* by Pegeen Snow
- **Activity:** Fun with Shakers: "We Shake Our Shakers Together" (adapted from "We Ring Our Bells Together," from week 4 of "The Three Bears"), "Pease Porridge Hot" (repeated from week 4 of "The Three Bears"), "I Eat My Peas with Honey," "Shakers Away" (adapted from "Scarves Away," from week 3 of "The Three Bears")
- **Developmental Tip:** Developing small and large motor skills

Story/Activity 4
- **Book:** *Eat Your Peas, Ivy Louise!* by Leo Landry
- **Activity:** YouTube video for "I Got a Pea" by Bryant Oden

Closing Ritual
- **Vote**
- **Fingerplay:** "Five Fat Peas in a Peapod Pressed" (repeated from weeks 1 and 2)

ITEMS NEEDED

- picture of a can of peas (Google Images has plenty!) or a real can of peas
- picture of a bag or box of frozen peas or a real bag or box of frozen peas
- toy pea or peapod (optional)
- 2 bowls (optional)
- fresh peas for tasting (optional)
- laminated green circles (peas)
- tote bag with enough chickitas or shakers for each storytime participant

Pea stuffed toys can be ordered online:

- Disney produces a Pixar *Toy Story 3* "Exclusive 7 Inch Plush Figure Peas in a Pod"
- www.etsy.com sells homemade crafts. Search online for "peas in a pod" and choose from a wide variety of items.
- Freemountain Toys from Bristol, Vermont, used to make peas in a zippered pod. These are occasionally available on eBay.

BOOKS NEEDED

Baker, Keith. 2010. *LMNO Peas.* New York: Beach Lane Books.

Landry, Leo. 2005. *Eat Your Peas, Ivy Louise!* Boston: Houghton Mifflin.

Snow, Pegeen, and Mike Venezia. 2011. *Eat Your Peas, Louise!* New York: Children's Press.

Stevens, Janet, and H. C. Andersen. 1982. *The Princess and the Pea.* New York: Holiday House.

Script

BEGINNING RITUAL

Introduction

Fingerplay: "Five Fat Peas in a Peapod Pressed"
Repeat from weeks 1 and 2.

STORY/ACTIVITY 1

Book: *The Princess and the Pea* adapted and illustrated by Janet Stevens

Tell the story while showing the illustrations. Have the children help you by frequently asking questions before turning the page. See if they can predict what is going to happen—ask, "What happened then?" At the end of the story, ask:

Who remembers what the queen put under the bed? A pea! Where did the queen get the pea? Do you know where peas come from? From here? (*Show a picture of a can of peas* or a real can of peas.) From here? (Show a picture of a bag or box of frozen peas or a real bag or box of frozen peas.) Peas grow in a garden! And they grow in pods, so in order to eat them, you have to open the pod first, and this is called shelling peas.

Show a picture of a pea from a nonfiction book. If you have a stuffed animal Pea or peapod, use that. Bring in a real pea. If your library does not have restrictions on food, let each child open a pod and taste a fresh pea. Bring in two bowls—one for the peas and one for their discarded pods.

Activity: "Making Pea Soup"

Hand out laminated green circles and pretend that they are big peas. Stand up.

Once you have your pea, stand up in a big circle and together we can make some pea soup. Pretend we are the outside rim of a big pot of soup. Let's put our peas in and mix them around. (*Move laminated peas from side to side.*) At first they fall to the bottom of the pot. (*Drop peas to the floor*), but when we add water, they rise. (*Raise peas to waist level.*) Keep stirring them! Then, as the water starts to boil, the peas circle around even faster and rise with the rising water. (*Raise peas to shoulder height.*) But when you turn the heat down, the water stops boiling and the peas sink. (*Put peas on the floor*).

Now that we have some delicious pea soup, let's do the hokey pea-okey.

Activity: "The Hokey Pea-okey"

Follow the directions in the song.

You put your pea in, you take your pea out.
You put your pea in, and you shake it all about.
You do the hokey pea-okey and you turn yourself around.
That's what it's all about. Peas!

Repeat.

Activity: "Head, Shoulders, Peas, and Toes"

Repeat from week 1. When finished, ask everyone to put their peas on the floor and to sit on their peas; then read your next story.

STORY/ACTIVITY 2

Book: *LMNO Peas* by Keith Baker
Read aloud.

Activity: "I Sat Next to the Princess at Tea"
Repeat from weeks 1 and 2.

STORY/ACTIVITY 3

Book: *Eat Your Peas, Louise!* by Pegeen Snow
Read aloud.

Activity: Fun with Shakers
Hand out shakers, chickitas, or appropriately-sized maracas.

"We Shake Our Shakers Together"
(by Barbara Cass-Beggs; to the tune of "The Farmer in the Dell")
We shake our shakers together. We shake our shakers together.
We shake our shakers together. Because it's fun to do.
Shake them up high. (*Shake them up high while singing this in a high voice.*)
Shake them down low. (*Shake them down low while singing in a low voice.*)
Shake them in the middle. (*Shake them directly in front of you using your normal
   singing voice.*)

Show the illustration of "Pease Porridge Hot" from Iona Opie's Here Comes Mother Goose
   (Candlewick Press, p. 74), while shaking shakers to the beat of the following rhyme.

"Pease Porridge Hot"
Pease porridge hot.
Pease porridge cold.
Pease porridge in the pot,
Nine days old.

Some like it hot.
Some like it cold.
Some like it in the pot,
Nine days old.

Show the illustration of "I Eat My Peas with Honey" from the Bill Martin Jr. Big Book
of Poetry *(Simon & Schuster Books for Young Readers, 2008), and shake shakers to the
beat while reciting the following rhyme.*

"I Eat My Peas with Honey"
I eat my peas with honey.
I've done it all my life.
It makes the peas taste funny,
But it keeps them on my knife!

   Can you imagine eating peas with a knife instead of a spoon or a fork? How silly!

Walk around with a tote bag and invite children to drop their chickitas in the bag while singing "Shakers Away."

"Shakers Away" (adapted from "Scarves Away," by Barbara Cass-Beggs)

Shakers away, shakers away,
Put your shakers away today.

>> DEVELOPMENTAL TIP

In many rhymes, children listen for certain phrases and respond to them with specific physical movements. In addition to being fun, these activities actually help to develop small and large motor skills, which make it easier for children starting school to accomplish tasks such as holding a pencil.

STORY/ACTIVITY 4

Book: *Eat Your Peas, Ivy Louise!* by Leo Landry
Read aloud.

Activity: YouTube video for "I Got a Pea" by Bryant Oden
Show the YouTube Video for the song "I Got a Pea" by Bryant Oden, found at www.youtube.com/watch?v=pSN5mu8RMKo&feature=related or www.youtube.com/watch?v=1Q6DdTcqGy8.

CLOSING RITUAL

Vote

Fingerplay: "Five Fat Peas in a Peapod Pressed"
Repeat from weeks 1 and 2.

MORE BOOKS ABOUT PEAS

Bardoe, Cheryl. 2006. *Gregor Mendel: The Friar Who Grew Peas.* New York: Harry N. Abrams.

Bonwill, Ann (author), and Simon Rikerty (illustrator). 2011. *I Don't Want to Be a Pea!* Oxford, UK: Oxford University Press.

Child, Lauren. 2003. *I Will Never Not Ever Eat a Tomato.* Boston: Candlewick Press.

Macdonald, Margaret Read (author), and Pat Cummings (illustrator). 1998. *Pickin' Peas.* New York: HarperCollins.

Potter, Beatrix. 1983. *Peter Rabbit, Lost in Mr. McGregor's Garden.* New York: Chatham River Press.

Potter, Beatrix. 2004. *The Tale of Peter Rabbit*. New York: Grosset and Dunlap.

Rosenthal, Amy Krouse. 2005. *Little Pea*. San Francisco: Chronicle Books.

BOOKS WITH PICTURES OF PEAS

Gibbons, Gail. 2007. *The Vegetables We Eat*. New York: Holiday House. Page 19.

Lockwood, Sophie. 2008. *Flies*. Mankato, MN: The Child's World. Page 25.

ADDITIONAL PEA GAMES

- Play the Duck, Duck, Goose game, substituting the words *carrot, carrot, pea*.
- Make a pea out of green felt. Ask the children to sit in a circle and pass the "pea" around while you play some recorded music. When the music stops, the child must do something silly with the pea (e.g., sit on it, put it on her head, flap it up and down). Repeat until each child has had a turn.

Week 4: Read the Same Story by a Different Adapter; Show Different Illustrations

Week 4 Outline

Repetition with Variety: Read the same story by a different adapter; show different illustrations

Theme: None

Beginning Ritual
- **Introduction**
- **Fingerplay:** "Five Fat Peas in a Peapod Pressed" (repeated from weeks 1–3)

Story/Activity 1
- **Book:** Same story as focus text, but by a different adapter and illustrator, *The Princess and the Pea* adapted by John Cech, illustrated by Bernhard Oberdieck, OR *The Princess and the Pea* adapted by Rachel Isadora
- **Activity:** "Making Pea Puppets"
- **Developmental Tip:** Exploring different materials
- **Activity:** "The Hokey Pea-okey," modified (repeated from week 3)
- **Activity:** "Head, Shoulders, Peas, and Toes," modified (repeated from weeks 1 and 3)

Story/Activity 2

- **Book:** Fractured version of focus text, *The Princess and the Pea-ano (Happily Ever After)* by Mike Thaler, illustrated by Jared D. Lee
- **Activity:** "Pease Porridge Hot" (repeated from week 3)

Story/Activity 3

- **Book:** *The Very Smart Pea and the Princess-to-Be* by Mini Grey
- **Activity:** Fun with Bells: "We Ring Our Bells Together" (repeated from week 4 of "The Three Bears"), "Pease Porridge Hot" (repeated from week 3), "It's Raining, It's Pouring" (repeated from week 1), "Frère Jacques" (repeated from week 4 of "The Three Bears"), "Grandfather's Clock" (repeated from week 4 of "The Three Bears"), "Bells Away" (repeated from week 4 of "The Three Bears")

Story 4

- **Book:** *Food: A Lift-the-Flap Shadow Book* by Roger Priddy (repeated from week 4 of "The Three Bears")

Closing Ritual

- **Vote**
- **Fingerplay:** "Five Fat Peas in a Peapod Pressed" (repeated from weeks 1–3)

ITEMS NEEDED

- enough construction paper to give 2 pages to each child
- laminated peas
- craft sticks (enough to have 1 for each child and adult)
- Glue Dots (can be purchased online from www.enasco.com as Craft Glue Dots)
- cutout pictures of a pea (1 for each person) from Google images, a round green circle, or dried peas
- bells

BOOKS NEEDED

Cech, John (adapter), Bernhard Oberdieck (illustrator), and H. C. Andersen (original author). 2007. *The Princess and the Pea.* New York: Sterling.

Grey, Mini, and H. C. Andersen. 2011. *The Very Smart Pea and the Princess-to-Be.* New York: Dragonfly Books.

Isadora, Rachel, and H. C. Andersen. 2007. *The Princess and the Pea.* New York: G. P. Putnam's Sons.

Priddy, Roger. 2010. *Food: A Lift-the-Flap Shadow Book.* New York: Priddy Books. (Board book)

Thaler, Mike (author), and Jared D. Lee (illustrator). 1997. *The Princess and the Pea-ano.* New York: Scholastic.

Script

BEGINNING RITUAL

Introduction

Fingerplay: "Five Fat Peas in a Peapod Pressed"
Repeat from weeks 1–3.

STORY/ACTIVITY 1

Book: *The Princess and the Pea* adapted by John Cech, illustrated by Bernhard Oberdieck OR *The Princess and the Pea* adapted by Rachel Isadora
Cech's book is a long version of the story for children who can pay attention. Isadora's is a bare-bones version set in Africa with lavish illustrations. Read aloud.

Activity: "Making Pea Puppets"
Hand out one craft stick, one marker, one Glue Dot, and one pea picture or dried pea to each child. Ask the adult to write the child's name on the stick—or if the child can, to write it himself. Ask everyone to put the Glue Dot on the top of the stick, and to press the picture/circle—or if you are adventurous, the dried pea—onto the Glue Dot. This is now a pea puppet.

>> DEVELOPMENTAL TIP
Giving children time to explore materials like different kinds of paper, cardboard, tape, glue, stickers, and scissors gives them the opportunity to see what can and cannot be done with them. This type of experimentation leading to making conclusions is a beginning form of problem solving. It addresses the question, "Can I make the materials do what I want them to do, and if not, how can I adjust things to get the result that I want?" Even the simplest craft project has value!

Activity: "The Hokey Pea-okey"
Repeat the activity from week 3, with modifications. Do the hokey pea-okey with the pea puppets. Add even more things to do with your pea! For instance, after singing the "regular" song once with peas, add new directions such as

- "You lift your pea UP, you put your pea DOWN. You lift your pea UP, and you TWIST it all around. You do the hokey pea-okey and you turn yourself around . . ."
- "Move your pea in a circle, put your pea on your nose. Move your pea in a circle, and drop it to your toes. You do the hokey pea-okey and you turn yourself around . . ."

Activity: "Head, Shoulders, Peas, and Toes"

Repeat from weeks 1 and 3. Sing this going faster and faster as the children get more proficient. Then give two pieces of construction paper to each child. Ask the children to put one piece of paper on the floor in front of them. This is a bedframe. Then ask everyone to put their pea on the bedframe, and cover it with the second piece of paper. Pretend it is a pile of mattresses and ask everyone to try climbing to the top! When finished, collect peas and construction paper and read the next story.

STORY/ACTIVITY 2

Book: *The Princess and the Pea-ano (Happily Ever After)* by Mike Thaler, illustrated by Jared D. Lee
Read aloud.

Activity: "Pease Porridge Hot"
Repeat from week 3, with clapping.

STORY/ACTIVITY 3

Book: *The Very Smart Pea and the Princess-to-Be* by Mini Grey
Read aloud.

Activity: Fun with Bells
Walk around with a canvas bag of bells, giving one to each person, adults as well as children. When you have returned to your seat, lead the group in ringing their bells to the beat of these songs from previous sessions.

"We Ring Our Bells Together"
(by Barbara Cass-Beggs; to the tune of "The Farmer in the Dell")
We ring our bells together. We ring our bells together.
We ring our bells together, because it's fun to do.
We ring our bells together. We ring our bells together.
We ring our bells together, because it's fun to do.

Ring them up high. *(Sing in a high voice while ringing the bell above your head.)*
Ring them down low. *(Sing in a low voice while ringing the bell way down low.)*
Ring them in the middle. *(Sing in a normal voice while ringing the bell in front of you.)*

"Pease Porridge Hot"
Repeat from week 3, using bells.

"It's Raining, It's Pouring"
Repeat from week 1.

"Frère Jacques"
Are you sleeping? Are you sleeping?
Brother John? Brother John?
Morning bells are ringing. Morning bells are ringing.
Ding, ding, dong. Ding, ding, dong.

Frère Jacques, frère Jacques,
Dormez vous? Dormez vous?
Sonnez les matines, sonnez les matines,
Ding, ding, dong. Ding, ding, dong.

"Grandfather's Clock"
Grandfather's clock goes, "Tick, tock, tick, tock." (*Ring bells slowly on the beat to "Tick, tock, tick, tock."*)
Mother's kitchen clock goes, "Tick, tock, tick, tock, tick, tock, tick, tock." (*Ring bells to a quicker beat on each "Tick, tock."*)
Brother's little watch goes, "Tick, tick, tick, tick, tick, tick, tick, tick, tick, tick, tick, tick . . . STOP!" (*Ring bells very quickly to each "Tick" and then STOP.*)

Walk around with a canvas bag and invite children to drop their bells in to the bag, while singing "Bells Away."

"Bells Away" (by Barbara Cass-Beggs)
Bells away, bells away,
Put your bells away today.

STORY 4

Book: *Food: A Lift-the-Flap Shadow Book* by Roger Priddy
Ask kids to shout out the name of the food: cupcake, banana, peas, apple, strawberry, broccoli, and cheese.

CLOSING RITUAL

Vote

Fingerplay: "Five Fat Peas in a Peapod Pressed"
Repeat from weeks 1–3.

RETELLINGS OF "THE PRINCESS AND THE PEA"

Boada, Francesc, Pau Estrada, and H. C. Andersen. 2004. *The Princess and the Pea / La princesa y el guisante*. San Francisco: Chronicle Books.

Child, Lauren (author), Polly Borland (illustrator) and Andersen, H. C. (author). 2006. *The Princess and the Pea*. New York: Hyperion Books for Children.

Galdone, Paul, and H. C. Andersen. 1978. *The Princess and the Pea*. New York: Seabury Press.

Stevens, Janet, and H. C. Andersen. 1982. *The Princess and the Pea*. New York: Holiday House.

Stockham, Jessica, and H. C. Andersen. 2009. *The Princess and the Pea*. Swindon [England]: Child's Play. Lift-the-flap book.

Walter, Anne, and Jane Cope. 2009. *The Princess and the Pea*. London: Franklin Watts.

Ziefert, Harriet, Emily Bolam, and H. C. Andersen. 1996. *The Princess and the Pea*. New York: Viking.

OTHER VERSIONS OF "THE PRINCESS AND THE PEA"

Auch, Mary Jane, and Herm Auch. 2002. *The Princess and the Pizza*. New York: Holiday House.

Blackaby, Susan, Charlene DeLage (illustrator), and H. C. Andersen. 2004. *The Princess and the Pea*. Minneapolis, MN: Picture Window Books.

Campbell, Ann-Jeanette (author), and Kathy Osborn Young (illustrator). 1993. *Once upon a Princess and a Pea*. New York: Stewart, Tabori & Chang.

Edwards, Pamela Duncan (author), and Henry Cole (illustrator). 2010. *Princess Pigtoria and the Pea*. New York: Orchard Books.

Johnston, Tony (author), and Warren Ludwig (illustrator). 1996. *The Cowboy and the Black-Eyed Pea*. New York: Putnam and Grosset.

Perlman, Janet, Debbie Rogosin (illustrator), and H. C. Andersen. 2004. *The Penguin and the Pea*. Toronto: Kids Can Press

Takayama, Sandi, Esther Szegedy (illustrator), and H. C. Andersen. 1998. *The Prince and Li Hing Mui*. Honolulu, Hawaii: Bess Press.

Vaës, Alain, and H. C. Andersen. 2001. *The Princess and the Pea*. Boston: Little, Brown.

Ward, Jennifer (author), and Lee Calderon (illustrator). 2011. *There Was an Odd Princess Who Swallowed a Pea*. Tarrytown, NY: Marshall Cavendish Children.

Williams, Brenda, Sophie Fatus (illustrator), and H. C. Andersen. 2008. *The Real Princess: A Mathemagical Tale*. Cambridge, MA: Barefoot Books.

Wilson, Tony, and Sue DeGenarro. 2012. *The Princess and the Packet of Frozen Peas*. Atlanta: Peachtree.

Young, Laurie (author), and Johanna Hantel (illustrator), with Matt Powers and H. C. Andersen. 2007. *Princess Polly and the Pea: A Royal Tactile and Princely Pop-Up*. Atlanta: Piggy Toes Press.

Week 5: Read More Versions of the Story; Dance with Peas

Week 5 Outline

Repetition with Variety: Read more versions of the story; dance with peas

Theme: Marriage and Counting

Beginning Ritual
- **Introduction**
- **Fingerplay:** "Five Fat Peas in a Peapod Pressed" (repeated from weeks 1–4)

Story/Activity 1
- **Book:** *Cinderella* by Max Eilenberg and Niamh Sharkley
- **Activity:** "1, 2, 3, 4, 5, Once I Caught a Fish Alive"

Story/Activity 2
- **Book:** Same story as focus text, but by a different adapter and illustrator, *The Princess and the Pea* retold by Janet Rieheck OR *The Princess and the Pea* retold by Susan Blackaby, illustrated by Charlene DeLage
- **Activity:** Dance with Peas: "I Got a Pea" (repeated from week 3), "The Hokey Pea-okey" (repeated from weeks 3 and 4), "Head, Shoulders, Peas, and Toes" (repeated from weeks 1, 3, and 4), "Put Your Pea in the Air!"

Story/Activity 3
- **Book:** *Princess Smarty-Pants* by Babette Cole
- **Developmental Tip:** Counting is fun
- **Activity:** "Ten in the Bed" (repeated from week 2)

Story/Activity 4
- **Book:** *Alligator Wedding* by Nancy Jewell, illustrated by Jonathan Rutland OR *Woof: A Love Story* by Sarah Weeks, illustrated by Holly Berry
- **Activity:** "Carrot, Carrot, Pea"

Closing Ritual
- **Vote**
- **Fingerplay:** "Five Fat Peas in a Peapod Pressed" (repeated from weeks 1–4)

ITEM NEEDED

- reversible doll (optional)

Reversible Dolls

- A Topsy Turvy Cinderella doll can be found online at North American Bear Co.
- Etsy (www.etsy.com) also has some knitted reversible Cinderella dolls. Search for "Cinderella doll" and see the wide selection.

BOOKS NEEDED

Blackaby, Susan (reteller), Charlene DeLage (illustrator), and H. C. Andersen. 2008. *The Princess and the Pea: A Retelling of the Hans Christian Andersen Fairy Tale.* Mankato, MN: Picture Window Books.

Cole, Babette. 2005. *Princess Smartypants.* New York: G. P. Putnam's Sons.

Eilenberg, Max, and Niamh Sharkey. 2008. *Cinderella.* Cambridge, MA: Candlewick Press.

Jewell, Nancy (author), and J. Rutland (illustrator). 2010. *Alligator Wedding.* New York: Henry Holt.

José, Eduard (adapter), Janet Riehecky (adapter), H. C. Andersen, and Francesc Rovira (illustrator). 1988. *The Princess and the Pea.* Chanhassen, MN: Child's World.

Weeks, Sarah (author), and Holly Berry (illustrator). 2009. *Woof: A Love Story.* New York: HarperCollins.

Script

BEGINNING RITUAL

Introduction

Fingerplay: "Five Fat Peas in a Peapod Pressed"
Repeat from weeks 1–4.

STORY/ACTIVITY 1

Book: *Cinderella* by Max Eilenberg and Niamh Sharkley
Read aloud or retell the story using a reversible doll.

The ball where Cinderella met the prince was a very fancy dance. Who remembers how many balls were held in the story we just read? Let's count by looking at the illustrations again. *(Count.)*

Activity: "1, 2, 3, 4, 5, Once I Caught a Fish Alive"
1, 2, 3, 4, 5, Once I caught a fish alive. *(Start with a closed fist and lift fingers one by one.)*

6, 7, 8, 9, 10, Then I threw him back again. *(Lift fingers from other fist one by one. Pretend to throw fish back in water.)*

Why did you let him go?

Because he bit my finger so. *(Pretend to bite finger.)*

Which finger did he bite?
This little finger on the right. (*Show pinky finger.*)
Waaaaaah! He bit my finger!

STORY/ACTIVITY 2

Book: *The Princess and the Pea* retold by Janet Riehecky, illustrated by Francesc Rovira OR *The Princess and the Pea* retold by Susan Blackaby, illustrated by Charlene DeLage
Here's another version of "The Princess and the Pea." Who can tell me what happened? (*Show illustrations and have the children tell you the story. When you arrive at the page with all the mattresses, count them aloud to make sure there are twenty-four.*)

Activity: Dance with Peas
Hand out the laminated peas, play the song "I Got a Pea" by Bryant Oden (from week 3), and have everyone dance with their peas. Also dance to "The Hokey Pea-okey" (from weeks 3 and 4) and "Head, Shoulders, Peas, and Toes" (from weeks 1, 3, and 4). Finish with "Put Your Pea in the Air," following the directions in the song.

"Put Your Pea in the Air!" (To the tune of "If You're Happy and You Know It")
Put your pea in the air, in the air.
Put your pea in the air, in the air.
Put your pea in the air, and wave it way up there.
Put your pea in the air, in the air.

Put your pea on your nose, on your nose.
Put your pea on your nose, on your nose.
Put your pea on your nose, then drop it to your toes.
Put your pea on your nose, on your nose.

Put your pea on the floor, on the floor.
Put your pea on the floor, on the floor.
Sit down on your pea, and sing along with me
With your pea on the floor, on the floor.

STORY/ACTIVITY 3

Book: *Princess Smarty-Pants* by Babette Cole
Read aloud and count how many suitors there were.

> **TIP:** Three good books about women who refused to marry when it did not seem right to them are *The Girl Who Wouldn't Get Married* by Ruth Belov Gross, illustrated by Jack Kent; *Helga's Dowry* by Tomie DePaola; and *The Paper Bag Princess* by Robert Munsch, illustrated by Michael Martchenko.

>> DEVELOPMENTAL TIP

Children love to count if it's done in a fun way! Point to picture book illustrations and encourage your children to help you count specific objects, or play a game together of counting items in a counting book.

Activity: "Ten in the Bed"

Repeat from week 2.

STORY/ACTIVITY 4

Book: *Alligator Wedding* by Nancy Jewell, illustrated by Jonathan Rutland OR *Woof: A Love Story* by Sarah Weeks, illustrated by Holly Berry

Read aloud.

Activity: "Carrot, Carrot, Pea"

If you have time, play this variation on Duck, Duck, Goose, substituting the words carrot, carrot, pea.

CLOSING RITUAL

Vote

Fingerplay: "Five Fat Peas in a Peapod Pressed"

Repeat from weeks 1–4.

> **A Pea Game!**
> Haba produces a Sleepy Princess and the Pea Game for ages 3 and up, that is suitable for one to four players

BOOKS ABOUT MARRIAGE AND WEDDINGS

DePaola, Tomie. 1999. *Helga's Dowry: A Troll Love Story*. Topeka, KA: Econo-Clad.

Gross, Ruth Belov (author), Jack Kent (illustrator), and Peter Christen Asbjørnsen. 1983. *The Girl Who Wouldn't Get Married*. New York: Four Winds Press.

LaRochelle, David (author), and Richard Egielski (illustrator). 2007. *The End: A Reverse Fairy Tale that Starts with the Wedding and Moves Backward!* New York: Arthur A. Levine.

Munsch, Robert N. (author), and Michael Martchenko (illustrator). 1980. *The Paper Bag Princess*. Toronto: Annick Press.

Wise, William (author), and Richard Egielski (illustrator). 1997. *Perfect Pancakes, If You Please*. New York: Dial Books for Young Readers. 1997.

Week 6: Invite the Children to Retell the Story in Their Own Words

Week 6 Outline

Repetition with Variety: Invite the children to retell the story in their own words

Theme: Rain and Climbing

Beginning Ritual
- **Introduction**
- **Fingerplay:** "Five Fat Peas in a Peapod Pressed" (repeated from weeks 1–5)

Story/Activity 1
- **Book:** *Rain* by Alice K. Flanagan
- **Activity:** "Making Rain"
- **Developmental Tip:** Learning through play

Story/Activity 2
- **Book:** *My Side of the Car* by Kate Feiffer, illustrated by Jules Feiffer
- **Activity:** Fun with Scarves: "We Wave Our Scarves Together" (adapted from "We Ring Our Bells Together," from week 4 of "The Three Bears"), "It's Raining, It's Pouring" (repeated from weeks 1 and 4), "Rain Rain, Go Away" (repeated from week 1), "Pitter Patter, Listen to the Rain" (repeated from week 1)
- **Activity:** "Decorate Crowns Craft"

Story/Activity 3
- **Book:** A kinesthetic presentation of the focus text, *The Princess and the Pea* adapted and illustrated by Janet Stevens
- **Activity:** Dance with Peas: "The Hokey Pea-okey" (repeated from weeks 3–5), "Head, Shoulders, Peas, and Toes" (repeated from weeks 1, 3, 4, and 5), "Put Your Pea in the Air" (repeated from week 5), "Peas Away" (adapted from "Scarves Away," from week 3 of "The Three Bears")

Story 4 (if there is time)
- **Book:** *While You Are Sleeping: A Lift-the-Flap Book of Time Around the World* by Durga Bernhard

Closing Ritual
- **Vote**
- **Fingerplay:** "Five Fat Peas in a Peapod Pressed" (repeat from weeks 1–5)

ITEMS NEEDED

- laminated peas
- tote bag with colored scarves
- crowns (1 per child)

- crayons (5 per child)
- colored scarves (at least 1 per attendee)

BOOKS NEEDED

Bernhard, Durga. 2011. *While You Are Sleeping: A Lift-the-Flap Book of Time Around the World.* Watertown, MA: Charlesbridge.

Feiffer, Kate (author), and Jules Feiffer (illustrator). 2011. *My Side of the Car.* Somerville, MA: Candlewick Press.

Flanagan, Alice K. 2003. *Rain.* Chanhassen, MN: Child's World.

Stevens, Janet, and H. C. Andersen. 1982. *The Princess and the Pea.* New York: Holiday House.

Script

BEGINNING RITUAL

Introduction

Fingerplay: "Five Fat Peas in a Peapod Pressed"
Repeat from weeks 1–5.

STORY/ACTIVITY 1

Book: *Rain* by Alice K. Flanagan
Show the cover of the book and ask the children what type of weather they see. After they answer, read the story aloud.

Activity: "Making Rain"
Ask everyone to sit in a big circle. Explain that you will be standing inside of the circle, facing out. You will be walking around the circle doing different things, and whoever you are facing should mimic what you are doing and continue making that motion until you come around again with a new one.

Now we are going to make our own rainstorm. In order to do this, everyone must sit in a circle. I am going to be in the center of the circle, facing you. Everyone should be looking at me, and it must be absolutely quiet if we are going to bring a rainstorm right here in the library. I am going to slowly walk around the circle, and when I am facing you, do EXACTLY what I am doing. Don't talk, just listen to the sounds. Keep repeating that motion until I am standing in front of you again, doing something else, and then stop doing the first thing and start doing the new movement with me. Continue doing this until everyone is silent. If you are quiet the entire time and listen to the sounds we are making, it will sound just like a rain storm in the library!

> Start by walking slowly around the circle snapping fingers slowly. Not all children can do this, but that is okay.
>
> Snap fingers more quickly.
>
> Rub palms of hands together.
>
> Tap hands together lightly.
>
> Clap loudly.
>
> Stamp your feet.
>
> Stamp and clap at the same time.
>
> Stamp without clapping.
>
> Clap without stamping.
>
> Tap.
>
> Rub palms together.
>
> Snap quickly.
>
> Snap slowly.
>
> Fold hands and put them in your lap.

>> DEVELOPMENTAL TIP

Scientific studies of the brain suggest that a child's natural approach to learning is through play. Playing games like the one above helps children learn to follow directions and use their imagination.

STORY/ACTIVITY 2

Book: *My Side of the Car* by Kate Feiffer, illustrated by Jules Feiffer
Read aloud.

Activity: Fun with Scarves
Walk around with a canvas bag. Reach in and give each person a colored scarf. Include adults too if they are attending your session. Sing!

"We Wave Our Scarves Together"
(by Barbara Cass-Beggs; to the tune of "The Farmer in the Dell")

We wave our scarves together, we wave our scarves together.

We wave our scarves together because it's fun to do.

Wave them up high. (*Up high in a high voice*)

Wave them down low. *(Down low in a low voice)*
Wave them in the middle. *(In the middle, in your normal voice)*

Ask the children to pretend their scarves are rain. Throw them up in the air, watch the colorful "raindrops" falling down, and catch them while singing the following songs: "It's Raining, It's Pouring" (from weeks 1 and 4), "Rain, Rain, Go Away" (from week 1), "Pitter Patter" (from week 1).

Now let's use our imaginations and pretend that our scarves are raindrops. We've been singing a few songs about rain during our past few storytimes, so let's sing the songs while we throw our scarves up in the air and try to catch the colored raindrops on their way down.

Activity: "Decorate Crowns Craft"

Inexpensive crowns can be purchased from Oriental Trading (www.orientaltrading.com) or made using the crown template. Hand each child a crown and five crayons or some stickers. Tell the children they will have five minutes to decorate their crown. When everyone has finished decorating, ask them to put their crowns on their heads. Give each person a laminated pea.

STORY/ACTIVITY 3

Book: *The Princess and the Pea* adapted and illustrated by Janet Stevens

We have been hearing this story *(hold up* The Princess and the Pea *by Janet Stevens)*, playing games with it, and acting out different parts for a few weeks now. Today, let's pretend that we are the characters in the story, and let's act out the entire thing. Raise your hand if you would like to be a narrator (those are the people who tell the story). *(Choose as many children as you like.)*

All narrators stand over here. *(Designate area.)*
Raise your hand if you would like to be the queen. *(Choose as many children as you like.)* All queens, stand over here. *(Designate area.)*
Raise your hand if you would like to be the prince. *(Choose as many children as you like.)* All princes, stand over here. *(Designate area.)*
And, raise your hand if you would like to be the princess. *(Choose as many children as you like.)* All princesses, stand over here. *(Designate area.)*
Parents, you will be the audience. Please sit in that area *(designate area)* and give your utmost attention to our group of actors and actresses.
Narrators, you can start by telling the story. *(Point to one narrator to start.)*
Once upon a time . . . *(When you get to the part about the rain, tell everyone to throw*

their scarves up in the air four times each and then collect them, leaving each child with one scarf.)

You may have to help the narrators along. The essential parts of the story are as follows:

Princess in the rain. (Scarves thrown up in the air.)

Princess knocks on door.

Princess drinks tea with queen and prince. (Sing the song "I Sat Next to the Princess at Tea.")

Queen hides pea under the mattress. (Put a pea down in the middle of the floor. Have each child put their colored scarf down on top of the pea.)

Princess gets ready for bed. (Play Raffi's "Brush Your Teeth.")

Princess climbs up mattresses.

Princess tosses and turns all night while the prince sleeps soundly and snores, and the queen sleeps soundly and snores.

Princess climbs down and joins the queen and the prince for breakfast.

Princess complains about her sleep. (Rubbing her back.)

Prince jumps up and shouts, "Yipeee! Will you marry me?"

Queen brings the pea to the museum curator. (You!)

That was a great version of "The Princess and the Pea."

Activity: Dance with Peas

Now let's dance with our peas.

Hand out peas. Do all the pea dances: "The Hokey Pea-okey" (from weeks 3–5), "Head, Shoulders, Peas, and Toes" (from weeks 1, 3, 4, and 5), "Put Your Pea in the Air" (from week 5), and "Peas Away."

"Peas Away" (adapted from "Scarves Away," by Barbara Cass-Beggs)

Peas away, peas away,

Put your peas away today.

STORY 4 (IF THERE IS TIME)

Book: *While You Are Sleeping: A Lift-the-Flap Book of Time Around the World* **by Durga Bernhard**

Now that the prince and princess and married, and the pea is safely in the museum, what do you think the princess is doing? *(Pause for answers.)* I think she must be catching up on all the sleep she missed when there was a pea under her mattresses. And what do you think other people are doing while the princess might be sleeping? Let's have a look in this book, *While You Are Sleeping: A Lift-the-Flap Book of Time Around the World* by Durga Bernhard. *(Read aloud.)*

CLOSING RITUAL

Vote

Fingerplay: "Five Fat Peas in a Peapod Pressed"
Repeat from weeks 1–5.

BOOKS ABOUT CLIMBING

Carle, Eric. 1972. *The Secret Birthday Message.* New York, Crowell.

——. 1986. *Papa, Please Get the Moon for Me.* Saxonville, MA: Picture Book Studio.

Crews, Nina. 2011. *Jack and the Beanstalk.* New York: Henry Holt.

Fancher, Lou, and Steve Johnson. 2006. *Star Climbing.* New York: Laura Geringer Books.

Fowles, Shelley. 2006. *Climbing Rosa.* London: Frances Lincoln.

Osborne, Mary Pope. 2000. *Kate and the Beanstalk.* New York: Atheneum Books for Young Readers.

Richards, Beah E. (author), and R. Gregory Christie (illustrator). 2006. *Keep Climbing, Girls.* New York: Simon & Schuster Books for Young Readers.

Walker, Richard (author), and Niamh Sharkey (illustrator). 1999. *Jack and the Beanstalk.* New York: Barefoot Books.

chapter 5

Series 3
I Ain't Gonna Paint No More

Focus Text:
I Ain't Gonna Paint No More!

by Karen Beaumont and David Catrow
(Orlando, FL: Harcourt, 2005)

Forbidden to paint anything after being caught painting parts of the house, an artistic child can't resist
painting every part of his body while singing "I Ain't
Gonna Paint No More."

Ways to Present *I Ain't Gonna Paint No More!* in Storytime Sessions

Week 1: Introduce *I Ain't Gonna Paint No More.* (painting)

Week 2: Inspire imagination with the aid of colored scarves. (houses)

Week 3: "Paint" body parts. (body parts)

Week 4: Discuss the silent story being told through the illustrations. (bathtubs)

Week 5: Discuss the book's illustrations. (colors)

Week 6: Examine other books by Karen Beaumont. (books by Karen Beaumont)

Week 1: Introduce *I Ain't Gonna Paint No More*

Read the story aloud. Sing the story with bells.

THEME

Painting

ITEM NEEDED

- bells (enough for each participant)

SUGGESTED CONTENT

Focus Text

Read (don't sing!) the book aloud at the beginning of storytime. Toward the end of storytime, hand out bells. This time, sing the book to the tune of "It Ain't Gonna Rain No More" and ask everyone to ring their bells to the beat as you sing the book. Invite them to sing along with you if they already know the words. The tune can be found on Fred Penner's CD The Cat Came Back, *track 8 (Casablanca Kids, 1991).*

>> DEVELOPMENTAL TIP

Even if you can't sing on key, be sure to sing to your child! Your child is not looking for a concert-quality song; she wants familiar sounds from a person who means a great deal to her. Singing together can be great fun, and it doesn't require any special equipment or cost any money.

SONGS

"Paint, Paint, Paint"
by Kathy Buchsbaum (to the tune "Row, Row, Row Your Boat")
Paint, paint, paint the house, *(Move arms up and down like painting.)*
Paint it all day long.
Paint, paint, paint, paint,
And sing this song!

Paint, paint the fence, *(Move arms up and down like painting.)*
Paint it all day long.
Paint, paint, paint, paint,
And sing this song!
(Then you can make it silly...)

Paint, paint, paint the dog—
No! We don't paint a dog!
What can we paint?

(Paper, wall, car, etc.)

"If You're Happy and You Know It, Paint Your House"

Sing "If You're Happy and You Know It." Add a verse: "If you're happy and you know it, paint your house," using appropriate motions.

PAINTING ACTIVITIES

Painting with Watercolors Craft

Put a plastic tablecloth on the floor or on a table. Place watercolor sets with brushes, bowls filled only slightly with water, and paper on top of the tablecloth, and invite children to do some painting of their own.

Makin' by Shakin' Craft

Materials
- secure plastic storage container (such as Ziploc brand Twist 'n' Loc containers)
- small, round, plastic balls with holes in them (such as practice golf balls) or marbles
- 4-by-8-inch pieces of paper
- paper plates
- paint
- wipes (for hands)
- garbage can

Setup
1. Pour four colors of paint into four different bowls.
2. Place the bowls on the table where the children will be working.
3. Place a plastic container, ball (or marble) and a piece of paper at each child's seat.

Activity *(Having adult assistance is best for this activity)*
1. Each child writes their name on the paper (or has the adult do it for them) and puts their piece of paper into the open plastic container.
2. Each child takes turns putting part of a ball (or marble) in a bowl of paint, so that the ball eventually has all four colors on it, but not in large quantities.

3. Each child puts a painted ball into a container and closes the lid.
4. Check to be sure the lids are securely fastened.
5. Ask the children to shake their containers vigorously.
6. Unscrew the lid and remove the painting. It may take a while to dry.

Paint in a Bag Craft

Materials
- zip-close sandwich bags
- masking tape
- permanent marker
- plastic spoons
- 1 paper plate
- finger paint (just 1 color is fine; 2 or 3 colors are also fine)
- wipes (for hands)
- garbage can

Setup
1. On a table, place a pile of plastic bags (enough for 1 per child), the masking tape, the permanent marker, the spoons, the jars of finger paint, the wipes, and the paper plate.
2. Place the garbage can next to the table.
3. Open the jars; dip a plastic spoon in each jar so that the spoon represents the color available. Place the spoons on the paper plate.

Activity *(Having adult assistance is best for this activity.)*
1. Sit at the table, and ask the children to form a line.
2. One by one, ask the children which color they would like in their bag.
3. Using a plastic spoon, put two scoops of color in the bag.
4. Place the bag on the table and show the children how to push the air out before sealing it. Make sure to explain what you are doing verbally as you do it.
5. Fold over the top of the seam, so that the zipper portion has flapped over the bag.
6. Cut or rip a piece of masking tape that is longer than the bag's width. Tape it over the folded seam to make sure that the bag will not open.
7. Ask the child to press on the masking tape to make sure it sticks well.
8. Turn the bag over and fold in the sides of the masking tape.
9. Ask the child or parent to write the child's name with the permanent marker on the masking tape.
10. On a display bag, show the children how to use both hands to smush the paint out to the sides of the bag.

11. Show how to use your finger to make a line.
12. Show how to use your finger to make a circle.
13. Show how to use your finger tips to make dots.
14. Show how to use your hand to create a clean slate.
15. Tell the children that they may keep this and continue playing with it at home.

BOOKS ABOUT PAINTING AND DRAWING

Try displaying books with painting projects that caregivers may want to check out.

Arnold, Katya. 2005. *Elephants Can Paint, Too!* New York: Atheneum Books for Young Readers.

Bridges, Shirin Yim. 2008. *The Umbrella Queen.* New York: Greenwillow.

Carle, Eric. 2011. *The Artist Who Painted a Blue Horse.* New York: Philomel.

Cousins, Lucy. 2009. *Maisy Goes to Preschool.* Somerville, MA: Candlewick Press.

Dewan. Ted. 2003. *Bing: Paint Day.* New York: David Fickling Books.

Henry, Sally. 2009. *Painting.* New York: PowerKids Press.

Hissey, Jane. 2001. *Old Bear's Surprise Painting.* New York: Philomel.

Larsen, Andrew (author), and Irene Luxbacher (illustrator). 2009. *The Imaginary Garden.* Toronto: Kids Can.

Markun, Patricia Maloney (author), and Robert Casilla (illustrator). 1993. *The Little Painter of Sabana Grande.* New York: Bradbury.

Micklethwait, Lucy. 2007. *I Spy Colors in Art.* New York: Greenwillow Books.

Pinkwater, Daniel Manus. 2008. *Bear's Picture.* Boston: Houghton Mifflin.

Reynolds, Peter H. 2004. *Ish.* Cambridge, MA: Candlewick Press.

Saltzberg, Barney. 2010. *Beautiful Oops!* New York: Workman Pub.

Seeger, Laura Vaccaro. 2008. *One Boy.* New York: Roaring Brook.

Snyder, Carol (author), and Lisa Jan-Clough (illustrator). 2002. *We're Painting.* New York: HarperFestival

Sweet, Melissa. 2005. Carmine: *A Little More Red.* Boston: Houghton Mifflin.

Wallace, Nancy Elizabeth. 2006. *Look! Look! Look!* Singapore: Marshall Cavendish Children

Walsh, Ellen Stoll. 1989. *Mouse Paint.* New York: Harcourt Brace Jovanovich.

Whatley, Bruce. 2001. *Wait! No Paint!* New York: HarperCollins.

Wiesner, David. 2010. *Art and Max.* Boston: Clarion Books.

Week 2:
Inspire Imagination with the Aid of Colored Scarves

Sing the story using colored scarves as paintbrushes.

THEME

Houses

ITEMS NEEDED

- colored scarves (enough for each child and each adult)
- flannelboard pieces from figures 5.1 and 5.2

SUGGESTED CONTENT

Focus Text

Do you remember this story from last week? I hope so! I am going to read it aloud again, but this time, I want you to use your imaginations and pretend that your scarves are paintbrushes. Every time the characters in the story paint something, I want you to paint it too! *(Read book aloud.)*

>> DEVELOPMENTAL TIP

Some children love to sit and listen to books, and some find other activities more interesting. Help your children enjoy books by having them participate in some way. This can be as simple as asking them to join in saying a repeated phrase—or as complicated as creating a new version of the story and acting it out!

SONG

"The Paintbrush Hokey Pokey"
Dance to this adapted version of the hokey pokey.

You put your paintbrush in, you take your paintbrush out.
You put your paintbrush in, and you paint it all about.
You do the hokey pokey and you turn yourself around.
That's what it's all about.
Hey!

Try adding in more body parts (e.g., nose, elbow, bottom).

ACTIVITIES

Painting with Scarves

Since we've used our scarves as paintbrushes, let's all stand up and paint the sky. What color should we use to paint the sky? *(Pause for answers.)* Reach up as high as you can and make big strokes from side to side with your paint brush. What else is in the sky? *(The moon, the stars, planets, the sun, spaceships, aliens, etc.)*

Scarf Toss

On the count of three, throw your scarves into the air and try to catch them before they reach the floor. One...two...three...WHEEEEeeee.

Discussion

Explain what a rhyme is. Ask the children what words they know that rhyme with house.

Discussion: Guess Which Paintbrush?

Make flannelboard pieces from figures 5.1 and 5.2. Put the pieces on the flannelboard and ask the children what is different about each and what is alike. Explain that they are both paintbrushes but one is for painting houses and the other is for painting pictures. Hold the flannelboard artist's paintbrush in your hand and pretend to paint a picture (with small movements). Pretend to use the large paintbrush to paint a house (with large movements).

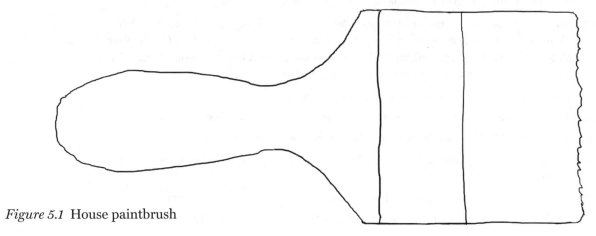

Figure 5.1 House paintbrush

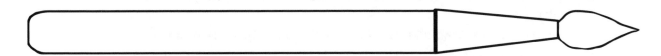

Figure 5.2 Artist's paintbrush

HANDOUT FOR PARENTS

Download and print out this house template for your child to decorate and assemble: www.thetoymaker.com/toyblanks/House.pdf.

BOOKS ABOUT HOUSES

Angelou, Maya. 2003. *My Painted House, My Friendly Chicken, and Me.* New York: Crown Books for Young Readers.

Banks, Kate (author), and Georg Hallensleben (illustrator). 2005. *The Great Blue House.* New York: Farrar Straus Giroux.

Barton, Byron. 1981. *Building a House.* New York: Greenwillow.

Beaumont, Karen (author), and David Catrow (illustrator). 2005. *I Ain't Gonna Paint No More!* Orlando, FL: Harcourt.

Beil, Karen Magnuson (author), and Mike Wohnoutka (illustrator). 2008. *Jack's House.* New York: Holiday House.

Edwards, Pamela Duncan. 2008. *Jack and Jill's Treehouse.* New York: Katherine Tegan.

Gibbons, Gail. 1996. *How a House Is Built.* New York: Holiday House.

Hoberman, Mary Ann (author), and Betty Fraser (illustrator). 1978. *A House Is a House for Me.* New York: Viking Press.

Kohara, Kazuno. 2008. *Ghosts in the House!* New York: Roaring Brook.

Komatsu, Yoshio (author), Akira Nishiyama (illustrator), Katy Bridges (translator), and Naoko Amemiya (translator). 2004. *Wonderful Houses around the World.* Bolinas, CA: Shelter. Do not read this aloud. Instead, show the pictures of different homes around the world from this book or any other nonfiction book about houses.

Moore, Max. 2009. *Homes Around the World.* New York: DK.

Pinkwater, Daniel Manus. 1977. *The Big Orange Splot.* New York: Scholastic.

Riphagen, Loes. 2011. *Animals Home Alone.* New York: Seven Footer Kids.

Seuling, Barbara (author), and Kay Chorao (illustrator). 2004. *Whose House?* Orlando, FL: Harcourt.

Spier, Peter. 1978. *Oh, Were They Ever Happy!* Garden City, New York: Doubleday.

Swanson, Susan Marie (author), and Beth Krommes (illustrator). 2008. *The House in the Night.* Boston: Houghton Mifflin.

Taback, Simms. 2002. *This Is the House That Jack Built.* New York: G. P. Putnam's Sons.

Wallace, Nancy Elizabeth. 2005. *Alphabet House.* New York: Marshall Cavendish.

Westcott, Nadine Bernard. 1991. *The House That Jack Built.* Boston: Little, Brown. Popup, pull-tab book.

Wood, Audrey, and Don Wood. 2000. *The Napping House.* San Diego: Harcourt.

Yolen, Jane (author), and Wendy Anderson Halperin (illustrator). 2005. *Soft House.* Cambridge, MA: Candlewick Press.

Week 3: "Paint" Body Parts; Review Vocabulary and Develop Fine Motor Skills

Mimic the actions of the child in the book by painting body parts while the story is being read.

THEME

Body parts

ITEMS NEEDED

- crayons (or, if you are ready for a challenge, watercolor paints and brushes) in these colors: red, green, black, blue, orange
- paper with an outline of a body (one for each child)

SUGGESTED CONTENT

Focus Text

Sing I Ain't Gonna Paint No More *aloud while children "paint" themselves.*

Hand out a paper with a body outline and five markers (or watercolor paint sets and a bowl or water and brushes) to each child. An image to download can be found at http:// media.photobucket.com/image/Body%20Outline%20To%20Color/emilycake84/body .gif. Make sure each child's name is on his paper. Read or sing the story and ask the children to paint the body part on the outline when the child in the book is painting his own body parts. When finished, collect the materials and put papers on a nearby table to dry if necessary.

>> DEVELOPMENTAL TIP

Knowing the names of your body parts helps build positive body awareness, which leads to heightened self-confidence. That's one reason children love books like this and songs like "Head, Shoulders, Knees, and Toes." Let's stand up and do it!

BODY PARTS ACTIVITIES

"Head, Shoulders, Knees, and Toes"

Sing "Head, Shoulders, Knees, and Toes." Start out slowly. Say the body parts and touch them while the children follow along. Then sing the song slowly. Then sing it faster. Then faster. Then faster. Then as fast as you can so it is almost impossible to follow along.

Labeling Body Parts

Give each child some paper and crayons or markers. Tell them to draw a picture of themselves. Once they have finished, ask their adult to work with them and help label the parts, such as "Susie's head," "Susie's eyes," and "Susie's hands." You may want to add a developmental tip for parents that naming parts of the body helps build self-awareness and positive body image. Suggest that the pictures be posted on refrigerators for at least a week, so the children can feel proud of their drawings and have time to look at the written words that name parts of themselves.

Musical Body Parts

Make musical instruments using your body. Lips can bibble; cheeks can pop or drum; hands can clap flat and cupped, or swish like cymbals; feet can stomp or tap, go from heel to toe, or slide.

BODY CONTROL ACTIVITIES

Balance

Talk about what the parts of the body help you do. For instance, What do you use your hands for? What do you use your feet for? What do you use your toes for? You might not think that toes are important, but without toes, you might have a lot of trouble balancing! *Use masking tape to make a line on the floor, and invite children to try to walk the full length of the "balance beam." Even if they cannot balance well, encourage them to continue practicing.*

>> DEVELOPMENTAL TIP

Balance is a basic part of physical fitness that develops with practice and experience. Balance helps people control and maintain their body position when standing still or moving. Doing balancing exercises helps your preschooler enjoy movement while developing motor skills.

Freeze Game

Play the freeze game with a tambourine.

And we walk, and we walk, and we walk, and we stop. *(Freeze.)*
And we walk, and we walk, and we walk, and we stop. *(Freeze.)*
And we walk, and we walk, and we walk, and we stop. *(Freeze.)*
And we all turn around! WHOOOO! *(Shake the tambourine vigorously while everyone turns around.)*

And we run . . .
And we jump . . .
And we paint!

BOOKS ABOUT BODY PARTS

Alda, Arlene. 2008. *Here a Face, There a Face.* Plattsburgh, NY: Tundra Books of Northern New York.

Arnold, Tedd. 1997. *Parts.* New York: Dial Books for Young Readers.

———. 2001. *More Parts.* New York: Dial Books for Young Readers.

———. 2004. *Even More Parts.* New York: Dial Books for Young Readers.

Bodkin, Odds. 2002. *Belly Button.* Watertown, MA: Perkins School for the Blind.
  This Perkins Panda Book has Braille writing in addition to the illustrations. It comes with audio cassette with the song "Belly Button" on the first track.

Butler, John. 2004. *Whose Nose and Toes?* New York: Viking.

Craig, Lindsey (author), and Marc Tolon Brown (illustrator). 2010. *Dancing Feet!* New York: Alfred A. Knopf.

Cronin, Doreen, and Scott Menchin. 2009. *Stretch.* New York: Atheneum Books for Young Readers.
  Read aloud; ask children to stretch along with the dog!

Fox, Mem (author), and Helen Oxenbury (illustrator). 2008. *Ten Little Fingers and Ten Little Toes.* New York: Harcourt.

Manushkin, Fran (author), and Tracy Dockray (illustrator). 2009. *The Tushy Book.* New York: Feiwel and Friends.

Mariotti, Mario, and Roberto Marchiori. 1980. *Hanimals.* La Jolla, CA: Green Tiger Press.
  This is a wonderful wordless book of painted hands that look like animals. Show the pictures to the children and ask them which animal it is. Other amazing books by Mariotti and Marchiori with painted hands include *Humands,* 1982, *Humages,* 1985, *Hanimations,* 1989, *Hands Off,* 1990.

Menchin, Scott. 2011. *What If Everything Had Legs?* Somerville, MA: Candlewick Press.

Munsch, Robert N. (author), and Hélène Desputeaux (illustrator). 1992. *Purple, Green and Yellow.* Toronto: Annick Press.

Prelutsky, Jack (author), and Brandon Dorman (illustrator). 2008. *Be Glad Your Nose Is on Your Face and Other Poems: Some of the Best of Jack Prelutsky.* New York: Greenwillow Books.

Randolph, Joanne. 2009. *Whose Toes Are Those?* New York: Rosen Pub. Group/ PowerKids.

Rockwell, Lizzy. 2004. *The Busy Body Book.* New York: Crown.

Rowe, Jeanette. 2000. *Whose Nose?* Southwood Books.
  Also from Jeanette Rowe: *Whose Feet?* 2000, and *Whose Ears?* 2000.

Stower, Adam. 2004. *Two Left Feet.* New York: Bloomsbury Children's Books.

Thomas, Jan. 2009. *Can You Make a Scary Face?* New York: Beach Lane Books.

Verdick, Elizabeth. 2003. *Teeth Are Not for Biting.* Minneapolis: Free Spirit Pub.

Yagyu, Genichiro. 1994. *The Holes in Your Nose.* Brooklyn: Kane/Miller.
  Children love this book. Great colorful illustrations accompany activities to go along with the book, such as hearing how your voice sounds different when holding your nose. Read ahead of time and paper clip together pages that you feel might be too much for your audience to handle—such as the bloody nose, the description of boogers, or the illustration of a child's bottom with a hole.

Week 4: Discuss the Silent Story Being Told by "Reading" the Illustrations to Convey Meaning

Find meaning in pictures while connecting visual representations with actions or objects.

THEME

Bathtubs

SUGGESTED CONTENT

Focus Text

I'm sure you all remember this book, *I Ain't Gonna Paint No More* by Karen Beaumont. *(Before reading or singing the book, have a short discussion about it. Hold up the book and display the cover while you are speaking.)* Before we sing and act it out, let's look at the illustrations. They were drawn by a man named David Catrow. Who do you see on the cover of the book? *("A boy.")* What is he doing? *("Painting himself.")* Which colors can you see? *("Red, green blue, yellow, orange, white.")*

Now let's turn to the end papers. *(Open book.)* Those are the pages at the very beginning and end of the book. Do you see any colors here that you did not see on the cover? *("Black, purple.")* What do those two black splotches look like? An ant? A spider?

(Turn and point to the different pieces of information on the title page.) This page is called the title page. It has the title of the book, *I Ain't Gonna Paint No More;* the author of the book, Karen Beaumont; and the name of the person who drew all the pictures, the illustrator, David Catrow. Look at the opposite pages. Are those the same two black splotches from the end papers? What do these look like?

(Turn to the first page.) Here's the first page of the story. What do you see here? *(Let the children describe what they see. You may want to walk around with the book and let each child point to one thing and describe it.)* Do you think that the boy's mother is happy that he is painting all over the house?

(Turn the page.) What did the mother do? *(Pause for answers.)* That's right! She put the boy AND the dog into the bathtub to wash themselves off. Do they look happy? *(Pause for answers.)* I don't think so! Look, his hands are crossed in front of him, like this . . . can you do that too? And his eyes are squinched up like this . . . can you do that too?

(Turn the page.) What's happening here? *("The mother is taking the paints and hiding them on the top shelf of the closet. But the boy is watching from the top of the stairs.")* Notice that the house is just black and white; the only colors you can see are the paints and the boy.

(Turn the page.) Now what? *("The boy has piled a bunch of things on top of one another and climbed up to get to the paints.")* Look! He's already spilled a bit of red on the top two boxes.

(Turn the page.) Uh-oh, what now? *("He's getting paint on the floor.")* Does he look happy or sad? What's he doing with his hands? *("Clasping his hands.")* Let's all try that. And what is he doing with his mouth? *("Smiling.")* Let's all do that. Where's the dog? *("Peeking around the corner.")*

(Turn the page.) Oh no! What's he doing now? *(Painting his face.)* What color is he using? *(Red!)* Does he look happy? *(Yes.)* How do you know he's happy? *(He has a big smile!)*

(Turn the page.) What's he doing here? *("Painting his neck and painting the dog.")* Does the dog look happy? *("No.")* How do we know? *("He's pulling out his collar, sticking out his tongue, and looking at the boy with very wide eyes.")* Let's try that!

(Turn the page.) What's he painting now? *("His chest.")* Put your finger in the air and let's try to make the same shape in the air that he is drawing on his chest. *(Do this.)* Where's the dog? *("Behind him.")*

(Turn the page.) What now? *("He's painted his arm.")* What does it look like he's painted? *("Ants.")* What colors did he use here? *("Red, green, black, orange, yellow, blue.")*

(Turn the page.) What now? *("He painted his hand.")* What's on his hand? *("A face.")* Is the face happy or sad? *("Happy.")* What's climbing out of the mouth? *("Ants.")* Ick!

(Turn the page.) What body part is he painting now? *("His back.")* What is he using to paint his back? *("A roller, not a paintbrush.")* Where's the dog? *("Climbing down the wall.")* What color are the dog's footprints? *("Red.")*

(Turn the page.) What now? *("He painted his leg.")* Who does the dog look like? *("The Easter Bunny!")*

(Turn the page.) Now what is the boy painting? *(His feet, the chair, the floor, the walls, the dog.)*

(Turn the page.) What's happening here? *("The boy is going crazy painting all over the walls with two paintbrushes. The dog is howling. The mother sees the mess and is startled.")*

(Turn the page.) And how does the story end? *("The boy and the dog are sitting in the bathtub washing off all the paint.")* What's on the boy's head? *("A washcloth.")* Where is the paint? *("In the water and on the floor, walls, and bathtub.")* Who doesn't have paint on them anymore? *("The boy and the dog.")*

(Turn the page.) These are the end pages. Do you see the black drawing that is not a splotch? What does that look like? *("A ladder, a chicken foot.")*

(Turn the page.) Here are the final end papers. If you look carefully, you'll see the picture is the same as on one of the papers at the front of the book.

Now that we've looked at all of the illustrations, I'm going to sing the book, and I want you to sing along with me! *(Read the book, singing all of the parts that can be sung. Pause before saying the name of the body parts—or don't say them at all—so the children will be encouraged to shout out the right word before you turn the page.)*

And that is the story of *I Ain't Gonna Paint No More* by Karen Beaumont, illustrated by David Catrow.

>> DEVELOPMENTAL TIP

By looking together at illustrations, finding a story there, and verbalizing the story with your children, you are helping them to find meaning in pictures and connect visual representations with actions or objects.

SONGS AND RHYMES

"Two Little Eyes to Look Around"

Point to the body parts of the face as you mention them in the following rhyme.

Two little eyes to look around.
Two little ears to hear a sound.
One little nose to smell what's sweet. *(Take a big sniff)*
And one little mouth that likes to eat . . . Mmmmmmmm. *(Rub tummy)*

"This Is the Way We Wash"
(to the tune of "Here We Go 'round the Mulberry Bush")

Use colored scarves. Tell the kids to pretend that the scarves are washcloths.

This is the way we wash our neck, wash our neck, wash our neck. *(Rub the scrunched-up scarf against your neck.)*
This is the way we wash our neck, so early in the morning.
Ask the children to call out other body parts that can be washed and choose appropriate ones for a few more verses.

HANDOUT FOR PARENTS

Create a playtime bathtub for your child:
> Start with a heavy cardboard box.
> Trim the box until it is only two feet high.
> Paint the outside of the box white.
> Cover a toilet paper roll with aluminum foil.
> Cut a hole near the top of the box and insert the foil-covered roll to be the faucet.
> Fill the tub with Styrofoam peanuts for bubbles.
> Add bath toys, washcloths, and empty shampoo bottles as desired.

BOOKS ABOUT BATHS

Andreasen, Dan. 2009. *The Treasure Bath*. New York: Henry Holt.

Andres, Kristina. 2010. *Elephant in the Bathtub*. New York: North-South.

Carle, Eric. 2005. *10 Little Rubber Ducks*. New York: HarperCollins.

Conrad, Pam (author), and Richard Egielski (illustrator). 1993. *The Tub People*. Illinois: HarperCollins.

Dougherty, Terri (author), and Hye Won Yi (illustrator). 2006. *The Bath*. Minneapolis: Picture Window Books.

Esbaum, Jill (author), and Mary Newell DePalma (illustrator). 2006. *Estelle Takes a Bath*. New York: Henry Holt.

Fernandes, Eugenie. 1996. *Waves in the Bathtub*. Buffalo, NY: Firefly Books.

Fox, Mem, and Olivia Rawson (authors), with Kerry Argent (illustrator). 2010. *A Giraffe in the Bath*. New York: Penguin/Viking.

Jenkins, Steve, and Robin Page. 2011. *Time for a Bath*. Boston: Houghton Mifflin Books for Children.
Learn the fascinating ways different animals bathe. Small pages make this a challenging storytime choice, but it works with small groups.

Kalman, Bobbie. 2011. *A Bath*. Ontario: Crabtree Pub. Co.
Fun photographs of different animals taking a bath. Ask the children to name the different animals that are bathing.

Krosoczka, Jarrett. 2003. *Bubble Bath Pirates!* New York: Viking.
Hand out towels or rug samples. Ask each child to pretend it is a bathtub and they are sitting in it in order to be part of the story. Hand out colored scarves. Ask the children to pretend the scarves are washcloths and also to pretend they are pirates in the bathtub while you are reading the book aloud.

Kudrna, C. Imbior. 1988. *To Bathe a Boa*. Minneapolis, MN: CarolRhoda Books.

Maizes, Sarah (author), and Michael Paraskevas (illustrator). 2012. *On My Way to the Bath*. New York: Walker and Company.

Medearis, Angela Shelf (author), and Jacqueline Rogers (illustrator). 1996. *We Eat Dinner in the Bathtub*. New York: Scholastic.

Rasmussen, Ann, and Marc A. Nemiroff (authors), with Kate Flanagan (illustrator). 2000. *The Very Lonely Bathtub*. Washington, DC: Magination Press.

Segal, John. 2011. *Pirates Don't Take Baths*. New York: Philomel Books.

Stevens, Kathleen (author), and Ray Bowler (illustrator). 1985. *The Beast in the Bathtub*. Milwaukee, WI: G. Stevens.

Westcott, Nadine Bernard. 2008. *The Lady with the Alligator Purse.* New York: Little, Brown.

Wood, Audrey, and Don Wood. 2010. *King Bidgood's in the Bathtub.* Boston: Sandpiper Books.

MUSIC AND POETRY ABOUT BATHS

Katz, Alan (author), and David Catrow (illustrator). 2001. *Take Me Out of the Bathtub and Other Silly Dilly Songs.* New York: Margaret K. McElderry. (The first poem in the book is "Take Me Out of the Bathtub.")

———. 2003. *I'm Still Here in the Bathtub: Brand New Silly Dilly Songs.* New York: Margaret K. McElderry.

Levy, Debbie (author), and Stephanie Buscema (illustrator). 2010. *Maybe I'll Sleep in the Bathtub Tonight and Other Funny Bedtime Poems.* New York: Sterling.

McMullan, Kate (author), and Janie Bynum (illustrator). 2005. *Bathtub Blues.* New York: Little, Brown. (Book with music)

Schwartz, Alvin, and Syd Hoff. 1989. *I Saw You in the Bathtub and Other Folk Rhymes.* New York: Harper & Row.

Week 5: Discuss the Book's Illustrations, Focusing on Colors, Lines, and Shapes

Promote positive physical interaction between adult caregivers and children while focusing on book illustration.

THEME

Colors

ITEMS NEEDED

- large stickers in these colors: red, yellow, purple, orange, green, black, and blue
- tote bag with colored scarves

PREPARATION

Cut small squares from sheets of large stickers; each square should have one or two stickers on it. Have two stickers of each color for each child in storytime.

SUGGESTED CONTENT

Focus Text

Hand out the big stickers to the parents and caregivers. Hand out colored scarves to the children. Ask the children to pretend the scarf is a paintbrush and to imagine that the stickers are the paint. As you sing the book together and each child is "painting" a part of the body with a scarf, parents will stick the stickers on that body part. Use red for the head, yellow for the neck, purple for the chest, orange for an arm (or both arms), green for a hand, black for the back, blue for a leg, and one of each color to cover the feet. When you have finished singing the story together, ask the children the following questions:

What color did we paint our head? *("Red.")*
What color did we paint our neck? *("Yellow.")*
What color did we paint our chest? *("Purple.")*
What color did we paint our arm? *("Orange.")*
What color did we paint our hand? *("Green.")*
What color did we paint our back? *("Black.")*
What color did we paint our leg? *("Blue.")*
What color did we paint our feet? *("All the colors!")*

SCARF ACTIVITIES

Scarf Toss

We're going to play a game. When I count to three, throw your scarves in the air. Then I will call out a body part and see if you can catch them using that part. For instance if I say "head," when your scarf is coming down, try to catch it with your head like this. *(Demonstrate.)* Let's go! *(Play game.)*

>> DEVELOPMENTAL TIP

Stories, games, and songs that focus on body parts and their actions increase children's awareness of how different parts of the body can start specific movements. By using their muscles to make the motions in a story, game, or song, children develop their gross motor skills and body self-awareness.

"Head, Shoulders, Knees, and Toes"

Let's sing "Head, Shoulders, Knees, and Toes," using our scarves to touch the parts of the body that we name. (Repeat from week 4.)

"Who Is Wearing Red Today?"

"Who Is Wearing Red Today?" is a song about the colors that we wear. If we sing about a color you're wearing, wave your scarf in the air. When the verse is over, follow the directions and sit down.

"Who Is Wearing Red Today?"
(to the tune of "London Bridge Is Falling Down")

Who is wearing red today? Red today? Red today?

Who is wearing red today? Wave your scarves and sit down.

Continue using the names of other colors until everyone is sitting down.

OTHER ACTIVITIES

Red Light, Green Light Game

You can be the stoplight for the first round of this game; afterward, the children should take turns being the stoplight. The objective of this game is for all the vehicles to be able to touch the stoplight.

How to play:

All children form a line about fifteen feet away from the stoplight. The stoplight's back is facing the children.

When the stoplight says, "Green light," the children can move toward the stoplight.

As soon as the stoplight says, "Red light," the children must stop moving.

The stoplight can turn around while saying, "Red light," and if any of the children are caught moving, they are out and must sit down.

The game continues when the stoplight turns around and says, "Green light," again.

If the game ends before anyone is able to touch the stoplight, then the stoplight is the winner.

If a player manages to touch the stoplight, that person wins the game and becomes the stoplight for the next game.

If you play this game, you may want to hand children a piece of paper with two large circles on it. Provide red and green crayons and ask the children to color in each circle with a different color. Invite them to take their picture home, and encourage parents to play red light, green light with them and their friends. This helps children develop self-regulation skills by learning how to stop and go according to someone else's directions.

BOOKS ABOUT COLORS

Allington, Richard L., and Noel Spangler. 1979. *Colors.* Milwaukee, WI: Raintree Children's Books. Nonfiction.

Brocket, Jane. 2011. *Ruby, Violet, Lime: Looking for Color.* Minneapolis: Millbrook. Nonfiction.

Crews, Donald. 2009. *Freight Train.* New York: Mulberry.

Hoban, Tana. 1978. *Is It Red? Is It Yellow? Is It Blue? An Adventure in Color.* New York: Greenwillow Books. Nonfiction.

Jonas, Ann. 1989. *Color Dance*. New York: Greenwillow.

Katz, Karen. 1999. *The Colors of Us*. New York: Henry Holt.

Kochan, Vera (author), and Viviana Garófoli (illustrator). 2011. *What If Your Best Friend Were Blue?* Tarrytown, NY: Marshall Cavendish Childrens.

Lionni, Leo. 1975. *A Color of His Own*. New York: Pantheon Books.

———. 1995. *Little Blue and Little Yellow*. New York: HarperCollins.
  Also available as an animated film by Contemporary Films.

Martin, Bill, Jr. (author), and Eric Carle (illustrator). 2010. *Brown Bear, Brown Bear, What Do You See?* New York: Henry Holt.
  Ask the children to recite the words of the book along with you as you read aloud.

Onyefulu, Ifeoma. *Chidi Only Likes Blue: An African Book of Colors*. 2006. London: Frances Lincoln Children's Books.

Rusch, Elizabeth (author), and Chad Cameron (illustrator). 2007. *A Day With No Crayons*. Flagstaff, AZ: Rising Moon.

Saltzberg, Barney. 2010. *Beautiful Oops!* New York: Workman.
  If you think you have made a mistake when creating a picture, it's natural to want to use an eraser to "fix" it. But erasers don't work when you are painting. And a mistake can be an asset; artists can make new and even better pictures out of something they thought was a mistake. This book is about just that.

Shahan, Sherry (author), and Paula Barragán (illustrator). 2004. *Spicy Hot Colors / Colores picantes*. Little Rock, AR: August House LittleFolk.

Stinson, Kathy (author), and Robin Baird Lewis (illustrator). 1982. *Red Is Best*. Toronto: Annick Press.

Stuve-Bodeen, Stephanie. 1998. *We'll Paint the Octopus Red*. Bethesda, MD: Woodbine House.
  A girl discusses the many things she can do with her new baby brother, born with Down syndrome.

Weeks, Sarah (author), and David Diaz (illustrator). 2006. *Counting Ovejas*. New York: Atheneum Books for Young Readers

Weeks, Sarah (author), and David A. Carter (illustrator). 2007. *Peek in My Pocket: A Lift-the-Flap Pop-Up Book*. San Diego: Harcourt.
  Ask the children to call out the names of the colors.

Yoo, Taeeun. 2007. *The Little Red Fish*. New York: Dial Books for Young Readers.

SONGS ABOUT COLORS

"Colors," sung by Hap Palmer, track 1 on *Learning Basic Skills through Music: Volume 1*, Educational Activities, 1969.

"Bumping Up and Down in My Little Red Wagon"
  Lyrics and a video with accompanying movements can be found at www.mamalisa.com/?t=es&p=2426&c=23.

Week 6: Examine Other Books by Karen Beaumont

Compare books by the same author; compare pictures drawn by different illustrations; find what is the same and what is different.

THEME

Books by Karen Beaumont

ITEMS NEEDED

- felt pieces representing body parts

PREPARATION

Make out of felt: three heads, three necks, three chests, six arms, six legs, six hands, six feet, and three big oval shapes out of a variety of colors.

SUGGESTED CONTENT

Focus Text

Give each child at least one flannel piece. Tell the children that you are all going to read or sing the story together. When the part they are holding is mentioned, they should come up to the flannelboard and put it on one of the bodies. At the end of the song, you will see how silly the bodies look! You may want to use fewer bodies and parts depending on how many children you have. If you don't mind a zany person with many body parts, then use them all!

We've been reading this book for the past five weeks. You know the book so well by now, you could probably recite it by heart. Instead of showing you the illustrations, this time when we sing the story, I will keep the book in my lap. However, look at the flannel piece you are holding and decide which part of the body it is. And when that part is named in the song, come up and put your piece on any one of these three bodies. For instance, I have a leg. So, when we get to the part of the story where he paints his leg, I will get up and put my piece on the flannelboard where I think his leg is supposed to be. I could put it on this body, or this body, or this body. The body parts are in different sizes, shapes, and colors, so when we are done with the song, we will have created a very interesting illustration!

>> DEVELOPMENTAL TIP

By comparing different books written by the same author, or the same story illustrated by different artists, you are helping children learn to distinguish between what is the same and what is different. Creative ideas often form when children are able to make connections between two totally different things they know, and to find a unique way to bring them together. This can also be a great strategy for problem solving.

MORE BOOKS BY KAREN BEAUMONT

Beaumont, Karen (author), and Daniel Roode (illustrator). 2012. *Dini Dinosaur.* New York: Greenwillow Books.

Beaumont, Karen (author), and David Catrow (illustrator). 2004. *I Like Myself!* Orlando: Harcourt.

———. 2011. *Where's My T-R-U-C-K?* New York: Dial Books for Young Readers.

Beaumont, Karen (author), and Eugene Yelchin (illustrator). 2008. *Who Ate All the Cookie Dough?* New York: Henry Holt.

Beaumont, Karen (author), and Jackie Urbanovic (illustrator). 2011. *No Sleep for the Sheep!* Boston: Houghton Mifflin Harcourt.

Beaumont, Karen (author), and Jane Dyer (illustrator). 2006. *Move Over, Rover.* Orlando: Harcourt.

Beaumont, Karen (author), and Jennifer Plecas (illustrator). 2004. *Baby Danced the Polka.* New York: Dial Books for Young Readers.

Beaumont, Karen (author), Jose Aruego (illustrator), and Ariane Dewey (illustrator). 2004. *Duck, Duck, Goose! A Coyote's on the Loose!* New York: HarperCollins.

Beaumont, Karen (author), and Joy Allen (illustrator). 2002. *Being Friends.* New York: Dial Books for Young Readers.

Beaumont, Karen (author), and LeUyen Pham (illustrator). 2011. *Shoe-La-La!* New York: Scholastic Press.

Beaumont, Karen (author), and Rosanne Litzinger (illustrator). 1997. *Louella Mae, She's Run Away!* New York: Holt.

chapter 6

Series 4
Buz

Focus Text: *Buz*

by Richard Egielski (New York: Laura Gerringer, 1985)

After being accidently swallowed by a boy, Buz the bug goes the wrong way. Chased by two pills on the hunt for "the bug," Buz manages to escape, but arrives home with a "bug" of his own. This book was chosen as a best illustrated children's book of 1995 by the *New York Times*, and a 1998 Young Reader's Choice Award (Pennsylvania).

Ways to Present *Buz* in Storytime Sessions

Week 1: Introduce *Buz*. (bugs)

Week 2: Explore the book through flashlight play and dramatization. (health)

Week 3: Tell *Buz* as a flannelboard story. (breakfast, nutrition)

Week 4: Narrate the tale while the children act it out. (size)

Week 5: Focus on the illustrations; compare pictures. (books illustrated by Egielski)

Week 6: Invite the children to go through an obstacle course to act out the story. (chase scenes)

Week 1: Introduce *Buz*

Read the story aloud.

THEME

Bugs

ITEMS NEEDED

- tote bags with colored scarves
- tambourine
- nonfiction book with photos of bugs
- CD player
- CD: Berkner, Laurie. *Whaddaya Think of That?* (Two Tomatoes, 2001). The song to be used is "Doodlebugs," track 2.

SUGGESTED CONTENT

Focus Text

This is a silly book about a bug, called *Buz*. The story and the pictures were created by the same person, Richard Egielski. It has great illustrations and uses words that we don't use in everyday conversation, such as molars, mashed, whirled, crept, surrender, commanded, and gurgled.

But before we read the book, let's act out some of the words.

Molars are teeth on the side of your mouth and when they *mash* something, that means they chew them and squish them. Let's all mash our molars.

To *whirl* is to turn around very quickly. Let's all stand up and whirl around.

To *creep* is to walk very quietly, hoping that no one will hear you. When people creep, they often bend over and take small steps. Let's stand up and creep around the circle.

To *command* is to give an order that you expect people to follow, and to *surrender* is to give up and let someone else win. Let's all raise both hands up high in the air, and say, "I surrender."

To *gurgle* is to make a funny sound in your throat, which almost sounds like gargling. It can sound like this. (Make gurgling sound.) Let's all try gurgling!

Now that you know what all these words mean, it's time to read the story!

Buz by Richard Egielski (*Read aloud while giving explanations, asking questions, and listening to answers.*)

First page: (With title and picture of bug only) What do you see on this page? *(A bug, named Buz)*

Second set of pages: The title of this book is *Buz* and the author is Richard Egielski. What do you see here? *(A box of cereal, milk, orange juice, a spoon, the bug flying over the cereal.)* It looks like Buz wants some cornflakes for breakfast.

Third set of pages: (Skip over.)

Fourth set of pages: (Read text.) Look! The bug is on top of the spoonful of cereal, and the boy is about to swallow it. YICK!

Fifth set of pages: (Read text.) Buz is in the boy's mouth now, and he's trying hard not to be bitten. The molars certainly are mashing around! Can you mash your molars?

Sixth set of pages: (Read text.) Oh no! Buz went down the boy's throat and up behind his eye. "Help! Get me out of here!"

Seventh set of pages: (Read text.) Someone must be shining a flashlight into the boy's eye!

Eighth set of pages: (Read text.) Did you know that germs or a virus is sometimes called a bug?

Ninth set of pages: (Read text and sing the bugle call for "CHARGE!" A version of this can be found on the Internet Archive in the Community Audio collection at http://archive .org/details/BugleCallCharge, performed by the USAF Heritage of America Band.)

Tenth set of pages: (Read text.)

Eleventh set of pages: (Read text.) But look, Buz is hiding right there!

Twelfth set of pages: (Read text.) They are being quiet, hoping Buz will appear. Is that water covering their feet?

Thirteenth set of pages: (Read text.) Do you see the water getting higher?

Fourteenth set of pages: (Read text.) Oh no! The water is getting very high. And the pills can't swim! But Buz can. *(FYI: This is a picture of an inner ear.)*

Fifteenth set of pages: It's the boy! He's in a bathtub with his toy boat. Buz must have floated out of the boy's ear!

Sixteenth set of pages: (Read text.)

Seventeenth set of pages: (Read text.) Do you see the germ in his eye?

And that's the story of *Buz* by Richard Egielski. *(Children often ask for this story to be read again. If so, read it a second time, but read only the text and do not add in any explanations. Give the children an extra bit of time to look at the illustrations on each page.)*

>> DEVELOPMENTAL TIP

Even if you don't talk about the meaning of unknown words in a book, children hear them and get an idea of their meaning from the story and illustrations. After you've read a book aloud to your child a number of times, when you mention one of those words, your child will most likely know exactly what it means.

SONGS AND RHYMES

"Here Is the Beehive"

Here is the beehive. Where are the bees? *(Make a fist.)*

Hidden inside where nobody sees. *(Move other hand around fist.)*

Watch and you'll see them come out of the hive. *(Point to fist.)*

One, two, three, four, five . . . *(Show fingers one at a time.)*

BUZZZZZZZZ! *(Tickle your tummy!)*

"One, Two, Three, Mother Caught a Flea"

One, two, three, *(Make a fist. Lift three fingers one at a time.)*

My mother caught a flea. *(Clap hands.)*

She put it in a teapot *(Drop flea in pretend teapot.)*

And made a cup of tea. *(Stir tea.)*

When the flea jumped out *(Lift both hands.)*

My mother gave a shout *(Put hand in front of mouth as if calling out.)*

And Daddy came running in. *(Roll hands.)*

His shirt was hanging out. *(Tug on shirt.)*

"I'm a Little Pill Bug" (to the tune of "I'm a Little Teapot")

I'm a little pill bug small and gray, *(Squat down.)*

I like to hide in the leaves all day. *(Put hands over head, as if hiding underneath them.)*

I have two antennae *(Use fingers as antennae.)*

And fourteen legs too, *(Run in place.)*

I can roll into a ball; *(Try as best as you can!)*

How about you? *(Point to someone else.)*

"Five Green and Speckled Frogs"

Five green and speckled frogs sitting on a speckled log *(Bend one arm at the elbow to make the log. Hold five fingers—frogs—on top of it.)*

Eating some most delicious bugs—YUM YUM! *(Rub belly.)*

One jumped into the pool where it was nice and cool. *(Jump one finger off log and dive down.)*

And now there are four green, speckled frogs—RIBBIT! *(Hold up four fingers.)*

Four green and speckled frogs sitting on a speckled log *(four fingers on log)*

Eating some most delicious bugs—YUM YUM! *(Rub belly.)*

One jumped into the pool where it was nice and cool. *(Jump one finger off log and dive down.)*

Then there were three green and speckled frogs—RIBBIT! *(Hold up three fingers.)*

Three green and speckled frogs sitting on a speckled log *(three fingers on log.)*
Eating some most delicious bugs—YUM YUM! *(Rub belly.)*
One jumped into the pool where it was nice and cool. *(Jump one finger off log and dive down.)*
Then there were two green and speckled frogs—RIBBIT! *(Hold up two fingers.)*

Two green and speckled frogs sitting on a speckled log *(two fingers on log)*
Eating some most delicious bugs—YUM YUM! *(Rub belly.)*
One jumped into the pool where it was nice and cool. *(Jump one finger off log and dive down.)*
Then there was one green and speckled frog—RIBBIT! *(Hold up one finger.)*

One green and speckled frog sitting on a speckled log *(one finger on log)*
Eating some most delicious bugs—YUM YUM! *(Rub belly.)*
One jumped into the pool where it was nice and cool. *(Jump one finger off log and dive down.)*
Then there were no green and speckled frogs—RIBBIT! *(Shake head.)*

If you use this song, there is a fun craft for bug-eating frogs on DLTK's Growing Together website: www.dltk-kids.com/animals/mfrogpouch.html or www.suite101.com/paper-plate-frog-puppet-a53188. FunFelt Stories sells a storytelling glove for this activity at www.funfeltstories.com/product/five-green-and-speckled-frogs-glove-puppet.

BUG ACTIVITIES

Bug Poetry

Do you like bugs? Here is a funny poem about a bug. *(Choose a poem—or two or three—to read aloud.)* The poems are all from this book *(Hold up book and show cover)*, *Bugs: Poems about Creeping Things* by David Lee Harrison.

Counting Bug Legs

Read I'm a Pill Bug *by Yukihisa Tokusa; illustrated by Kiyoshi Takahashi.* Although pill bugs have fourteen legs, insects have just six legs, three on each side. *Display the illustration of Buz that clearly shows his legs and ask the children to count how many legs he has.*

The Animal Walk

Can you walk like a bug? How would you walk if you had six legs?
How do cows walk? They are so big!

How do frogs walk? *(Pause while children act like frogs.)* Do they walk or jump?

Snakes don't have legs. How do they get around? *(Pause while children act like snakes.)* They slither!

What about horses? *(Pause while children act like horses)* They gallop!

Do fish walk? *(Pause for answers)* No, they swim! Show me how you can swim.

Do bees walk? *(Pause for answers)* No, they fly! Show me how you can fly.

Bug Freeze Game

Now let's form a big circle that's going to move in this direction, and we'll play the Bug Freeze Game. *(Shake the tambourine, choose a direction, and point.)*

Let's be flies! *(Flap pretend wings up and down)*
And we fly and we fly and we fly and we STOP.
  (Tap hard on tambourine and freeze at "STOP.")
And we fly and we fly and we fly and we STOP.
  (Tap hard on tambourine and freeze at "STOP.")
And we fly and we fly and we fly and we STOP.
  (Tap hard on tambourine and freeze at "STOP.")
And we all fly around, BUZZZZZZZ . . .
  (Fly around the circle while shaking tambourine vigorously.)

Let's hop like fleas! *(Hop.)*
And we hop and we hop and we hop and we STOP.
  (Tap hard on tambourine and freeze at "STOP.")
And we hop and we hop and we hop and we STOP.
  (Tap hard on tambourine and freeze at "STOP.")
And we hop and we hop and we hop and we STOP.
  (Tap hard on tambourine and freeze at "STOP.")
And we all hop around—FLEAS!
  (Hop around in a circle while shaking tambourine vigorously.)

Let's walk like pill bugs (even though we only have two legs and they have more!)
  (Walk.)
And we walk and we walk and we walk and we STOP.
  (Tap hard on tambourine and freeze at "STOP.")
And we walk and we walk and we walk and we STOP.
  (Tap hard on tambourine and freeze at "STOP.")
And we walk and we walk and we walk and we STOP.
  (Tap hard on tambourine and freeze at "STOP.")
And we all turn around—PILL BUGS!
  (Turn around while shaking tambourine vigorously.)

Show Photographs of Bugs

You may want to show photographs of bugs from a nonfiction bug book from your collection. One possible choice is Backyard Bugs *by Robin Kittrell Laughlin.*

>> DEVELOPMENTAL TIP

We often want to build on our children's curiosity, but don't always know how to answer their questions. We can often discover the answers together in books. Knowledge about the world, even in very young children, is key to understanding. Combining a story and a factual book on nature or science helps expand children's scientific knowledge.

"Shoo Fly"

Hand out scarves before leading the children in this song.

Shoo, fly, don't bother me, *(Whip out scarf as if using a fly swatter.)*
Shoo, fly, don't bother me,
Shoo, fly, don't bother me,
For I belong to somebody. *(Point to self and smile.)*
I feel, I feel, I feel like a morning star, *(Hold each end of the scarf, lift scarf over your
    head and pull tightly. Move scarf from side to side.)*
I feel, I feel, I feel like a morning star.
I feel, I feel, I feel like a morning star.
I feel, I feel, I feel like a morning star.
So . . .
Shoo, fly, don't bother me, *(Whip out scarf as if using a fly swatter.)*
Shoo, fly, don't bother me,
Shoo, fly, don't bother me,
For I belong to somebody. *(Point to self and smile.)*

Doodlebugs

Give each person a second colored scarf. Play track 2, "Doodlebugs," from the Laurie Berkner CD Whaddaya Think of That? *and ask everyone to wave their scarves along with the music.*

Thumbprint Bugs Craft

Use giant color stamp pads (which can be purchased through Oriental Trading (www .orientaltrading.com), paper, and dark markers to create bug pictures. Simply place your thumb on an inkpad and then press your thumb onto a piece of paper. Use a marker to add feet and perhaps antennae to your thumbprint body, and you have created a bug. Encourage the children to be as creative as they want. For examples of fingerprint bugs, see Ed Emberley's Fingerprint Drawing Book, *listed below.*

HANDOUT FOR PARENTS

Many young children are fascinated by bugs. Building upon their interest is easy—simply go outdoors, find some bugs, and ask questions about them. Doing this with children increases their interest in the natural world and the life sciences. In the early years, science is about investigating everyday experiences, experimenting, and trying to figure out what is going on and why it is happening. Below are a few examples of what you can do to nurture your child's sense of wonder and early interest in science:

Walk outdoors with your child and take a closer look at bugs.
Do you know what kind of bug it is? Is it an ant? How do you know?
See if you can both discover where the bug is coming from.
Where is bug going to?
What is the bug doing?
Is the bug carrying anything?
Does this bug have six legs? Let's count them!
Are there many of the same bugs in one area, or is the bug you see there by itself?
Is the bug moving slowly or quickly?

Here are some online resources you can explore with your children:

- Create a lovely bug box
    www.thetoymaker.com/Toypages/05Bugbox/05Bugbox.html
- Hear a bug
    www.naturesongs.com/insects.html
- See photographs of bugs by visiting the Entomology Image Gallery
    www.ent.iastate.edu/imagegal/coleoptera/
- Make an insect mask
    www.pbs.org/wnet/nature/fun/mask.html.
- Go on a bug hunt by looking for answers to questions
    http://projects.edtech.sandi.net/brooklyn/insects/bughunt.htm
- Play bug games with the Magic School Bus
    www.scholastic.com/magicschoolbus/games/bugs/index.htm.
- Learn more about bugs
    www.ars.usda.gov/is/kids/insects/story8/piratebugs2.htm

BOOKS ABOUT BUGS

Arnold, Tedd. 2006. *Super Fly Guy.* New York: Scholastic.

Beccaloni, George. 2010. *Biggest Bugs Life-Size.* Richmond Hill, Ontario: Firefly Books. Nonfiction.

Carter, David A. 1997. *Bugs in Space: A Pop-Up Journey*. New York: Simon & Schuster.

———. 2008. *The Big Bug Book: A Pop-Up Celebration*. New York: Little Simon.

Cyrus, Kurt. 2010. *Big Rig Bugs*. New York: Walker and Co.

De Groat, Diane. 2011. *Ants in Your Pants, Worms in Your Plant! (Gilbert Goes Green)*. New York: Harper.

Dodd, Emma. 2010. *I Love Bugs!* New York: Holiday House.

Dussling, Jennifer. 2011. *Bugs! Bugs! Bugs!* New York: DK Readers. Nonfiction.

Emberley, Ed. 2000. *Ed Emberley's Fingerprint Drawing Book*. Boston: Little, Brown.

———. 2007. *Bye-Bye, Big Bad Bullybug!* New York: LB Kids.

Fischer, Scott M. 2010. *Jump!* New York: Simon & Schuster Books for Young Readers.

Harrison, David Lee (author), and Rob Shepperson (illustrator). 2007. *Bugs: Poems about Creeping Things*. Honesdale, PA: Boyds Mills.

Jarman, Julia (author), and Guy Parker-Rees (illustrator). 2011. *Ants in Your Pants!* East Sussex, UK: Gardners Books.

Jenkins, Steve, and Robin Page. 2008. *How Many Ways Can You Catch a Fly?* Boston: Houghton Mifflin.

Laughlin, Robin Kittrell. 1996. *Backyard Bugs*. San Francisco: Chronicle Books. Nonfiction.

Martin, Bill, Jr. (author), Michael Sampson (author), and Patrick Corrigan (illustrator). *The Little Squeegy Bug*. 2001. Tarrytown, New York: Marshall Cavendish Children.

Nielson, Clare (author), Dug Steer (author), Derek Matthews (illustrator), Richard Hawke (paper engineer), and Janie Louise Hunt (designer). 1999. *Snappy Little Bugs: Pop-Up Fun*. Brookfield, CT: Millbrook.

Prasadam, Smriti (author), and Emily Bolam (illustrator). 2010. *Hello Bugs*. Wilton, CT: ME Media.

Rosen, Michael (author), and Kevin Waldron (illustrator). 2010. *Tiny Little Fly*. Somerville, MA: Candlewick Press.

Samton, Sheila White. 1995. *Frogs in Clogs*. New York: Crown.

Spinelli, Eileen (author), and Dan Andreasen (illustrator). 2008. *Hug a Bug*. New York: HarperCollins.

Steig, Jeanne (author), and Britt Spencer (illustrator). 2008. *Fleas!* New York: Philomel Books.

Stevens, Kathryn. 2008. *Bugs Rule!* Mankato, MN: Child's World.
  Not for reading aloud, but for showing some of the great illustrations.

Tokuda, Yokihisa (author), and Kiyoshi Takahashi (illustrator). 2006. *I'm a Pill Bug*. La Jolla, CA: Kane/Miller.

Wilson, Karma (author), and Joan Rankin (illustrator). 2003. *A Frog in the Bog*. New York: Margaret K. McElderry.

MUSIC AND POETRY ABOUT BUGS

Berkner, Laurie. 1998. *Buzz Buzz*. New York: Two Tomatoes. Sound recording. "Bumblebee" is track 5.

——. 2000. *Whaddaya Think of That?* New York: Two Tomatoes. Sound recording. "Doodle-bugs" is track 2.

Cornwell, Tom, and Dan Merrill. 2006. *Bug Songs.* Windsor, CO: Bug Biz, LLC.

Milne, A. A. (1927) 2009. *Now We Are Six.* "Forgiven." New York: Dutton Children's Books.

Minor, Pam. 2004. *Just for Kids.* Maryland: Kindersinger. "Insect Tango" is track 16.

Music Together. 2007. *Family Favorites.* Princeton, NJ: Music Together. "One Little Owl" is track 12.

Polisar, Barry Louis (author), and David Clark (illustrator). *Insect Soup: Bug Poems.* Silver Spring, MD: Rainbow Morning Music.

Raffi. 1996. *The Singable Songs Collection.* Cambridge, MA: Rounder Records. Sound recording. "Five Little Frogs" is track 5.

Sunseri, MaryLee. 2008. *Grasshoppers Three Bug Songs.* Pacific Grove, CA: Piper Grove Music.

Week 2: Explore the Book through Flashlight Play and Dramatization

Dramatize swallowing a bug, and being swallowed as a bug.

THEME

Health

ITEMS NEEDED

- flashlights with batteries that work (enough for at least half of the children; the flashlights can be different sizes)
- tote bag for the flashlights
- tote bag with colored scarves

SUGGESTED CONTENT

Focus Text

How are you feeling today? Raise your hands if you are feeling happy! *(Pause for answers.)* Hands down. Are you feeling itchy? Sniffly? Tired? Excited? *(Use words to describe different ways a child might feel.)*

Raise your hand if you have ever accidentally swallowed a bug. *(Pause for answers.)*

How would you feel if you swallowed a bug by mistake? *(Pause for answers)*

Who would like to come up to the front of the room and act out what it might to be like if you swallowed a fly, mosquito, or bee by mistake? *(Choose a child and encourage her to ham it up as much as possible. Choose a few other children to act out the boy swallowing the bug.)* We've seen a few examples of how the boy might react to accidentally swallowing a bug; how do you think a bug would feel if he was swallowed by a boy? Who would like to come up to the front and act THAT out? *(Choose one child or more to take turns and act it out. Encourage each one to use his imagination.)*

Now that we've put ourselves in the place of both the boy and the bug, let's have another look at the story, *Buz* by Richard Egielski. *(Read the book aloud.)*

SONGS

"The Ants Go Marching One by One"
(to the tune of "When Johnny Goes Marching Home Again")

Sing only one or two verses of this song as you march around the library. Alert librarians to wave at the ants as they march by. Be sure to stay close to your storytime space, so you can be back by the time the verse ends.

The ants go marching one by one, hurrah, hurrah! *(March with knees high; pump arm for hurrahs.)*
The ants go marching one by one, hurrah, hurrah!
The ants go marching one by one.
The little one stops to suck his thumb. *(Pretend to suck thumb.)*
And they all go marching down into the ground
To get out of the rain, boom, boom, boom,
Boom, boom, boom, boom.

The ants go marching two by two, hurrah, hurrah!
The ants go marching two by two, hurrah, hurrah!
The ants go marching two by two,
The little one stops to tie his shoe. *(Pretend to tie shoe.)*
And they all go marching down into the ground
To get out of the rain, boom, boom, boom,
Boom, boom, boom, boom.

"I Think I'm Going to Sneeze" (to the tune of "The Farmer in the Dell")

I think I feel a breeze. *(Sway back and forth.)*
It makes me want to sneeze. *(Take a deep breath and hold tummy.)*
A-a-a-a chu! *(Bring tissue up to nose.)*
"Excuse me, please!" *(Fold hands.)*

>> DEVELOPMENTAL TIP

Covering one's nose with a tissue when sneezing prevents germs from spreading. Practicing this response—by using the paper plate doll or singing a song—teaches your child good health and manners in a fun and easy way.

Figure 6.1 Paper plate face template

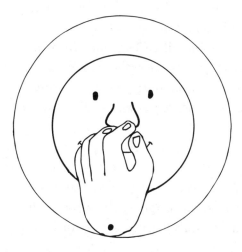

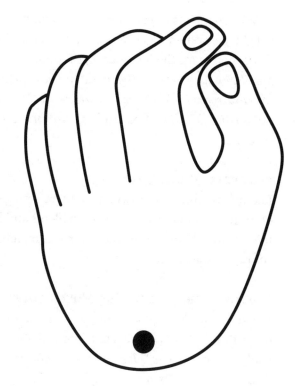

Figure 6.2 Blow your nose activity template

ACTIVITIES

Flashlight Play

Raise your hands if you can tell me what the doctor did when the boy came to visit him, and what the bug doctor did when Buz went to visit? *("They shined a light in their eyes.")* Doctors use a special instrument to look in the eyes of their patients. Theirs is not a regular flashlight; if you are not a doctor and do not have the right equipment, it is not safe to shine a light in anyone's eyes. However, I do have some flashlights here, and we can do some experimenting with them. I can hand the flashlights only to children who promise me that they will not shine the flashlights AT anyone. Will you promise? *(Wait for everyone to reply in the affirmative. Then, from a tote bag filled with flashlights, hand out one flashlight per child or one for every two children, depending on how many you have. As you distribute them, turn them on and off to make sure they work while saying, "This turns it on; this turns it off.")*

Everyone stand up and make a big circle.

Turn your flashlights on. Turn them off.

Turn them on again and place them face down on the floor, like this.

If you don't have a flashlight, don't worry, you can have the next turn. Just stand next to someone who does have one.

I'm going to turn off the lights for a few seconds so we can see what happens with our flashlights.

Hold onto your flashlight and pretend it is a rocket ship. Let's countdown to blastoff together;

Ten, nine, eight, seven, six, five, four, three, two, one . . . BLAST OFF!

Lift your flashlights gently in the air. Keep the light facing the floor, though.

What happens as you lift the flashlight up? ("The light gets dimmer, the circle of light gets bigger. When it gets to a certain height, the light is almost not visible at all.")

Let's go in for the landings. Let's count together: Five, four, three, two, one. *(Bring the flashlight back to floor. If you did not have enough flashlights for everyone, give a turn to the children who have been waiting. Let the children try this activity two or three times. Collect the flashlights by walking around with the open tote bag singing, "Flashlights Away.")*

>> DEVELOPMENTAL TIP

Looking for different uses of an item encourages creativity and inventiveness; these skills help children find ways to solve problems and be ready to learn. You will be surprised by how many different things children can imagine and do with a flashlight. They thrive on your encouragement.

Creative Dramatics: "Bug Movements"

We know that mosquitoes and flies like to fly around. But there are other bugs that do other things. Let's act out some bug activities. *(You may want to play some music in the background, such as "Flight of the Bumblebee" by Nikolai Rimsky-Korsakov.)*

Let's start out by being a fly that is flying around a delicious looking piece of cake. Buzzzzz.

Flies rub their front legs together, so let's rub our legs together too!

Now we're all fleas, jumping around in a shaggy dog's fur.

Buzzy bees, fly from flower to flower.

Inchworms, crawl along the ground.

Pillbugs, walk with all fourteen legs!

Crickets, hop across the yard.

Okay, ants, pick up that piece of sugar and carry it across the room. Wow! It's so heavy!

BOOKS ABOUT GERMS AND VISITS TO THE DOCTOR

Albee, Sarah (author), and Tom Brannon (illustrator). 2003. *Elmo Says Achoo!* New York: Random House.

Berger, Melvin. 1995. *Germs Make Me Sick!* New York: HarperCollins.

Buckley, Charley (author), and Dave A. Santillanes (photo illustrator). 2007. *Show Jo How to Wash Your Hands.* Indianapolis: Literary Architects. Out of print.
This enchanting picture book is suitable for children with autism. It's out of print but worth finding through interlibrary loan.

Charlip, Remy (author and illustrator), and Burton Supree (author). 2001. *Mother, Mother, I Feel Sick; Send For the Doctor, Quick Quick Quick.* Berkeley: Tricycle Press.

Cole, Joanna. 2005. *My Friend the Doctor.* New York: HarperCollins.

Cousins, Lucy. 2001. *Doctor Maisy.* Cambridge, MA: Candlewick Press.

Gordon, Sharon. 2002. *Keeping Clean.* New York: Children's Press. (nonfiction)

Gorman, Jacqueline L. 2011. *Doctors.* New York: Gareth Stevens Pub.

Hallinan, P. K. 1996. *My Doctor, My Friend.* Nashville, TN: Ideals Children's Books.

Katz, Bobbi (author), and Steve Björkman (illustrator). 1996. *Germs! Germs! Germs!* New York: Scholastic.

Keller, Laurie. 2000. *Open Wide.* New York: Henry Holt.

Landau, Elaine. 1999. *The Common Cold.* Tarrytown, NY: Marshall Cavendish Benchmark. Although this nonfiction book is meant for older children, choose one or two of the full color illustrators and a fact or two to read aloud.

London, Jonathan (author), and Frank Remkiewicz (illustrator). 2002. *Froggy Goes to the Doctor.* New York: Viking.

Maccarone, Grace (author), and Betsy Lewin (illustrator). 1998. *I Have a Cold.* New York: Scholastic.

———. 2009. *Itchy, Itchy Chicken Pox.* Paw Prints.

Robinson, Deborah, and Carla Perez. 1984. *Your Turn, Doctor.* New York: Puffin. In this oldie but goodie, a girl fantasizes about changing places with her doctor and giving him a checkup and injection instead of the other way around!

Rowan, Kate (author), and Katharine McEwen (illustrator). 1998. *I Know How We Fight Germs.* Cambridge, MA: Candlewick Press.

Schecter, Ellen, and Gioia Fiammenghi. 1992. *I Love to Sneeze.* New York: Bantam Books.

Simon, Charnan (author), and Dorothy Handelman (photographer). 1998. *The Good Bad Day.* Brookfield, CT: Millbrook Press.

Singer, Marilyn (author), and David Milgrim (illustrator). 2009. *I'm Getting a Checkup.* New York: Clarion.

Slegers, Liesbet. 2011. *Katie Goes to the Doctor.* New York: Clavis.

Smee, Nicola. 1999. *Freddie Visits the Doctor.* Hauppauge, NY: Barron's Educational Series.

Wells, Rosemary. 2001. *Felix Feels Better.* Cambridge, MA: Candlewick Press.

Ziefert, Harriet. 2004. *You Can't Take Your Body to the Repair Shop: A Book about What Makes You Sick.* Maplewood, NJ: Blue Apple Books. Select parts to read—there are funny poems about illnesses such as tummy aches, colds and flu, as well as rhymes about vomiting and allergies.

MUSIC ABOUT GERMS AND VISITS TO THE DOCTOR

Gill, Jim. 1993. *Jim Gill Sings the Sneezing Song and Other Contagious Tunes.* Chicago: Jim Gill Music.

Week 3: *Buz* Flannelboard

Use flannelboard pieces and props to tell the story; focus on the breakfast scene in the book.

THEME

Breakfast, nutrition

ITEMS NEEDED

- flannelboard
- pictures of different kinds of food that have been glued onto pieces of felt
  (Some of the food pictures should be taken directly from a color copy of the illustrations in *Seven Silly Eaters*. Others can be drawings or photographs from magazines, but two types of food should be portrayed: breakfast food, and food for the rest of the day. Breakfast foods can include: cold cereal, hot cereal, eggs of any kind, pancakes, waffles, frittatas, toast, English muffins and orange juice.)
- the written phrases *Breakfast Foods* and *Other Foods* on flannel pieces
  (Put each phrase on the top, opposite sides of the flannelboard.)

PREPARATION

Set up a flannelboard at a height that children can reach. Attach a strip of felt down the middle to divide the flannelboard into two sections. At the top of one section, place a picture of the spoon with cornflakes from Buz, and on the other side, place a picture of a hamburger.

SUGGESTED CONTENT

Focus Text

(*Hold up* Buz *by Richard Egielski.*) Does anyone remember what kind of food the boy in this story had for breakfast? (*If the children don't know the answer, show them the picture with the cornflakes and the glass of orange juice and ask what they see.*) I'm going to read this story aloud; it is really short and I've already read it in some earlier storytimes, so if you know the words, feel free to say them along with me! (*Read aloud.*)

>> **DEVELOPMENTAL TIP**

Children don't usually get bored when a good story is read over and over. Instead, they notice new things each time the story is being read, and it is a great way for them to learn new vocabulary words.

RHYME

Cereal Rhyme

Give each child an empty bowl and spoon. Have an empty cornflakes box. Make crunching sounds as you pretend to eat breakfast. Recite the rhyme about cereal and act it out.

So many kinds of cereal!
You may already know.
Let's say a poem and act them out,
We'll do it nice and slow.
There are:
Rounds ones,
Square ones,
Flaky ones, too.
Mushy ones,
Crunchy ones,
And some are even blue!
Oatmeal's hot, Kix are cold,
Captain Crunch is sweet.
So take a bit of cereal,
It sure is fun to eat!

ACTIVITIES

"I Like Cereal"

If you like rap music, you may want to play the song "I Like Cereal" from the album Ping Pong Playa *by Chops. Listen to the lyrics first to be sure this song is appropriate for your audience. Invite children to tap their wooden spoons to the beat on an overturned empty cereal bowl.*

Breakfast Food Choices

(Give each child a flannel piece with a picture of food on it. Point to the flannelboard.)
Today, the flannelboard has a line down the middle of it. Over here it says "Breakfast Foods," and on the other side of the line it says, "Other Foods." I have given each of you a picture of a kind of food, and I would now like you to come up to the flannelboard one at

a time and put your picture where it belongs. For instance, where would I put a picture of pizza? *(Pause for answers.)* That's right! I'd put it over here, on the side for "Other Foods." Once you've put your picture on the flannelboard, sit back down so someone else can have a turn to come up. Who's going to be first?

Make a Mouth Craft

Materials
- "mouth" pictures made from template 6.3, copied onto red paper, and cut out
- white beans (uncooked)
- white glue or glue sticks

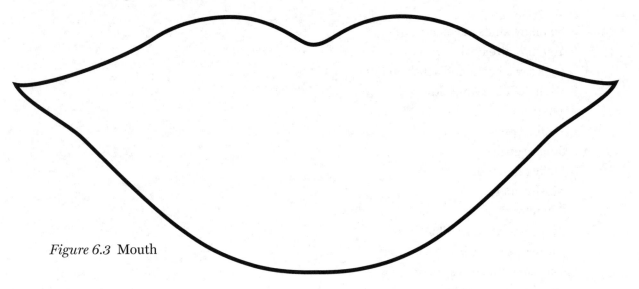

Figure 6.3 Mouth

Activity
1. Give each child a red paper mouth.
2. Give each child a large handful of white beans and some glue or a glue stick.
3. Ask them to pretend the beans are teeth and they need to attach them using the glue.
4. See how realistic the picture can look!

BOOKS ABOUT BREAKFAST

Broad, Jackie J., Shielaugh V. Divelbiss, and Lauren B. Costello. 2010. *Eat Your Breakfast or Else!* Mill Valley, CA: Three Puppies Press.

Brown, Calef. 2008. *Soup for Breakfast: Poems and Pictures.* Boston: Houghton Mifflin.

Farber, Erica (author), and Huck Scarry (illustrator). 2011. *Ice Cream for Breakfast.* (Richard Scarry's Great, Big Schoolhouse, Level 3.) New York: Sterling.

Hoberman, Mary Ann (author), and Marla Frazee (illustrator). 1997. *The Seven Silly Eaters.* San Diego: Harcourt Brace.

Schories, Pat. 2004. *Breakfast for Jack.* Asheville, NC: Front Street.
Wordless.

Sobol, Richard, and Leonardo DiCaprio. 2008. *Breakfast in the Rainforest.* Somerville, MA: Candlewick Press.
Shows photographs of African mountain gorillas eating breakfast in Uganda's national parks.

Tafuri, Nancy. 2006. *Five Little Chicks.* New York: Simon & Schuster Books for Young Readers.

Weeks, Sarah (author), and Betsy Lewin (illustrator). 2003. *Two Eggs, Please.* New York: Atheneum Books for Young Readers.

Wells, Rosemary. 1985. *Max's Breakfast.* New York: Dial Books for Young Readers.
Board book.

Week 4: Narrate the Tale while the Children Act It Out

Ask the children to act out the story as you are telling it.

THEME

Size (big and small)

ITEMS NEEDED

- 2 hula hoops OR 1 hula hoop and 1 collapsible fabric tunnel
- blue piece of shiny satin or silk, or a blue sheet, or a blue towel
- white coat, a stethoscope, or something to signify "doctor"
- 3 craft sticks
- chair
- Glue Dots (can be purchased online from www.enasco.com as Craft Glue Dots)
- pictures of two pills and a bug
- plastic container, lined with a piece of dark construction paper and with a tablespoon of sugar inside
- magnifying glass

PREPARATION

Draw a picture of Buz or use a color copier with enlargement. Draw a picture of the two pills or use a color copier. Cut out the pictures and attach each one to a craft stick to make puppets.

SUGGESTED CONTENT

Focus Text

Hold up the book and ask whoever remembers this story to raise their hands. If there are many new children at storytime, consider reading the story aloud again.

Depending on the size of your group, choose one child to be Buz, two children to be the pills, and one child to be the doctor. Select one or two children to be the mouth and the eyes, one or more to be the teeth, and two or more to be the bathtub.

One or two children hold a hula hoop vertically (the mouth).

One or more children stand in a half-circle behind the hula hoop (molars).

One or two children connect both hands over their head, making a circle. The circle is moved to the side of the body (eyes).

One or two children hold another hula hoop (the ear) OR a tunnel is placed on the ground and no one needs to hold it!

Two children hold a blue strip of shiny satin, or a blue sheet, or a blue towel (the bath water).

"Buz" holds the craft stick puppet of Buz or an actual puppet of a bug.

"The pills" hold craft stick puppets of the pills.

"The doctor" wears a white coat or a pretend stethoscope.

As you give a loose narration of the story below, you may need to give some physical prompts as well.

Buz *(the child with the Buz puppet)* walks through the boy's mouth *(hula hoop)* as he is eaten.

The molars mash up and down and all around, but they don't touch Buz at all. *(Teeth shake and squirm.)*

Instead, Buz ends up behind one of the boy's eyes. He peeks out to see what's there and how he can get back home. *(Buz peeks through one circle of arms and then the other.)*

Meanwhile, since the boy isn't feeling well, his mother takes him to the doctor. The doctor checks the boy's stomach (use stethoscope) and looks into the boy's eyes, but the light is so strong, it knocks Buz back. *(Doctor shines the light into the eye, and Buz falls onto the floor gently.)*

The doctor gives the boy two pills to cure his bug. *(Two children with pill puppets go through the mouth. The molars shake again without touching the pills. The pills go over to where Buz is lying on the floor.)*

The pills look for the bug, but they don't see him. *(Pills look in front, above, and around, but not down.)*

Just then, some water starts flowing into the boy's body. *(Water moves to the area where Buz and the pills are, and gently begins shaking the blue fabric.)*

The pills catch Buz! *(Each pill gently takes hold of one of Buz's arms.)*

But the water is rising *(blue fabric is shaken vigorously)* and the pills let go of Buz. They start to sink *(pills lie on the floor)* and Buz starts to swim.

He comes out of the boy's mouth *(go out—molars stay still)* and flies home.

But he is sneezing *(Buz sneezes)*, so his mother takes him to a doctor.

The doctor asks him to sit on a chair *(the doctor pulls up the chair; Buz sits down)* and looks in his eyes. *(Turn flashlight on and off, but do not shine it in Buz's face.)*

The doctor says, "I'm going to give you some pills to take care of that germ."

And Buz answers *(everyone says this together)*: "Bzzzzzzz."

SIZE ACTIVITIES

Two Bad Ants

Read aloud Two Bad Ants *written and illustrated by Chris Van Allsburg. Since the story is told from the ants' point of view, everything that might seem normal size to us seems gigantic to them. While reading the story aloud, ask if the children can figure out what all the items are.*

>> DEVELOPMENTAL TIP

Noticing patterns and relationships between objects is an aspect of mathematical thinking that children will use when they learn math in school. The previous book helps children see the relationship between the size of ants and the objects around them.

Magnification

Although we think sugar is made of tiny crystals, to the ants they seemed to be big and heavy objects. I have a magnifying glass here *(show magnifying glass)* and some sugar crystals *(hold up plastic container with sugar)*. The magnifying glass helps you look at things and see them much, much bigger. I'm going to take the cover off of the plastic container, and then I'm going to come around and give each child a turn to look at the sugar crystals through the magnifying glass. Feel free to describe what you are seeing.

>> DEVELOPMENTAL TIP

Although adults think of technology as things such as computers and smartphones, technology is really just another name for "tools that do a job." Magnifying glasses are tools, and by looking at things through a magnifying glass, you are using technology with your child!

Balloon Sizes

Slowly blow up a balloon and then let the air out. Ask the children to call out whether it is bigger or smaller. Repeat.

BOOKS ABOUT SIZES

Alborough, Jez. 1992. *Where's My Teddy?* Cambridge, MA: Candlewick Press.

Brown, Margaret Wise, and Clement Hurd. 2006. *Bumble Bugs and Elephants: A Big and Little Book.* New York: HarperCollins.

Coffelt, Nancy. 2009. *Big, Bigger, Biggest!* New York: Henry Holt.

Connio Sylviane. 2007. *I'd Really Like to Eat a Child.* New York: Random House.

Emberley, Rebecca, and Ed Emberley. 2011. *The Lion and the Mice.* New York: Holiday House.

Fleming, Denise. 1993. *In the Small, Small Pond.* New York: Henry Holt.

Graves, Keith. 2010. *Chicken Big.* San Francisco: Chronicle Books.

Hoban, Tana. 1976. *Big Ones Little Ones.* New York: Greenwillow Books.

Jenkins, Steve. 2004. *Actual Size.* Boston: Houghton Mifflin.
   In colorful collage, the actual sizes of animals are shown—from the complete picture of a small animal to the only part of a big animal that will fit on the page, such as African elephant's foot.

Kolar, Bob. 2008. *Big Kicks.* Cambridge, MA: Candlewick Press.

Lewis, J. Patrick (author), and Bob Barner (illustrator). 2007. *Big Is Big (and Little Little): A Book of Contrasts.* New York: Holiday House.

Miller, Margaret. 1998. *Big and Little.* New York: Greenwillow Books.

Nakagawa, Chihiro (author), and Junji Koyose (illustrator). 2008. *Who Made This Cake?* Asheville, NC: Front Street.

Pinkney, Jerry, and Aesop. 2009. *The Lion and the Mouse.* New York: Little, Brown Books for Young Readers. Wordless.

Rayner, Catherine. 2009. *Ernest, the Moose Who Doesn't Fit.* New York: Farrar Straus Giroux.

SAMi. 2007. *Big Little.* Maplewood, NJ: Blue Apple Books. Board book.

Seeger, Pete (author), and Michael Hays (illustrator). 1986. *Abiyoyo.* New York: Macmillan.

Sherry, Kevin. 2007. *I'm the Biggest Thing in the Ocean.* New York: Dial Books for Young Readers.

Trivizas, Eugenios (author), and Helen Oxenbury (illustrator). 1993. *The Three Little Wolves and the Big Bad Pig.* New York: Margaret K. McElderry.

Van, Allsburg C. 1988. *Two Bad Ants.* Boston: Houghton Mifflin.

MUSIC ABOUT SIZES

Palmer, Hap. 1994. *So Big: Activity Songs for Little Ones.* Topanga, CA: Hap-Pal Music.

Seeger, Pete. 1989. *Abiyoyo and Other Story Songs for Children.* Washington, DC: Smithsonian/Folkways.

Week 5: Focus on the Illustrations; Compare Pictures

Compare illustrations.

THEME

Books illustrated by Richard Egielski

ITEMS NEEDED

- parachute
- yellow construction paper, ripped into fist-sized pieces

SUGGESTED CONTENT

Focus Text

Remember this story? (*Hold up* Buz *by Richard Egielski.*) Today we are going to use a parachute to be the boy's mouth from the story of Buz.

Lay a big parachute outstretched on the floor and state that it is the mouth of the boy. Ask everyone to take hold of the edges with a child in between each adult and shake them up and down as if the boy is chomping on his cornflakes.

Let's pretend that this parachute is the boy's mouth. Everyone hold on to the edge of the parachute, with each child standing next to his or her adult. Walk back as far as you can until the parachute is taut. Let's move it up and down as if the mouth is eating breakfast.

Throw some small balls or pieces of yellow construction paper on top of the parachute and say they are the cornflakes being mashed and munched by the molars.

Look, the molars are mashing and crunching!

Ask the children to stay in their places but to let go of the parachute. On the count of three, adults should lift the parachute as high as they can, and all the children should run underneath it and sit on the floor. They are becoming bugs that were swallowed by mistake! Adults should swiftly bring the parachute down while walking toward the center of the circle. By holding the parachute down on the floor, they will be creating a tent for the children. Let the children stay in their tent for a few minutes, then ask the adults to lift the parachute and ask the children to run out, just like Buz exited the boy's body through his ear.

Now that we've been the boy's mouth, let's read the book aloud one more time. Feel free to recite the words with me! (*Read the book aloud again.*)

>> DEVELOPMENTAL TIP

Pretending fosters your child's imagination. Pretending that the parachute is a mouth encourages your child to think outside the box.

ACTIVITIES

The Whistle on the Train

Here's another story that was illustrated by Richard Egielski, even though the book was written by someone else. *The Whistle on the Train* was written by Margaret McNamara, illustrated by Richard Egielski, and paper engineered by Gene Vosough. Please sing along with me to the tune of "The Wheels on the Bus." *(Sing together.)*

Comparing Illustrations

Assemble all the books illustrated by Richard Egielski that are currently in your library. Include works by other illustrators that have very different artistic styles. Invite the children to look through the books and see if they can recognize the ones that were illustrated by Egielski. Ask questions such as:

- How did you know these books were illustrated by Richard Egielski?
- Does he use only bright colors?
- Why do you think he chose those colors?
- What are the details that make it an Egielski book?
- Do you see any things or any characters that are in more than one book?

BOOKS ILLUSTRATED BY RICHARD EGIELSKI

Arkin, Alan (author), and Richard Egielski (illustrator). 1999. *One Present from Flekman's.* New York: HarperCollins.

Broach, Elise (author), and Richard Egielski (illustrator). 2010. *Gumption.* New York: Atheneum Books for Young Readers.

Brown, Margaret Wise (author), and Richard Egielski (illustrator). 2003. *The Fierce Yellow Pumpkin.* New York: HarperCollins.

Burgess, Gelett (author), and Richard Egielski (illustrator). 1985. *The Little Father.* New York: Farrar Straus Giroux.

Conrad, Pam (author), and Richard Egielski (illustrator). 1990. *The Tub People.* Berkeley Heights, NJ: Library Learning Resources, Inc.

——. 1992. *The Lost Sailor.* New York: HarperCollins.

——. 1993. *The Tub Grandfather.* New York: HarperCollins.

———. 1995. *Call Me Ahnighito.* New York: HarperCollins.

DiPucchio, Kelly S. (author), and Richard Egielski (illustrator). 2004. *Liberty's Journey.* New York: Hyperion Books for Children.

Egielski, Richard. 1997. *The Gingerbread Boy.* New York: Laura Geringer.

———. 1998. *Jazper.* New York: HarperCollins.

———. 2001. *Slim and Jim.* New York: Laura Geringer/HarperCollins.

———. 2005. *Saint Francis and the Wolf.* New York: Laura Geringer.

———. 2007. *The Sleepless Little Vampire.* New York: Arthur A. Levine.

———. 2010. *Captain Sky Blue.* New York: Michael Di Capua Books/Scholastic.

———. 2011. *Itsy Bitsy Spider.* New York: Atheneum Books for Young Readers.

LaRochelle, David (author), and Richard Egielski (illustrator). 2007. *The End: A Reverse Fairytale That Starts with the Wedding and Moves Backward!* New York: Arthur A. Levine.

Martin, Bill, Jr. (author), and Richard Egielski (illustrator). 1996. *Fire! Fire! Said Mrs. McGuire.* San Diego: Harcourt Brace.

McKelvey, Douglas Kaine (author), and Richard Egielski (illustrator). 2001. *Locust Pocus! A Book to Bug You.* New York: Philomel.
Creepy crawly rhymes.

McNamara, Margaret (author), Richard Egielski (illustrator), and Gene Vosough (paper engineer). 2008. *The Whistle on the Train.* New York: Hyperion Books for Children.

Palatini, Margie (author), and Richard Egielski (illustrator). 2001. *The Web Files.* New York: Hyperion Books for Children.

———. 2005. *Three French Hens: A Holiday Tale.* New York: Hyperion Books for Children.

Wells, Rosemary (author), and Richard Egielski (illustrator). 2003. *The Small World of Binky Braverman.* New York: Viking.

Wise, William (author), and Richard Egielski (illustrator). 1997. *Perfect Pancakes, If You Please.* New York: Dial Books for Young Readers.

Yorinks, Arthur (author), and Richard Egielski (illustrator). 1980. *Louis the Fish.* New York: Farrar Straus Giroux.

———. 1983. *It Happened in Pinsk.* New York: Farrar Straus Giroux.

———. 1986. *Hey Al.* New York: Farrar Straus Giroux.
Recipient of the Caldecott Medal for illustration in 1987.

———. 1988. *Bravo, Minski.* New York: Farrar Straus Giroux.

———. 1989. *Oh, Brother.* New York: Farrar Straus Giroux.

———. 1990. *Sid and Sol.* New York: Farrar Straus Giroux.

———. 1990. *Ugh.* New York: Farrar Straus Giroux.

———. 2008. *What a Trip!* New York: Michael di Capua Books/Scholastic.

———. 2009. *Homework.* New York: Walker.

Week 6: Invite the Children to Go Through an Obstacle Course to Act Out the Story

What is the same and what is different about chase scenes in different books? Children choose masks, act out the story.

THEME

Chase scenes

ITEMS NEEDED

- flannelboard
- color copies of pages from *Buz* with flannel backing
- collapsible tunnel (such as the Caterpillar Tunnel sold by Kaplan Educational)
- 3 chairs
- 3 beanbag cushions
- hula hoop
- small blanket
- masking tape

PREPARATION

Make color copies of all pages from *Buz*. Use tacky glue to attach each page to a piece of felt. Choose "chase scene music" from the selections below or any other source.

SETUP

Set up the room with a hula hoop to lift up and walk through, some chairs to walk around, beanbag cushions to climb over, a small blanket to climb under, a tunnel to climb through (or any other "safe" obstacles), and a blanket, sheet, rug, or area delineated with masking tape. Use masking tape to mark an obstacle course trail between all the stations.

SUGGESTED CONTENT

Focus Text

Begin your storytime by reading aloud The Gingerbread Boy *by Richard Egielski.*

Something the same happened in the books that we just read and the story of Buz. Can anyone tell me what it was? *(Pause for answers, but if no one answers or gives the correct answer, by saying the following.)* Both books had a chase scene! In *Buz*, the pills were trying to find Buz and then were trying to chase and catch him before the water kept rising. *(Show the appropriate illustration.)* In *The Gingerbread Boy*, everyone was chasing him because they wanted to eat him!

Now we are all going to use our imaginations. Let's pretend that we are the pills in the story of Buz. We are supposed to find Buz, but it's not easy! Buz is hiding in the boy's mouth and there are lots of things in there for him to hide behind! So, we have to go very carefully through the obstacle course of his throat in order to do our jobs. Let me show you how the obstacle course works. *(Show how the obstacle course works.)*

To go into the mouth, climb through the hula hoop. *(Point to the hula hoop.)*

To avoid being chomped by the molars, walk around the chairs. *(Walk around the chairs.)*

To go underneath the tongue, go under the blanket on this side and exit on the other side. *(Point to both sides of the blanket.)*

Climb over the tonsils. *(Point to beanbag cushions.)*

To be swallowed down the throat, crawl through the tunnel. *(Point to the tunnel.)*

And end up in the bathtub! *(A rug or sheet or area delineated with masking tape on the floor.)*

I'm going to put on some music that will add to the feeling of a chase scene. We are not running, however—we are just trying to be careful and find that hiding Buz! I'm going to pretend to be the spoon of cereal, so I will bring each of you to the "mouth" one at a time.

Start playing some "chase scene music." Gently encourage one child at a time to go on the obstacle course, pretending that they are pills chasing after Buz. Monitor the movement to make sure that there is enough space between children that they do not get on top of each other. Reinforce that this is obstacle course and not a race course; running is not an option.

›› DEVELOPMENTAL TIP

Music can help convey a mood. Peppy music helps us move faster; soft and slow music often relaxes us. Adding music to an already existing connection between words and pictures contributes to a child's depth of expression.

MUSIC TO ACCOMPANY CHASE SCENES

Rimsky-Korsakov, Nikolai. 1991. "Flight of the Bumblebee." Track 11, *Classics Greatest Hits.* New York: RCA Victor.

Tchaikovsky, Pyotr Illyich. "1812 Overture." Recorded by the Skidmore College Orchestra. This can be downloaded for free from http://commons.wikimedia.org/wiki/File:Pyotr_Ilyich _Tchaikovsky_-_1812_overture.ogg.
Cue to the chase scene music at 15:35.

A Google search on the Internet will result in many links to videos and music clips of the following songs:

Bizet, Georges. "Les Toreadors" or "Carmen Overture" from *Carmen Suite No. 1.*

Kabalevsky, Dmitri. "The Comedians Gallop" op. 26, no. 2

Khachaturian, Aram. "Sabre Dance."

Rich, James Q. "Spider," "Yakety Sax."

Strauss, Johann II. "Tritsch Tratsch Polka"

CHASING ACTIVITIES

Stop That Pickle!

Another book with a great chase scene is Stop That Pickle! *by Peter Armour, illustrated by Andrew Shachat. After reading this aloud, give all storytime participants (adults as well as children) a colored scarf. Ask everyone to scrunch up their scarves and pretend that it is a pickle. Before playing the song "I'm in a Pickle" by Duncan Wells (which can be purchased and downloaded from the Internet), give the following instructions:*

For "I'm in a pickle," wave your scarf at yourself.
For "He's in a pickle," swish your scarf out toward someone else.
Any other time you hear the word pickle, tap the top of your head with your scarf.

Car, Train, Plane Game

Play this transportation game, similar to Duck, Duck, Goose.

Ask children to sit in a circle.
Select a person to be the traffic controller.
The traffic controller walks around the outside of the circle, tapping each child on the head and randomly naming some form of transportation, such as car, train, and bus.
It the traffic controller says, "Plane," the child who was tapped jumps and chases the traffic controller around the circle, trying to tag her.
If the traffic controller manages to sit down in the tapped child's place before being tagged, the tapped child becomes the new traffic controller. If the traffic controller gets tagged before sitting down, the child must play another round.

Magnet Chase

Collect two metal matchbox cars.

Obtain four bar magnets with N (north) and S (south) printed on them.
Use masking tape to tape a bar magnet on top of each car.
Hand out the remaining bar magnets to children.
Explain to the children that a magnet is a piece of metal that attracts some metals.

There are different magnetic poles on each end of a magnet; one for north and one for south. The opposite ends attract each other, so when north and south are near each other, the metals try to connect. Metals with the same poles push each other away.

Ask the children to take turns holding their bar magnets near the car. What happens when north and north are near each other? Does the car move forward or run away?

HANDOUTS FOR PARENTS

Instead of a chase, have a race!

Download and print this Racing Turtle, follow the instructions, and see who is the fastest! www.thetoymaker.com/Toypages/37turtleraces/37turtle.html.

BOOKS ABOUT CHASE SCENES

Armour, Peter (author), and Andrew Shachat (illustrator). 1993. *Stop That Pickle!* Boston: Houghton Mifflin.

Axtell, David. 2000. *We're Going on a Lion Hunt.* New York: Holt.

Cuyler, Margery (author), and Joseph Mathieu (illustrator). 2008. *We're Going on a Lion Hunt.* Tarrytown, NY: Marshall Cavendish Children.

Egielski, Richard. 1997. *The Gingerbread Boy.* New York: Laura Geringer Book.

Funke, Cornelia Caroline (author), Kerstin Meyer (illustrator), and Anthea Bell (translator). 2004. *The Princess Knight.* New York: Chicken House.

Harper, Jessica, and Lindsay Harper Dupont. 2000. *I'm Not Going to Chase the Cat Today!* New York: HarperCollins.

Hill, Eric. 1980. *Where's Spot?* New York: Putnam.

Hurd, Clement. 2005. *The Merry Chase.* San Francisco: Chronicle Books.

Lewis, Kevin (author), and S. D. Schindler (illustrator). 2003. *The Runaway Pumpkin.* New York: Orchard Books.

Luna, James (author), Laura Lacámara (illustrator), and Carolina Villarroel (Spanish translator). 2010. *The Runaway Piggy / El Cochinito Fugitive.* Houston, TX: Piñata Books.

Many, Paul (author), and Scott Goto (illustrator). 2002. *The Great Pancake Escape.* New York: Walker & Company.

Pilkey, Dav. 1999. *Big Dog and Little Dog Making a Mistake.* San Diego: Harcourt.

Rosen, Michael, and Helen Oxenbury. 1989. *We're Going on a Bear Hunt.* New York: Margaret K. McElderry.

Thomson, Bill. 2010. *Chalk.* Tarrytown, New York: Marshall Cavendish Children.
    A dinosaur chases the children in the book.

chapter 7

Series 5
Muncha! Muncha! Muncha!

Focus Text: *Muncha! Muncha! Muncha!*
by Candace Fleming, illustrated by G. Brian Karas
(New York: Atheneum Books for Young Readers, 2002)

Mr. McGreely plants a vegetable garden and finds
himself plagued by persistent bunnies who hop over a
fence, splash through a trench, and climb a wall to get
to his vegetables.

Ways to Present *Muncha! Muncha! Muncha!* in Storytime Sessions

Week 1: Introduce *Muncha! Muncha! Muncha!* (planting)
Week 2: *Muncha! Muncha! Muncha!* flannelboard. (gardens)
Week 3: Use creative dramatics to build a garden and surrounding walls. (building)
Week 4: Compare books by the same author and illustrator. (persistence)
Week 5: Use ICDL to compare *Muncha! Muncha! Muncha!* with a similar book. (animals in gardens)
Week 6: Invite the children to act out the story (bunnies)

Week 1: Introduce *Muncha! Muncha! Muncha!*

Developing an awareness of nature and the environment

THEME

Planting

SUGGESTED CONTENT

Focus Text

Raise your hand if you have ever worked in a garden or if you have a garden of your own. What do you grow in your gardens? Flowers? Vegetables?

(*Give children the opportunity to share what's in their gardens.*) Thanks for sharing.

Our first story today is called *Muncha! Muncha! Muncha!* Candace Fleming, the author, wrote this book and G. Brian Karas, the illustrator, drew the pictures. (*Read the story aloud.*)

SONG

"Oats, Peas, Beans, and Barley Grow"

Just like Mr. McGreely planted a garden, we are going to plant one too. Let's all stand up and make a circle, and we'll sing a very old planting song. Listen to words and act it out. If you're not sure what to do, just watch me!

Chorus:
Oats, peas, beans, and barley grow.
Oats, peas, beans, and barley grow.
Do you, or I, or anyone know
How oats, peas, beans, and barley grow?

First the farmer plants the seed,
Stands up tall and takes his ease.
Stamps his feet and claps his hands,
And turns around to view the land.
CHORUS

Then the farmer waters the ground,
Watches the sun shine all around.
Stamps his feet and claps his hands,
And turns around to view the land.
CHORUS

Next the farmer hoes the weeds,
Stands up tall and quite at ease.
Stamps his feet and claps his hands
And turns around to view the land.
CHORUS

Last the farmer harvests the seeds,
Stands up tall and takes his ease.
Stamps his feet and claps his hands,
And turns around to view the land.
CHORUS

After weeks of sun and air
The farmer picks the crops right there.
Stamps his feet and claps his hands,
And turns around to view the land
CHORUS

Although the music to this song can be found at www.musick8.com/html/current_tune
.php?numbering=95&songorder=5, we recommend you download the music from
iTunes or play a faster recorded version of it while you are doing the activity.

See Raffi. "Oats, Peas, Beans, and Barley." On Baby Beluga. *Rounder, 1980. CD.*

ACTIVITY

Make Vegetable Prints Craft

Materials
- some vegetables, such as carrots, celery, turnips
- plastic container
- child-sized table
- newspaper or plastic tablecloth
- sharp knife (for cutting vegetables before the program)
- pencils
- paper (enough to give 1 piece of blank paper to each child)
- different colors of paint and some plastic plates OR nontoxic, color stamp pads

Setup
1. Cut vegetables in half and store them in a plastic container.
2. Cover a child-sized table with newspaper or plastic tablecloth.
3. Pour different colors of paint onto a few shallow plates OR set out nontoxic, washable ink pads of different colors.

Activity

1. Invite children and their parents to sit at the table.
2. Hand out one piece of paper to each child and ask parents to write their children's names on the paper.
3. Invite the children to make vegetable prints by using the cut vegetables as stampers.
4. When the pictures are dry, invite families to take them home and proudly display them there.

>> DEVELOPMENTAL TIP

This activity encourages creativity by showing children that there are more ways to paint than simply by using a paintbrush! When using paint rather than ink pads, children experience the concepts of wet and dry in an artistic context. Holding the vegetables and seeing the different patterns they can make encourages artistic awareness.

HANDOUT FOR PARENTS

When you bring your child's picture home, take some time to talk together about it. You may want to talk about the colors used, the shapes that were created, or patterns that are similar and different. Tacking the picture up on a bulletin board or attaching it with magnets on the refrigerator will show your children that their picture matters to you. Without saying, "Good job," or giving compliments of any kind, the simple fact that you spoke together about the picture and then put it up for display sends a message of encouragement to your child.

BOOKS ABOUT PLANTING

Ayres, Katherine (author), and Nadine Bernard Westcott (illustrator). 2007. *Up, Down and Around*. Cambridge, MA: Candlewick Press.

Butterworth, Christine (illustrator), and Lucia Gaggiotti (illustrator). 2011. *How Did That Get in My Lunchbox?* Cambridge, MA: Candlewick Press.

Hester, Denia (author), and Jackie Urbanovic (illustrator). 2005. *Grandma Lena's Big Ol' Turnip*. Morton Grove, IL: Albert Whitman.

Muldrow, Diane (author), and Bob Staake (illustrator). 2010. *We Planted a Tree*. New York: Golden Books.

Perez, Monica, Margret Rey, H. A. Rey, and Anna Grossnickle Hines (illustrator). 2009. *Curious George Plants a Tree*. Boston, MA: Houghton Mifflin.

Segal, John. 2006. *Carrot Soup*. New York: Margaret K. McElderry.

Vagin, Vladimir. 1998. *The Enormous Carrot*. New York: Scholastic.

Wallace, Nancy Elizabeth. 2010. *Planting Seeds*. Tarrytown, NY: Marshall Cavendish.

Week 2: Tell *Muncha! Muncha! Muncha!* as a Flannelboard Story

Children recognize clues and chime in responsively.

THEME

Gardens

ITEMS NEEDED

- script cards
- flannelboard
- *Muncha! Muncha! Muncha!* flannel pieces arranged in order as listed with extra bunnies (for at least 1 flannel piece per child)

PREPARATION

Create script cards: Make script cards (index cards) with the text of the story to help you tell the story with the flannel pieces. These cards can have the exact text on them, cue words, or key points that will help you retell the story

Create flannel pieces for *Muncha! Muncha! Muncha!* These can be easily made by using a color copier to enlarge and replicate illustrations from the book. Or, enlarge and photocopy the templates below and color them in. Always use tacky glue to attach illustrations to felt backings.

Figure 7.1 Bunny #1

Figure 7.2 Bunny #2

Figure 7.3 Bunny #3

Figure 7.4
Mr. McGreely

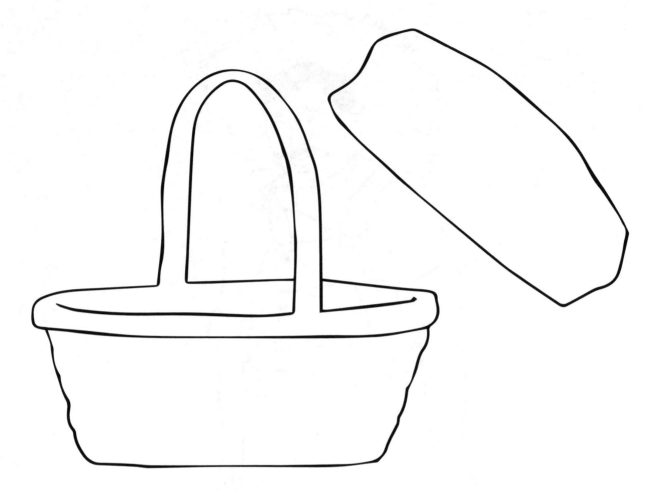

Figure 7.5
Basket with cover

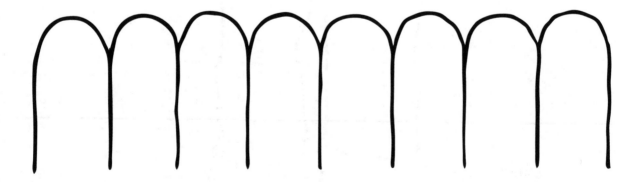

Figure 7.6 Small wire fence

Figure 7.7
Brick wall

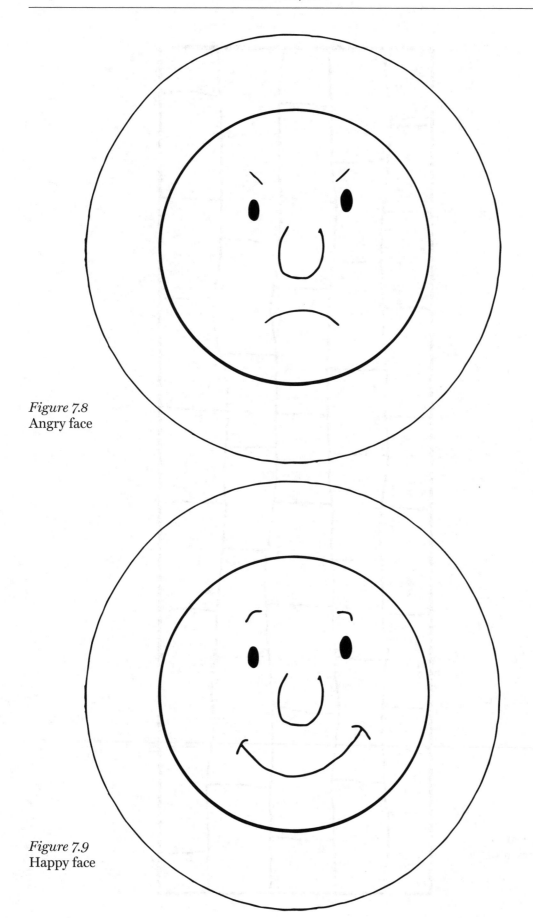

Figure 7.8
Angry face

Figure 7.9
Happy face

- Mr. McGreely (figure 7.4)
- garden plot (small piece of green felt)
- basket of vegetables (figure 7.5)
- small wire fence (figure 7.6)
- tall wooden wall (large brown felt rectangle)
- trench with water (long blue felt oval)
- brick wall (figure 7.7; enlarge this as much as possible)
- angry face (figure 7.8)
- happy face (figure 7.9)

The following phrases photocopied from the book, in color if possible:

- *Muncha! Muncha! Muncha!*
- *Tippy-tippy-tippy, pat*
- *Spring-hurdle, Dash! Dash! Dash!*
- *Dig-scrabble, Scratch! Scratch! Scratch!*

SUGGESTED CONTENT

Focus Text

At our last storytime, we read a story called *Muncha! Muncha! Muncha!* by Candace Fleming with illustrations by G. Brian Karas. Raise your hands if you remember the story! *(Pause while everyone raises their hands.)* Good. Today, we're going to use the same story, but instead of reading it aloud, I'm going to use pictures on the flannelboard. As I hold up each piece, I'll say its name and you can repeat it after me. Let's see what pieces we have. *(Hold up each piece and name it, have the children repeat the name of the piece.)*

Three little bunnies *(Pause while they repeat after you.)*
Mr. McGreely *(Pause while they repeat after you.)*
Garden plot *(Pause while they repeat after you.)*
Basket of vegetables *(Pause while they repeat after you.)*
Small wire fence *(Pause while they repeat after you.)*
Tall wooden wall *(Pause while they repeat after you.)*
Huge brick wall *(Pause while they repeat after you.)*
Angry face *(Pause while they repeat after you.)*
Happy face *(Pause while they repeat after you.)*

Here are some words that also have flannel pieces:
"Muncha! Muncha! Muncha!" *(Pause while they repeat after you.)*
"Tippy-tippy-tippy, pat." *(Pause while they repeat after you.)*
"Spring-hurdle, Dash! Dash! Dash!" *(Pause while they repeat after you.)*

"Dig-scrabble, Scratch! Scratch! Scratch!" *(Pause while they repeat after you.)*

Now I'm going to hand out one flannelboard piece to each child. I'll read the story again, and when your piece is mentioned, come up and put it on the flannelboard, or move it around on the flannelboard if it is already up there. Here we go!

(Hand out pieces, at least one per child. Make additional bunnies if needed so that all children have an opportunity to put a flannel piece on the board. Use script cards to tell the story. Pace yourself to give children the opportunity to put their pieces on the flannelboard while you are reading the story aloud.)

ACTIVITIES

Making Vegetable Salad

All this talk of different kinds of vegetables makes me hungry. I'd like to eat some vegetables too. In fact, I'd like to eat some vegetable salad. But before we can eat vegetable salad, we have to make it. Let's get some chairs and put them all in a big circle.

Put chairs in a circle with enough chairs for each child.

Walk around the circle tapping each child on the head and giving them the name of a vegetable. Use a maximum of five vegetables; this game can only be played if there are more than one of each vegetable.

Call out the name of one of the vegetables—for instance, "Carrots." All the carrots then need to stand up and exchange seats.

Practice calling out the name of each vegetable separately.

Then call out, "Vegetable salad," and everyone must exchange seats.

Play a few rounds of this and then ask one of the children to be the chef, calling out the names of the vegetables in the salad.

If the group likes competition, you may try removing a seat each time "vegetable salad" is called. The person who does not get to sit down becomes the next chef.

Rhyme Time

A rhyme is a word that has the same ending sound as another word. For instance, *house* rhymes with *mouse*. What words can you think of that rhyme with *bunny*? ("funny, money, honey, sunny, runny")

Make Garden Hats Craft

Materials

- ruler
- black marker
- paper plates (1 per child)
- 1 mat knife and a safe surface to cut on
- crayons or washable markers
- enough photocopies of the 4 vegetables, 3 bunnies, and Mr. McGreely from the templates above to make 1 complete set for each child
- Glue Dots (8 per child) or glue sticks (1 per child)

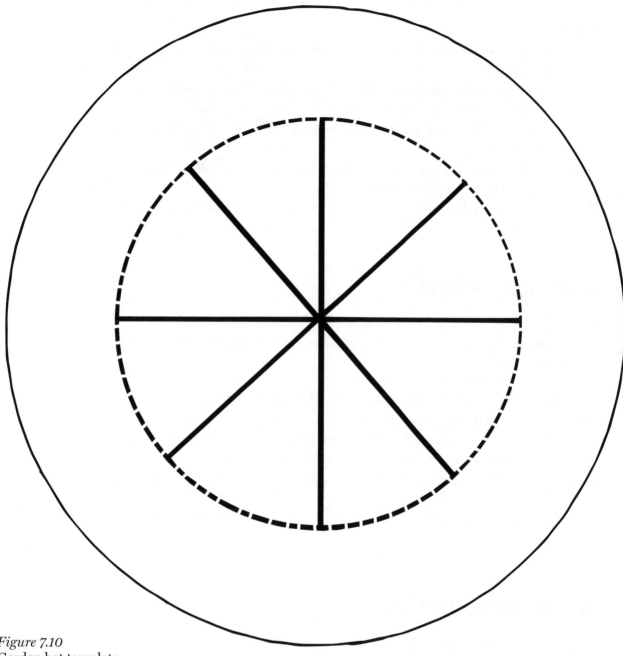

Figure 7.10
Garden hat template

Preparation
- Copy the bold lines on the garden hat template (figure 7.10) onto all of the paper plates (using the rule and marker).
- Use the mat knife to cut on all of the bold lines.

Activity

1. Hand a precut paper plate, 3 bunnies, 1 Mr. McGreely, and 4 vegetable pictures to each child.
2. Ask each child to fold up each of the "slices." (The children should now be able to stick their heads through the hole and wear the paper plate as a hat.)
3. Give the children crayons or markers and ask them to gently color the characters and vegetables.
4. Ask the children to glue each piece (with Glue Dots or glue sticks) onto the point of each "slice" of the crown.
5. Hold a garden hat show where each child can stand up one at a time to display her creation.

BOOKS ABOUT GARDENS

Aliki. 2009. *Quiet in the Garden*. New York: Greenwillow Press.

Arnold, Caroline (author), and Mary Peterson (illustrator). 2007. *Wiggle and Waggle*. Watertown, MA: Charlesbridge.
Two earthworms have adventures in a garden.

Davis, Nancy. 2009. *A Garden of Opposites*. New York: Schwartz & Wade.

Henkes, Kevin. 2010. *My Garden*. New York: Greenwillow Press.
A little girl uses her imagination to plan a garden of her own.

Mayer, Mercer. 2011. *A Green, Green, Garden*. New York: Harper.

Stewart, Sarah (author), and David Small (illustrator). 2007. *The Gardener*. New York: Square Fish.

Wallace, Karen (author), and Jon Berkeley (illustrator). 2002. *Scarlette Beane*. New York: Puffin.

POETRY ABOUT GARDENS

Brenner, Barbara (editor), and S. D. Schindler (illustrator). 2002. *Earth Is Painted Green*. New York: Bryon Preiss.

Havill, Juanita (author), and Christine Davenier (illustrator). 2006. *I Heard It from Alice Zucchini: Poems about the Garden*. San Francisco: Chronicle Books.

Shannon, George (author), and Sam Williams (illustrator). 2006. *Busy in the Garden*. New York: Greenwillow Books.

Ward, Jennifer (author), and Kenneth Spengler (illustrator). 2002. *Over in the Garden*. Flagstaff, AZ: Rising Moon Books.

Week 3: Use Creative Dramatics to Build a Garden and Surrounding Walls

Recognizing positions (up, over, under, beside, below)

THEME

Building

ITEMS NEEDED

- cardboard boxes of various sizes (e.g., shoeboxes, empty cereal boxes, packing boxes,)
- brown or green towel
- box of large paper clips
- pieces of blue construction paper (1 per child)

SUGGESTED CONTENT

Focus Text

Divide the children into two groups, the builders and the bunnies. Repeating this activity twice will give each child a chance to be both a builder and a bunny.

Let's pretend that this towel is Mr. McGreely's garden plot. (*Lay the towel on the floor and hand out pretend seeds to all the builders.*)

Let's hoe the garden. (*Encourage builders to pretend to hoe.*)

Let's sow the garden; that means planting the seeds. (*Builders pretend to plant seeds.*)

Let's pour a bit of water on the seeds. (*Builders pretend to pour water on seeds.*)

Look! Our vegetables are growing!

But here come those pesky rabbits! They're hopping AROUND the garden. Oh no! They've eaten the vegetables. And now they've hopped away. (*Rabbits follow spoken directions.*)

Let's build a wall around the garden. First a little wire wall BESIDE the edges of the garden. (*Hand the builders one paper clip each and ask them to place it around the towel.*)

The rabbits have climbed UP over the fence. They're eating the vegetables. And now they are hopping away. (*Rabbits follow spoken directions.*)

That's not high enough! We need a tall wooden wall. (*Encourage the builders to pile the boxes around the edges of the paper clips.*)

Oh no, it's still not good enough. The rabbits dug UNDERNEATH the wall. They're eating the vegetables. And now they're hopping away. (*Rabbits follow spoken directions.*)

We need to dig a trench and fill it with water. (*Encourage the builders to dig and place blue construction paper on the floor around the boxes.*)

The bunnies swam ACROSS the water. They CLIMBED UP the wall wooden wall, went OVER it, and DOWN on the other side. They ate the vegetables, and now they are hopping away. *(Rabbits follow spoken directions.)*

We need a big brick wall to keep the bunnies out! *(Encourage the builders to stand in a circle around the blue construction paper—the children are the wall.)*

Here I come with my basket into my PRIVATE garden. *(Invite bunnies to follow you in.)*

Wait a minute, there are bunnies in my basket . . . But you know what? I'd rather share my vegetables with the rabbits than eat them all by myself, especially when I have so many!

DOWN with the brick wall. *(Builders fall down.)*

Drain the moat. *(Everyone collects blue construction paper and put it in a bag.)*

Knock down the wooden wall. *(Everyone knocks over the boxes.)*

Pick up the wire fence. *(Everyone collects the paper clips and put them back in the box.)*

Now let's all sit in the garden and eat some carrots. *(Pretend to do so.)*

Muncha! Muncha! Muncha! . . . YUM!

>> DEVELOPMENTAL TIP

Building something is not just a physical activity; it involves thinking and problem solving too. Children who want to build something start with a problem ("How can we build the thing we want to build?"). Children then think about how to solve their problem by coming up with an idea of what to do and how to do it. Then, they test out their plan by actually building something. Or, if they build something once and it falls down immediately, they often experiment by building it in different ways in order to create something sturdier. This entire process is the beginning of engineering skills.

BOOKS ABOUT BUILDING

Caviezel, Giovanni (author), and Cristina Mesturini (illustrator). 2009. *Builder.* New York: Barron's Educational Series.

Champney, Jan (author), and Chris Fairclough (photographer). 2008. *Building.* London: Franklin Watts.

Cooper, Sharon Katz (author), and Amy Bailey Muehlenhardt (illustrator). 2006. *Whose Hat Is This? A Look at Hats Workers Wear—Hard, Tall, and Shiny.* Minneapolis, MN: Picture Window Books.

Dahl, Michael (author), and Todd Ouren (illustrator). 2004. *One Big Building: A Counting Book about Construction.* Minneapolis, MN: Picture Window Books.

Macken, JoAnn Early. 2009. *Building a House.* Mankato, MN: Capstone Press.

Murphy, Stuart J. (author), and Michael Rex (illustrator). 2006. *Jack the Builder.* New York: HarperCollins.

Week 4: Compare Books by the Same Author and Illustrator

Discuss the value of persistence and do the bunny hop.

THEME

Persistence

SUGGESTED CONTENT

Focus Text

We've read, heard, and acted out the story of *Muncha! Muncha! Muncha!* by Candace Fleming, illustrated by G. Brian Karas. Here's another book written by the same author, Candace Fleming, and also illustrated by G. Brian Karas: *Tippy-Tippy-Tippy, Hide!* It's now wintertime, and Mr. McGreely gets involved with those bunnies again . . . *(Read* Tippy-Tippy-Tippy, Hide! *aloud.)*

What was the same about *Tippy-Tippy-Tippy, Hide!* and *Muncha! Muncha! Muncha!?* What was different? *(Engage children in brief discussion about the books. You may want to mention the characters, the noises, the illustrations, and the idea that Mr. McGreely never wants to share what he has. Following are some questions you may want to ask.)* Was Mr. McGreely mean, or did he just want to have what was his? Were the bunnies being bad by eating his vegetables, or just doing what bunnies do? Why do you think he shared the carrots at the end of *Muncha! Muncha! Muncha!?* Did they look happy in the picture at the end of that book? What happened to Mr. McGreely at the end of *Tippy-Tippy-Tippy, Hide!* when he did not want to share his house with the rabbits? Does he look happy at the end of that book?

In both of these stories, the bunnies were very persistent. That means they kept trying to get what they wanted and they did not give up. Have you ever been persistent about something? What other stories do you know about animals or people who are persistent and just won't give up? *(A few examples are* The Carrot Seed *by Ruth Kraus,* The Three Little Pigs, *and* The Little Engine That Could *by Watty Piper.)*

>> DEVELOPMENTAL TIP

Persistence is a valuable trait! Trying to do something new can be difficult and frustrating. Children might find it easier to give up rather than to continue doing something challenging. As long as a task is not developmentally impossible, encourage your child to persist. Sticking with the task helps children accomplish their goals, leading to feelings of independence and self-confidence.

ACTIVITY

The Bunny Hop

Did you know that bunnies have their own dance? They do—it's called the bunny hop! Everyone stand up and let's practice the steps before the music begins.

Do the bunny hop. Find a CD with the song on it or play music from the Internet. It can also be downloaded from Amazon or iTunes at a minimal cost. Use music from the old bunny hop (1959) rather than the newer version. Consider attaching cotton ball "bunny tails" to each child with tape or safety pins. Follow the steps below:

Line children up.

Stand at the front as the leader of the line.

Have each child place their hands on the hips of the person in front of them. Show the children how the steps go along with the music. Then, turn the music off and practice the steps below with the children before starting the music again.

Stand with feet together.

Bring your right foot out to the side and then bring it back.

Repeat.

Bring your left foot out to the side and then bring it back.

Repeat.

Hop forward once.

Hop backward once.

Hop forward three times.

Repeat all steps while the music plays.

Now that you know all the steps, I'm going to turn on the music and we can all dance to the bunny hop! *(Turn on music and dance until the song ends.)*

See if you can all hop back to your seats as quietly as rabbits!

BOOKS ABOUT PERSISTENCE

Galdone, Paul. 1998. *The Three Little Pigs.* New York: Houghton Mifflin/Clarion Books.

Howe, James (author), and Amy Walrod (illustrator). 2005. *Horace and Morris Join the Chorus (But What about Dolores?).* New York: Atheneum Books for Young Readers.

Keller, Holly. 2005. *Pearl's New Skates.* New York: Greenwillow Books.

Krauss, Ruth (author), and Crockett Johnson (illustrator). 1945. *The Carrot Seed.* New York: Harper.

McCully, Emily Arnold. 1999. *Mouse Practice.* New York: Arthur A. Levine Books/Scholastic Press.

Palatini, Margie (author), and Bruce Whatley (illustrator). 2003. *The Perfect Pet.* New York: HarperCollins.

Penner, Fred, and Renee Reichert. 2005. *The Cat Came Back*. New Milford, Conn: Roaring Brook Press.

Piper, Watty (author), and Loren Long (illustrator). 2005. *The Little Engine That Could*. New York: Philomel Books.

Week 5: Use ICDL to Compare *Muncha! Muncha! Muncha!* with a Similar Book

Take advantage of the International Children's Digital Library to view an old copy of *The Tale of Peter Rabbit* to compare with *Muncha! Muncha! Muncha!*

THEME

Animals in gardens

ITEMS NEEDED

- computer or laptop with Internet access set up
- projector
- screen

SUGGESTED CONTENT

Focus Text

Use The Tale of Peter Rabbit *or find a similar book on the International Children's Digital Library (www.childrenslibrary.org) to screen.*

The last few weeks we've worked with this book (*hold up* Muncha! Muncha! Muncha!*).* We've read it, told the story using puppets, and used the flannelboard; you've placed pieces from the story on the flannelboard and you've acted it out.

This week I've got a book that is similar to *Muncha! Muncha! Muncha!* It's an old story, so instead of reading it to you from a book, I am going to show it to you on a screen, projected from my computer. Because the entire book has been scanned into the computer, you can see that it is very old. There are even scribbles on some of the pages! But I think the story is still interesting, and so are the illustrations. This is *The Tale of Peter Rabbit* by Beatrix Potter, illustrations by Wendy Rasmussen. (*Read aloud as it is screened.*)

Raise your hand if you think it would have been better if Little Peter Rabbit had listened to his mother and stayed out of Farmer McGregor's garden. (*Pause to see how many people raise their hands.*) Hands down.

What was the same about *The Tale of Peter Rabbit* and *Muncha! Muncha! Muncha!?* What was different? *(You may want to bring up story line, characters in the book, food mentioned, illustrations, language, length of the story, or any other factor.)*

SONG

"Here We Go 'Round the Mulberry Bush"

Everyone, stand up and make a big circle. We're going to create a garden of our own!

Chorus:
Here we go 'round the mulberry bush, *(Walk around the circle)*
The mulberry bush, the mulberry bush.
Here we go 'round the mulberry bush,
So early in the morning.

This is the way we hoe the ground, *(Stop in place and pretend to dig.)*
Hoe the ground, hoe the ground.
This is the way we hoe the ground,
So early in the morning.
CHORUS

This is the way we sow our seeds, *(Pretend to drop seeds in hole and cover them up.)*
Sow our seeds, sow our seeds.
This is the way we sow our seeds,
So early in the morning.
CHORUS

This is way we water our seeds, *(Pretend to use a watering can.)*
Water our seeds, water our seeds.
This is way we water our seeds,
So early in the morning.
CHORUS

This is the way we pick our sprouts, *(Pretend to pick vegetables from the garden.)*
Pick our sprouts, pick our sprouts.
This is the way we pick our sprouts,
So early in the morning.
CHORUS

ACTIVITY

Make Bunny Ears Craft

Materials
- 8½-by-14-inch construction paper (sheets of gray and sheets of pink)
- Scotch tape or masking tape
- glue sticks (1 per child)
- crayons

Preparation
1. Cut some of the construction paper into lengthwise strips to wrap around each child's head (1 or 2 per child).
2. Cut large oval-ish bunny ears out of the gray construction paper (2 per child).
3. Cut medium-size, oval-ish bunny ear inserts out of the pink construction paper (2 per child).

Activity
1. Take a long strip of construction paper and wrap it around each child's head. Tape it at the appropriate length.
2. Give each child two gray oval-ish bunny ears, and two smaller pink ovals (for the inside).
3. Tell the children to glue each pink oval to the inside of a larger gray oval.
4. Attach them to the inside of the crown base with tape.
5. Encourage the children to color them, if crayons are provided.

HANDOUT FOR PARENTS

Animals can be found in many places, not just in the garden! Go for a walk with your child and see how many different animals you can see. Find very small animals by turning over rocks; you may see bugs and worms. Look up in trees for birds and squirrels. Visit the zoo, go to the beach, or even go to a local park and have fun finding as many animals as you can.

BOOKS ABOUT ANIMALS IN GARDENS

Gerstein, Mordicai, and Susan Yard Harris. 1995. *Daisy's Garden*. New York: Hyperion Books for Children.

Gliori, Debi. 2003. *Flora's Surprise*. New York: Orchard Books.

Grant, Judyann Ackerman (author), and Sue Truesdell (illustrator). 2008. *Chicken Said "Cluck!"* New York: HarperCollins.

Potter, Beatrix (author), and Wendy Rasmussen (illustrator). 2012. *The Tale of Peter Rabbit*. London: Frederick Warne.

Week 6: Invite the Children to Act Out the Story

Improve verbal and nonverbal communication skills; express emotions.

THEME

Bunnies

ITEMS NEEDED

- Post-It notes or flags

PREPARATION

Put Post-It notes or flags on all pages of the book that mention the word *angry*.

SUGGESTED CONTENT

Focus Text

In *Muncha! Muncha! Muncha!* Mr. McGreely got very angry. In fact, when the bunnies first came, he was "angry" *(show page)*, then he was "really angry" *(show page)*, then he was "really, really, angry," *(show page)*, and finally, he was "FURIOUS!" *(show page)*. But at the end, when they are all eating carrots together, they look happy.

Who would like to come up to the front of the room and show us what angry looks like? *(Choose a volunteer. Help by asking questions such as "Where would your hands be if you were angry? How would you be standing? What might your face look like?" Choose other volunteers for "really angry," "really, really, angry," and "furious." "What did all three volunteers do that was the same? What did they do differently? Who would like to come up and show us what a happy face looks like?" Comment on the facial expression, the way the child is standing, what the hands are doing.)*

We have used this book for six weeks now *(hold up* Muncha! Muncha! Muncha!*)*. We've heard it, we've done it as a flannelboard story, we've danced to it, and today we explored the emotions of Mr. McGreely. Now I'm going to read (or tell) the story while you act out the parts of the bunnies and Mr. McGreely. Everyone who wants to be a bunny, go on this side of the room. *(Point to area.)* Everyone who wants to be Mr. McGreely go to this side of the room. *(Point to area.)*

When the bunnies tippy-tippy-tippy, pat, you bunnies will creep like sneaky bunnies. Try it! When I read the words "Muncha! Muncha! Muncha!" you will act like you are eating vegetables.

When Mr. McGreely gets angry, show your angry face. Let's practice. *(Have children practice the actions from the story.)* Now it's time for the story.

Read aloud and watch as the children act it out. Invite parents to make a video recording of it to play at home. If the children know the book really well, instead of reading the book or telling the story, invite the children to create their own dialogue while you sit back and watch. It does not have to be a faithful retelling; simply letting the children create their own dramatic reenactment is a valuable activity.

ACTIVITIES

Serve Salad

If there are no food allergies in the group and your library allows programs with food, consider making a vegetable salad with diced cucumbers, tomatoes, and red peppers. Put a small spoonful into paper cups, and give each child a cup and a plastic spoon. Discuss nutritious foods.

Bunny Head, Shoulders, Knees, and Toes

Wait a minute! I think we need some bunnies in our garden! Let's become bunnies.

Touch your head.

Touch your shoulders.

Touch your knees.

Touch your toes.

Touch your bunny eyes.

Touch your bunny ears.

Touch your fluffy little bunny cottontail!

Touch your bunny nose.

Now let's sing the bunny version of "Head, Shoulders, Knees, and Toes." We're going to start slowly, but we'll sing it a couple of times and go faster and faster. *(Sing the song several times.)*

What Time Is It, Mr. McGreely?

In this adaptation of the traditional game What Time Is It, Mr. Fox? Children will try to sneak up on Mr. McGreely.

One person is chosen to be Mr. McGreely. That person stands at the front of the room with his or her back toward the other children.

When the game begins, all of the children stand behind a masking tape line on the floor. In a chorus, the children ask, "What time is it, Mr. McGreely?"

If he answers, "One o'clock," they take one hop toward him.

If he answers, "Two o'clock," they take two hops toward him, and so on.

If Mr. McGreely thinks they are getting too close to him, he can answer "Lunchtime." The bunnies can then try to hop home immediately as Mr. McGreely turns around and tries to tag a bunny before she gets back behind the starting line. A bunny who is tagged becomes Mr. McGreely.

Also, if a bunny manages to hop close enough to tag Mr. McGreely before lunchtime, that bunny can exchange places with him.

HANDOUT FOR PARENTS

Being able to name emotions will help your child express himself. Making a game board and playing this game with your child can help him learn the names of different emotions and show how they look on faces.

1. Take a piece of paper and fold it in half lengthwise, then fold it in half sidewise.
2. Open up the paper and cut along the folded lines. There should now be four cards.
3. Draw a big circle on each card.
4. In each circle draw a simple face with two eyes and a mouth. (For a great video on easily drawing emotions on faces, see http://blip.tv/communication-nation/drawing-facial-expressions-4327711.)
   › In one circle, draw a smile with eyebrows up on the sides—happy.
   › In one circle, draw a frown with eyebrows down on the side—sad.
   › In one circle, draw a straight line with eyebrows forming a **V**—angry.
   › In one circle, draw a big open circle with eyebrows curved—surprised.
5. Play a game with your child where you mimic the expression from the cards you created. The other person has to guess what emotion you are feeling. You may want to add other cards and other emotions.

BOOKS ABOUT BUNNIES

D'Amico, Carmela, and Steven D'Amico. 2011. *Suki, the Very Loud Bunny.* New York: Dutton Children's Books.

Durant, Alan (author), and Guy Parker-Rees (illustrator). 2001. *Big Bad Bunny.* New York: Dutton Children's Books.

Fleming, Candace (author), and G. Brian Karas (illustrator). 2007. *Tippy-Tippy-Tippy, Hide!* New York: Atheneum Books for Young Readers.

Loomis, Christine (author), and Ora Eitan (illustrator). 1997. *Cowboy Bunnies.* New York: G. P. Putnam's Sons.

Novak, Matt. 2005. *Too Many Bunnies.* Brookfield, CT: Roaring Brook Press.

Steigemeyer, Julie (author), and Laura J. Bryant (illustrator). 2010. *Seven Little Bunnies.* Tarrytown, NY: Marshall Cavendish Children.

chapter 8

Series 6
Duck Soup

Focus Text: *Duck Soup*

by Jackie Urbanovic
(New York: HarperCollins, 2008)

Missing one last ingredient for his soup, Max
runs out to the garden to find it. Pandemonium
strikes when his friends arrive, think he's fallen
into the soup, and take desperate measures to get
him out.

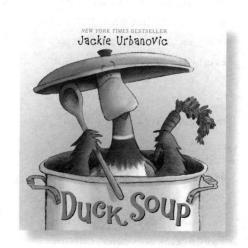

Ways to Present *Duck Soup* in Storytime Sessions

Week 1: Introduce *Duck Soup*. (ducks)
Week 2: Make an imaginary pot of soup. (soup, food, and eating)
Week 3: Use soup to test scientific concepts. (friendship)
Week 4: Reenact the search for Max with puppets. (animals)
Week 5: Compare similar stories. (birds)
Week 6: Invite the children to act out the story. (accidents and mistakes)

Week 1: Introduce *Duck Soup*

Introduce the selected book and read it aloud.

THEME

Ducks

SUGGESTED CONTENT

Focus Text

This story lends itself very well to over-the-top reading. It is a harrowing story fraught with peril and should be read as such. Be as dramatic as you can when reading the parts where Brody and the other animals are trying to find Max in the soup.

>> DEVELOPMENTAL TIP

When reading aloud to your child, stopping occasionally, pointing to a word, and then pointing to the related illustration helps your child understand the meaning of printed words. Running your finger under words as you read them shows that printed words go from left to right, familiarizes your child with some capital and small letters, and may even help her to recognize some simple printed words.

SONGS AND RHYMES

"Six Little Ducks"

Display a large flannel duck as a visual. Have children stand up and act this out with you.

Six little ducks that I once knew. *(Hold up six fingers.)*
Fat ones, skinny ones, tall ones too.
But the one little duck with the feather on his back,
He led the others with a "Quack, quack, quack, *("Quack" with hands and voices.)*
Quack, quack, quack."
He led the others with a "Quack, quack, quack!"

Down to the river they would go,
Wiggle-waggle-wiggle-waggle, all in a row. *(Wiggle-waggle around the storytime space.)*
But the one little duck with the feather on his back,
He led the others with a "Quack, quack, quack, *("Quack" with hands and voices.)*
Quack, quack, quack."
He led the others with a "Quack, quack, quack!"

Up from the river they did come.

Wiggle-waggle-wiggle-waggle, ho-hum-hum. *(Wiggle-waggle around the storytime space.)*

But the one little duck with the feather on his back,

He led the others with a "Quack, quack, quack, *("Quack" with hands and voices.)*

Quack, quack, quack."

He led the others with a "Quack, quack, quack!"

"Be Kind to Your Web-Footed Friends" (to the tune of "The Stars and Stripes Forever!")

Sing this song in an exaggerated, humorous way with lots of gestures and facial expression. Display a stuffed animal duck or a large flannel duck for a visual. Music can be found here: http://kids.niehs.nih.gov/games/songs/childrens/bekindmid.htm or can be downloaded from iTunes.

Be kind to your web-footed friends,

For a duck may be somebody's mother.

Be kind to your friends in the swamp,

Where the weather is always damp.

You may think that this is the end.

Well, it is!

"Five Little Ducks"

Music can be found here: http://kids.niehs.nih.gov/games/songs/childrens/5ducksmid .htm. The site states that the tune you hear won't work with the Aldis poem, but it does. Give it a try!

Five little ducks went out one day, *(Hold up five fingers on one hand.)*

Over the hill and far away. *(Move hand in arc and hide behind back.)*

Mother Duck said, "Quack, quack, quack, quack." *(Touch four fingers to thumb and "quack" with the other hand.)*

But only four little ducks came back. *(Bring forward first hand with four fingers showing.)*

Four little ducks went out one day, *(Hold up four fingers.)*

Over the hill and far away. *(Move hand in arc and hide behind back.)*

Mother Duck said, "Quack, quack, quack, quack." *("Quack" with the other hand.)*

But only three little ducks came back. *(Bring forward first hand with three fingers showing.)*

Three little ducks went out one day, *(Hold up three fingers.)*

Over the hill and far away. *(Move hand in arc and hide behind back.)*

Mother Duck said "Quack, quack, quack, quack." *("Quack" with the other hand.)*
But only two little ducks came back. *(Bring forward first hand with two fingers showing.)*

Two little ducks went out one day, *(Hold up two fingers.)*
Over the hill and far away. *(Move hand in arc and hide behind back.)*
Mother Duck said, "Quack, quack, quack, quack." *("Quack" with the other hand.)*
But only one little duck came back. *(Bring forward first hand with one finger showing.)*

One little duck went out one day, *(Hold up one finger.)*
Over the hill and far away. *(Move hand in arc and hide behind back.)*
Mother Duck said, "Quack, quack, quack, quack." *("Quack" with the other hand.)*
But none of the five little ducks came back. *(Keep hand behind back. Shake head sadly.)*

Sad Mother Duck went out one day, *(Raise "quacking" hand.)*
Over the hill and far away. *(Direction.)*
The sad mother duck said, "Quack, quack, quack." *("Quack" with hand.)*
And all of the five little ducks came back! *(Bring forward first hand with all five fingers and smile.)*

ACTIVITIES

Make Your Own Duck Puppets

Did you know that all of you have a duck with you right now?
> Put all of your fingers together.
> Put your thumb below your fingers.
> Touch your fingers to your thumb and do it again.
> Quack, quack!

"Boom, Boom, Ain't It Great to Be Crazy"

Sing this song, which includes a lyric about a duck! Music and lyrics can be found here: http://kids.niehs.nih.gov/games/songs/childrens/boomboommid.htm, or on any of the CDs listed in the box. And, of course, it can also be downloaded from iTunes.

Recordings of "Boom, Boom, Ain't It Great to Be Crazy"

All Aboard! 2003. Plattsburgh, NY: Direct Source. Track 13.

Delman, Elliott. 2004. 25 *Silly Songs.* Lincolnwood, IL: Publications International. Track 17.

I Love to Sing with Barney. 1998. [United States]: Lyons Partnership. Track 12.

McGrath, Bob. 1996. *If You're Happy and You Know It . . . Sing Along with Bob.* #2. Teaneck, NJ: Bob's Kids Music. Track 10.

Music for Little People. 2006. *100 Toddler Favorites.* Redway, CA: Music for Little People. Track 39.

BOOKS ABOUT DUCKS

Bedard, Michael. 2001. *Sitting Ducks.* New York: Puffin Books.

Costello, David. 2010. *I Can Help.* New York: Farrar Straus Giroux.

Emberley, Rebecca, and Ed Emberley. 2009. *Chicken Little.* New York: Roaring Book Press.

Enderle, Judith Ross (author), Stephanie Gordon Tessler (author), and Brian Floca (illustrator). 1997. *Where Are You, Little Zack?* Boston: Houghton Mifflin.

Gravett, Emily. 2009. *The Odd Egg.* New York: Simon & Schuster Books for Young Readers.

Hills, Tad. 2006. *Duck and Goose.* New York: Schwartz & Wade.

———. 2007. *Duck, Duck, Goose.* New York: Schwartz & Wade.

Kasza, Keiko. 2009. *Ready for Anything!* New York: G. P. Putnam's Sons.

Long, Ethan. 2006. *Tickle the Duck.* New York: Little, Brown.

Manning, Mick (author), and Brita Granstrom (illustrator). 2006. *SNAP!* London: Frances Lincoln.

McBratney, Sam (author), and Charles Fuge (illustrator). 2007. *Yes We Can!* New York: HarperCollins.

McPhail, David. 2011. *Waddles.* New York: Abrams Books for Young Readers.

Urbanovic, Jackie. 2009. *Duck and Cover.* New York, NY: HarperCollins.

———. 2007. *Duck at the Door.* New York, NY: HarperCollins.

Week 2: Make an Imaginary Pot of Soup

Read the book aloud and then use imagination and colored scarves to make a pot of special soup.

THEME

Soup, food, and eating

ITEMS NEEDED

- wooden spoons or colored scarves
- empty soup pot (as large as possible)

SUGGESTED CONTENT

Focus Text
Read the book aloud.

Some of the soups that Max made did not sound delicious. Would YOU want to eat Fish Soup with Curry and Pickled Lemon, or Cracker Barrel Cheese and Marshmallow Soup? What about Way, Way Too Many Beans Soup? I wouldn't want to eat them. But here's a chance for us to make our own soup, and you can use your imaginations to put into it whatever you want!

Have a pot in front of you. Give each child a wooden spoon or a colored scarf and ask them to stir their own bowl of soup with it. The swirling colors of the scarves look magnificent! Invite each child to come up and add something to go into the soup pot one at a time. Sing the song, inserting the child's name each time.

"Stir the Soup" (to the tune of "Pat-a-Cake")
Stir the soup, stir the soup. *(Act like you are stirring a pot.)*
Keep it nice and hot. *(Wave hands in front of face as if hot.)*
(Child's name) comes up to add to the pot. *(Point and beckon children to come up.)*
Spoken: *(Child's name)* chose *(whatever is chosen)!*
We stir it, and we stir it until it's done. *(Keep "stirring" and lick your lips for sweet.)*
Then we take a sip . . . oh, what fun! *(Dip in a spoon, take a sip, and make a face related to how you think the soup might taste.)*

>> DEVELOPMENTAL TIP
Singing games and playing music in groups helps children feel comfortable in a group setting and encourages social responsiveness. When children begin school, these types of positive associations will help them adjust to being part of a class.

SONGS AND RHYMES

"Pizza Song"
Since all the friends ate pizza at the end of the book, let's clap along to the pizza song!

Pizza, pizza hot.
Pizza, pizza cold.
Pizza, pizza in the box,
Nine days old.

Some like it hot.
Some like it cold.
And some like it in the box,
Nine days old!

"If You'd Like to Be a Duck" (to the tune of "If You're Happy and You Know It")

Before you begin this activity, practice quacking, waddling, shaking tails, flapping wings, and doing all four together so that children will be comfortable participating.

If you'd like to be a duck, say "Quack, quack."
If you'd like to be a duck, say "Quack, quack."
If you'd like to be a duckie, then you're very, very lucky!
If you'd like to be a duck, say "Quack, quack."

If you'd like to be a duck, waddle, waddle . . .
If you'd like to be a duck, shake your tail . . .
If you'd like to be a duck, flap your wings . . .
If you'd like to be a duck, do all four . . .

ACTIVITIES

Teamwork/Soup

Since teamwork is also a theme of this book, use teamwork to make soup.

Ask the children to stand in a circle and pretend that they are the soup pot.

Then ask them to pretend they are a vegetable or herb and to gently add themselves into the pot (into the middle of the circle).

They all sink to the bottom of the pot.

When the soup is just heating, the vegetables don't move. But when the water starts to simmer, they start moving.

When the water starts to boil, they move quickly while staying inside the pot.

Turn up the heat and turn it down again a number of times to change the level of the children's movement.

Pour out the soup and ask all the vegetables to slide out of the pot onto the floor!

Sheet Soup

For this activity you will need a large sheet or a parachute and construction paper shapes of various colors and sizes.

Place a sheet on the ground and tell the children to pretend it is a soup bowl.

Give children different shapes cut out of construction paper, representing different vegetables.

Ask the children to throw their vegetables in the pot and then pick up an edge of the sheet.

As it is getting hotter, the sheet starts to shake (watch the vegetables move up and down).

Turn the heat up, and the vegetables move even more vigorously.

Turn the heat down, and the vegetables don't move much.

When the pot is boiling, ask the children if they feel the wind.

Move the sheet from side to side as the friends look for Max inside the soup. Shake the sheet as hard as you can to push all the vegetables out!

BOOKS ABOUT SOUP, FOOD, AND EATING

Child, Lauren. 2003. *I Will Never Not Ever Eat a Tomato*. Cambridge, MA: Candlewick Press.

Cooper, Helen. 2007. *Delicious*. New York: Farrar Straus Giroux.

Davis, David (author), and Galbraith, Ben (illustrator). *Fandango Stew*. 2011. New York: Sterling.

Fleming, Denise. 1992. *Lunch*. New York: Henry Holt.

Kimmel, Eric A. (author), and Valeria Docampo (illustrator). 2009. *The Three Little Tamales*. New York: Marshall Cavendish.

Rodman, Mary Ann (author), and G. Brian Karas (illustrator). 2009. *Surprise Soup*. New York: Viking.

Sierra, Judy (author), and Edward Koren (illustrator). 2009. *Thelonius Monster's Sky-High Fly Pie*. New York: Knopf.

Soto, Gary (author), and Susan Guevara (illustrator). 1995. *Chato's Kitchen*. New York: Putnam.

Yolen, Jane (author), and Mark Teague (illustrator). 2005. *How Do Dinosaurs Eat Their Food?* New York: Blue Sky Press.

Week 3: Use Soup to Test Scientific Concepts

Discover what foods sink and float; learn about bay leaves.

THEME

Friendship

ITEMS NEEDED

- big pot filled halfway with water
- a few bay leaves
- some carrots (mini ones are fine)
- some potatoes
- shoebox with a cover
- tray
- dish towel

SETUP

Cover the pot and put it out of sight behind the storytelling chair. Put vegetables and bay leaves on a tray covered with a dish towel under or behind the storytelling chair.

SUGGESTED CONTENT

Focus Text

Raise your hand if you remember this story. *(Hold up the book.)* What were some of the ingredients that went into the soup? *("Pepper, salt, parsley, potato, carrots.")*

(Show the picture of the bay leaf floating at the top of the soup.) This is the herb that Dakota thought was Max's feather. Does anyone know what it really is! *(Pause for answers.)* It's a bay leaf. I have some bay leaves here.

SONG

"The More We Get Together"

Since Max, Brody, Dakota, and Bebe were such good friends, you might want to sing this song about friendship. Music can be found at www.songsforteaching.com/jimrule/themorewegettogether.htm.

The more we get together, together, together,
The more we get together, the happier we'll be.
For your friends are my friends,
And my friends are your friends.
The more we get together, the happier we'll be.

The more we get together, together, together,
The more we get together, the happier we'll be.
There's Timmy and Will and Yoella and Maya . . .
The more we get together, the happier we'll be.

Point to each child and have them say their name. Continue until all children have had a turn.

ACTIVITIES

What's Missing? Game

Bring out the tray of vegetables and take off the dish towel. Invite everyone to have a good look at what is on the tray for a minute. Then cover it up, put it behind your back, and take something off. Show the tray to the children again and see if they can correctly tell you what is now missing.

Vegetable Guessing Game

In this shoebox, I am going to put some carrots, potatoes, and bay leaves. One at a time I will invite you to come up and put your hand under the cover and into the box with NO PEEKING! Grab onto something, pull your hand out, and see if you guessed correctly. Who would like to go first? *(Play the game.)*

>> DEVELOPMENTAL TIP

Young children are able to absorb an amazing amount of information on topics of interest to them. They become experts, often knowing more than we do on some subjects. By taking advantage of their eagerness to learn, you can build their scientific knowledge.

Making Soup Science Experiment

Put the pot on the floor in front of you and take off the lid. Hand each child an item such as a bay leaf, potato, or carrot. Ask the children which items they think will float and which will sink: "What do you think is going to happen?" Tell them that you are all going to make some soup like the kind Max made. Invite children up one by one. Before they put each item into the pot, ask them if they think it is going to sink or float. Once a child drops in their item, have the child tell the group what actually happened. The children will learn that the bay leaves float but the potatoes and carrots do not, which explains why the bay leaf was floating at the top of the soup in the book.

You can also make felt representations of the bay leaves and the vegetables. Put a big flannel pot on the flannelboard and ask the children to put their flannel piece either in the bottom of the pot or on the top, depending on whether it sinks or floats.

>> DEVELOPMENTAL TIP

Determining what will sink and what will float involves looking at the items involved and forming a hypothesis about how buoyant each one is. Testing out the hypothesis not only teaches about sinking and floating, but also helps to exercise problem-solving skills while exposing children to some of the properties of water.

Exploring the Properties of Bay Leaves

Bring in enough bay leaves to give one to each child.

Ask the children to smell them and try to describe the smell.
Give each child a piece of cardboard (for backing) a sheet of copy paper, a crayon, and a bay leaf. Show them how to place the paper over the bay leaf and turn crayon on its side to do a rubbing with a crayon.
Ask parents to write bay leaf and their child's name on the paper.
Encourage the children to take the bay leaf and their rubbing home in a zip-close bag.

Connecting with Fine Arts

Download pictures (or show illustrations from a book of illustrations by Arcimbolo) of heads made out of vegetables, and ask questions about them.

What kinds of fruits and vegetables do you see?

Which ones were in the soup that Max made?

How do they look? Are they scary? Funny? Serious?

What do you see in them?

Hot Potato Game

Play this classic game with the kids to help them strengthen their self-regulation skills. Consider using the Wiggles "Hot Potato" song for the music. However, any child-friendly music will do. The object of the game is to be the last one standing.

Children stand in a circle. Have some object that represents the potato. This item could be an actual potato, a shoe, or a stuffed animal, for example.

Explain to the children that while the music is playing, they will pass the object from one child to the next very quickly, as if it really were a very hot potato. When the music stops, whoever is holding the object is out. So the idea is not to be the one holding the item when the music stops.

The last child standing gets a high five!

Counting and Matching Game

Make paper or flannel vegetables using the template from figure 8.2. Use the flannel-board for counting and matching games with soup ingredients.

Put an orange piece of flannel on the flannelboard, and ask everyone who has an orange vegetable to put it on the square.

Put a brown felt square on the flannelboard and ask for the potatoes. Use red for tomato and green for celery and bay leaf.

BOOKS ON FRIENDSHIP

Bloom, Suzanne. 2005. *A Splendid Friend Indeed.* Honesdale, PA: Boyds Mills Press.

Cannon, Janelle. 1993. *Stellaluna.* New York: Scholastic.

Cooper, Helen. 2005. *A Pipkin of Pepper.* New York: Farrar Straus Giroux.

David, Jacky (author), and David Soman (author, illustrator). 2009. *Ladybug Girl and Bumblebee Boy.* New York: Dial Books for Young Readers.

Gravett, Emily. 2010. *Blue Chameleon.* New York: Simon & Schuster Books for Young Readers.

Hillenbrand, Will. 2011. *Spring Is Here!* New York: Holiday House.

Hills, Tad. 2007. *Duck, Duck, Goose.* New York: Schwartz & Wade.

Howe, James (author), and Amy Walrod (illustrator). 1999. *Horace and Morris but Mostly Delores*. New York: Atheneum Books for Young Readers.

Hutchins, Pat. 1986. *The Doorbell Rang*. New York: Greenwillow.

McBratney, Sam (author), and Charles Fuge (illustrator). 2007. *Yes We Can!* New York: HarperCollins Publishers.

Russo, Marisabina. 2010. *A Very Big Bunny*. New York: Schwartz & Wade.

Wilson, Karma (author), and Jane Chapman (illustrator). 2003. *Bear Wants More*. New York: Margaret K. McElderry.

Winstead, Rosie. 2006. *Ruby and Bubbles*. New York: Dial Books for Young Readers.

Week 4: Reenact the Search for Max with Puppets

Take on challenges; become aware of physical space and use observation skills.

THEME

Animals

ITEMS NEEDED

- paper lunch bags (1 per child)
- pictures of dogs, cats, and parrots (1 of each picture per lunch bag)
- images of ducks (at least 10)
- tape
- bag with enough musical instruments for 1 per storytime participant (bells, maracas, rhythm sticks, or tambourines)

PREPARATION

Create paper bag puppets: dogs, cats, birds (Paper bag puppet instructions can be found here: www.dltk-kids.com/type/paper_bag.htm. Or photocopy figures 8.4 [Bebe], 8.5 [Brody], and 8.6 [Dakota]. Cut them out and attach them to lunch-size paper bags.) Use duck template (figure 8.3) or photocopy 10 colorful pictures of ducks (or as many as you'd like to use in the "find Max" activity).

SETUP

Hide the duck images in different places around the room. If needed, tape them down to avoid them moving around. The children are going to be looking for Max, so make some really easy to find and others more difficult.

SUGGESTED CONTENT

Focus Text

Read the story aloud, and then hand out the paper bag puppets. Explain that Max came to visit you earlier and that he brought some soup to share as well as many of his family and friends. However, just like in the book they all disappeared! You need the children to help find them. You have looked and looked, but you're pretty sure that the animals in the book are frightened of you. They will only come out if they see a friendly face. Since all of the children have Brody, Dakota, and Bebe puppets, lead them on a scavenger hunt around the room to find Max and his duck friends.

SONGS

"Hokey Pokey with Puppets"

You put your Brody in, you take your Brody out,
You put your Brody in, and you shake him all about . . .

Continue, using all the puppets.

"There Was a Great Big Moose"

Max is a duck who loves to drink soup; here's a song about a moose who loves to drink juice. Music for this can be found on Mary Lambert's Sing Out Summer Fun. *The single song can also be downloaded from Amazon. Have children stand and perform actions with you. This is a sing-and-response song, so the children should be encouraged to repeat the words after you.*

There was a great big moose! *(Hands up over head to show "big," then hold open hands
    up to head, thumb tips pressed against temples to look like moose antlers.)*
He liked to drink a lot of juice. *(Drink from an imaginary glass.)*
There was a great big moose! *(Repeat above actions.)*
He liked to drink a lot of juice. *(Repeat above actions.)*

Chorus:
Singin' oh way oh, *(Sway arms above head from side to side for rest of chorus. Feel free to
    dance or create your own actions.)*
Way oh way oh way oh way oh.
Way oh way oh,
Way oh way oh way oh way oh

The moose's name was Fred. (*Point to self.*)
He liked to drink his juice in bed. (*Drink from an imaginary glass.*)
The moose's name was Fred. (*Repeat above actions.*)
He liked to drink his juice in bed. (*Repeat above actions.*)
CHORUS

He drank his juice with care, (*Make drinking actions but hold out pinky and drink carefully.*)
but he spilled some in his hair. (*Rub the front of your shirt like something spilled.*)
He drank his juice with care, (*Repeat above actions.*)
but he spilled some in his hair. (*Repeat above actions.*)
CHORUS

Now he's a sticky moose (*Hold hands and arms out from the sides of body as if you're very sticky and don't want to be touched.*)
Because he's all covered in juice! (*Run hands down body from shoulders to knees to show you're covered in juice.*)
Now he's a sticky moose (*Repeat above actions.*)
Because he's all covered in juice! (*Repeat above actions.*)
CHORUS

>> DEVELOPMENTAL TIP

Learning through play is relaxed, fun, and creative. Through a single enjoyable activity, your child can learn about following directions, taking turns, and showing appreciation to others—all skills that are necessary for healthy development.

ACTIVITIES

Looking for a Moose

Max's friends went looking for him when they thought he was lost. Here's another book about looking for someone, called *Looking for a Moose* by Phyllis Root, illustrated by Randy Cecil. (*Read aloud. Consider being interactive with this book. Have children perform the actions along with the story. For example, have them roll up their sleeves, pull up their backpacks, and shield their eyes when "looking" for a moose.*)

Act Out the Story with Stuffed Animals

Try going to a secondhand store such as Goodwill and buying stuffed animals for each character in Duck Soup: *ducks, bunnies, dogs, and bugs. Give each child an animal. Read the story aloud and when the part of each animal comes up, prompt them to respond with the actions their character took in the book.*

BOOKS ABOUT ANIMALS

Bachelet, Gilles. 2006. *My Cat Is the Silliest Cat in the World.* New York: Abrams Books for Young Readers.

Carle, Eric. 2011. *The Artist Who Painted a Blue Horse.* New York: Philomel Books.

Fleming, Candace (author), and Sally Anne Lambert (illustrator). 2004. *Gator Gumbo: A Spicy-Hot Tale.* New York: Farrar Straus Giroux.

Fore, C. J. 2010. *Read to Tiger.* New York: Viking.

Gibbs, Edward. 2011. *I Spy with My Little Eye.* Somerville, MA: Templar Books/Candlewick Press.

Mayer, Mercer. 2010. *What Do You Do with a Kangaroo?* New York: Scholastic Paperbacks.

McKee, David. 2011. *Elmer and the Rainbow.* Minneapolis, MN: Andersen Press USA.

Rayner, Catherine. 2011. *The Bear Who Shared.* New York: Dial Books for Young Readers.

Root, Phyllis (author), and Randy Cecil (illustrator). 2006. *Looking for a Moose.* Cambridge, MA: Candlewick Press.

Rosen, Michael (author), and Kevin Waldron (illustrator). 2010. *Tiny Little Fly.* Somerville, MA: Candlewick Press.

Ward, Jennifer (author), and Steve Gray (illustrator). 2007. *There Was a Coyote Who Swallowed a Flea.* Flagstaff, AZ: Rising Moon.

Wildsmith, Brian. 2006. *Jungle Party.* New York: Star Bright Books.

Week 5: Compare Similar Stories

Tell the story using flannel pieces and script cards; compare similar stories to see what is the same and what is different.

THEME

Birds

ITEMS NEEDED

- flannel pieces
- large picture or illustration of a duck missing its tail, taped on a surface low enough so the children can reach it for pin-the-tail-on-the-duck. The picture also needs to be large enough for multiple children to have space to try to pin their tail up.
- tail feathers (actual feathers, or construction paper feathers), 1 per child
- blindfold
- flannelboard characters from the story that can either be made from templates or can be made from copies directly taken from the book.

- soup pot (figure 8.1)
- vegetables (figure 8.2)
- duck (Max) (figure 8.3)
- bird (Bebe) (figure 8.4)
- dog (Brody) (figure 8.5)
- cat (Dakota) (figure 8.6)

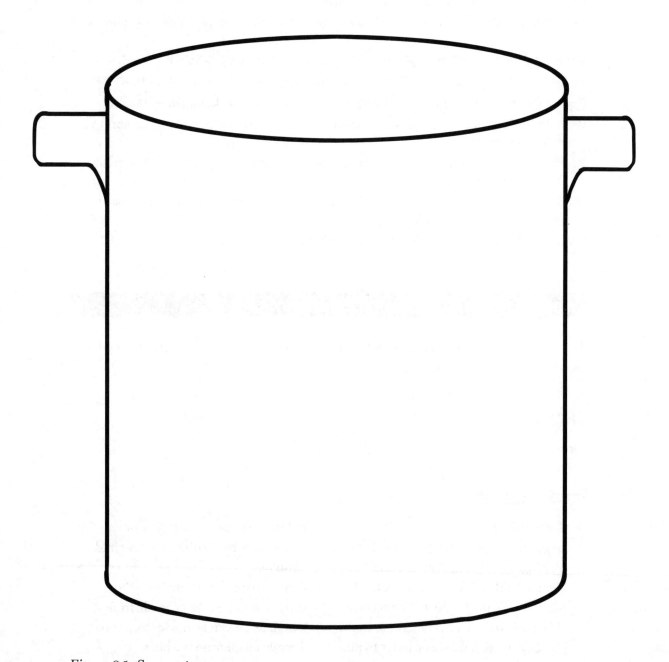

Figure 8.1 Soup pot

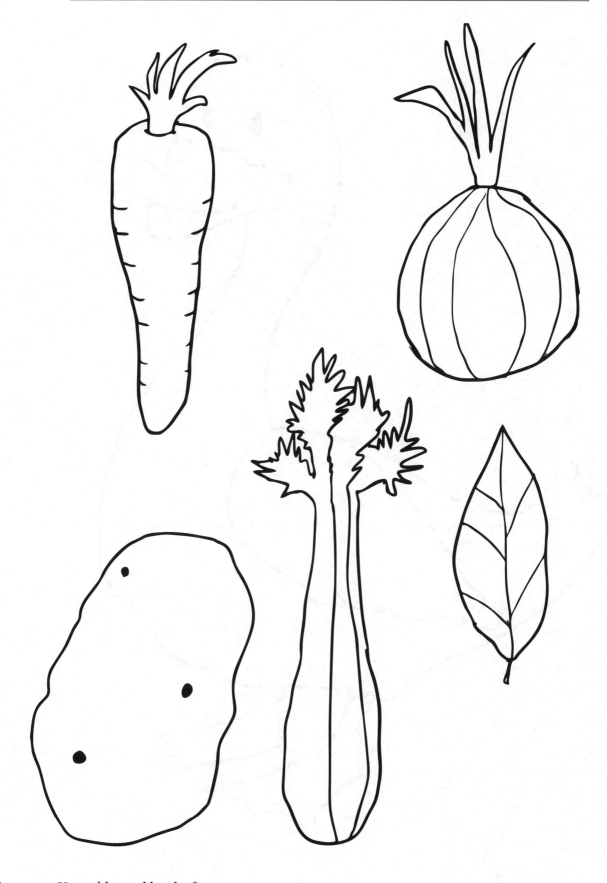

Figure 8.2 Vegetables and bay leaf

Figure 8.3 Duck

Figure 8.4 Bird

Figure 8.5 Dog

Figure 8.6 Cat

SUGGESTED CONTENT

Focus Text

Tell the story via flannelboard and script cards. Do an activity and then read aloud "The Lost Button," a chapter in Arnold Lobel's classic book, Frog and Toad Are Friends. *Ask the children to help you compare the two books.*

What is the same about "The Lost Button" and *Duck Soup*? *("In both stories, something is lost.")* What is lost in both stories? *("The button and Max.")* What is different? *("Frog has one friend, Max has three friends; different style of illustrations.")*

RHYME

"Two Little Dicky Birds" (first verse adapted by Barbara Cass-Beggs)

Two little dicky birds sitting on a cloud. *(Both hands out in front, index fingers extended. Bounce fingers up and down to rhythm.)*
One named Soft, one named Loud. *(Bring Soft finger forward, speak softly. Bring Loud finger forward, speak loudly.)*
Fly away, Soft; fly away, Loud. *("Fly" soft finger behind back; "fly" loud finger behind back.)*
Come back, Soft; come back, Loud. *(Bring soft finger back in front; bring loud finger back in front.)*

Two little dickie birds sitting in the snow, *(Both hands out in front, index fingers extended. Bounce fingers up and down to rhythm.)*
One named Fast; the other named Slow. *(Bring Fast finger forward quickly; Bring Slow finger forward slowly.)*
Fly away, Fast; fly away, Slow. *(Fly Fast finger behind back quickly; fly Slow finger behind back slowly.)*
Come back, Fast; come back, Slow. *(Bring Fast finger back in front quickly; bring Slow finger back in front slowly.)*

ACTIVITIES

Flight Freeze Game

Music needed: "Flight of the Valkyries" by Richard Wagner. See if your library has a CD with this song on it. It can also easily be found on many different CDs available through Amazon and other sites.

Ask the children to stand up. Explain that while the music is playing they can "fly" around the room like birds, but when the music stops, they must freeze. Children who do not freeze are out. The last person standing gets a high five!

>> DEVELOPMENTAL TIP

All children must learn how to respond to the word *stop*. Children enjoy playing freeze games or games that ask participants to stop at a certain point. In addition to being fun, these types of games teach children how to listen and give them practice at stopping when asked to do so.

Pin the Tail on the Duck Game

Hang up the large picture of the duck without a tail. Hand each child a tail feather to pin up. Blindfold each child in turn, put a piece of tape on their tail feather, spin them one to three times, point them toward the duck picture, and let them pin their tail feather on the duck. The child who gets the closest gets a high five!

BOOKS ABOUT BIRDS

Auch, Mary Jane (author), and Mary Jane and Herm Auch (illustrators). 2007. *Beauty and the Beaks*. New York: Holiday House.

Berne, Jennifer (author), and Keith Bendis (illustrator). 2010. *Calvin Can't Fly: The Story of a Bookworm Birdie*. New York: Sterling.

Fox, Mem (author), and David Miller (illustrator). 1998. *Boo to a Goose*. New York: Dial Books for Young Readers.

Gravett, Emily. 2009. *The Odd Egg*. New York: Simon & Schuster Books for Young Readers.

Horacek, Petr. 2008. *Silly Suzy Goose*. Cambridge, MA: Candlewick Press.

Kasbarian, Lucine (author), and Maria Zaikina (illustrator). 2011. *The Greedy Sparrow: An Armenian tale*. Tarrytown, NY: Marshall Cavendish Children.

Montes, Marisa (author), and Marsha Winborn (illustrator). 2002. *Egg-napped!* New York: HarperCollins Publishers.

Palatini, Margie (author), and Henry Cole (illustrator). 2009. *Bad Boys Get Henpecked!* New York: Katherine Tegen Books.

Sattler, Jennifer. 2009. *Sylvie*. New York: Random House Children's Books.

Schaefer, Lola M (author), and Donald Crews (illustrator). 2000. *This Is the Sunflower*. New York: Greenwillow Books.

Waddell, Martin (author), and Patrick Benson (illustrator). 1996. *Owl Babies*. Cambridge, MA: Candlewick Press.

Willems, Mo. 2003. *Don't Let the Pigeon Drive the Bus*. New York: Hyperion Books for Children.

Winstead, Rosie. 2006. *Ruby and Bubbles*. New York: Dial Books for Young Readers.

Week 6: Invite the Children to Act Out the Story

Act out the story.

THEME

Accidents and mistakes

ITEMS NEEDED

- flannelboard templates 8.1 and 8.2
  Make 1 pot and enough vegetable flannelboard pieces for 1 per child.

SUGGESTED CONTENT

Focus Text

We've been using this book in circle time for a few weeks, so if you've been here before, you probably know what happens. Who remembers the name of the main character? *(Pause for answers.)* What type of animal is he? *(Pause for answers.)* Who are his friends? *(Pause for answers.)* What is he making? You know this story so well, it's time for us to act it out!

Invite the children to act the story. Everyone who wants to be Max goes in one place, all Brodys in another, and so on. Make a circle on the floor with masking tape to be the pot. Read the story aloud and ask the children to act it out—you may need to prompt them, but they already should be able to recite the dialogue without any help.

SONG

"I'm a Nut"

Music and additional lyrics can be found here: http://kids.niehs.nih.gov/games/songs/childrens/imanutmid.htm.

Do you think Max tried to put nuts in his soup? If he did, he might have sung this silly song:
I'm an acorn small and round,
Lying on the cold, cold ground.
Everyone walks over me,
That is why I'm cracked, you see.
I'm a nut, click, click. *(Make clicking noise with tongue.)*
I'm a nut, click, click.
I'm a nut, I'm a nut, I'm a nut, click, click.

ACTIVITY

Math and Measuring

In Duck Soup, *Max only mentions measuring by using a "pinch." Hold up a measuring cup, pour in half a cup of colored water, and show the children where it reaches the line. Use the word measuring.*

Talk about math and measurements and introduce simple fractions by using a round rug or creating a masking tape circle on the floor. Ask the children to pretend that the circle on the floor is the pizza that all the characters ate at the end of the story. It is a WHOLE pizza. But since there is more than one friend to share the pizza, it needs to be divided.

Make a masking tape line down the middle of the circle. Tell the children it is now divided in half, but when both halves are put together, it makes a whole. Ask them stand on one half, to stand on the other, and then spread out on the whole. Ask questions such as, "Which is smaller, the half or the whole?" ("The half.") "When you put both halves together, what do you get?" ("The whole.") "How many parts of the circle are there?" (Two.) "If you cut a carrot in half, how many parts of the carrot would there be?" ("Two.")

>> DEVELOPMENTAL TIP

Through this simple activity, children are learning that there are parts to a whole, and the more parts you have, the smaller the parts are. But, when added up, they still make a whole.

>> DEVELOPMENTAL TIP

Having your children cook with you at home exposes them to the basics of fractions and math skills. Talk as you cook together and describe the different amounts you are measuring.

BOOKS ABOUT ACCIDENTS AND MISTAKES

Grey, Mini. 2009. *Egg Drop.* New York: Alfred A. Knopf.

Himmelman, John. 2006. *Chickens to the Rescue.* New York: Henry Holt.

Horowitz, Dave. 2008. *Humpty Dumpty Climbs Again.* New York: G. P. Putnam's Sons.

Huneck, Stephen. 2004. *Sally Goes to the Vet.* New York: Harry N. Abrams.

Luján, Jorge (author), Piet Grobler (illustrator), and Elisa Amado (translator). 2007. *Sky Blue Accident / Accidente celeste.* Toronto: Groundwood Books. Poetry.

MacLean, Christine Kole (author), and Cynthia B. Decker (illustrator). 2005. *Everybody Makes Mistakes.* New York: Dutton Children's Books.

Pett, Mark (author and illustrator), and Gary Rubinstein (author). 2011. *The Girl Who Never Made Mistakes.* Naperville, Ill: Sourcebooks Jabberwocky.

Shaw, Nancy, and Margot Apple. 1986. *Sheep in a Jeep.* Boston: Houghton Mifflin.
Pause at the end of each paragraph and see if the children can name the rhyming word after looking at the picture.

chapter 9

Series 7
Bark, George

Focus Text: *Bark, George*

by Jules Feiffer
(New York: HarperCollins, 1999)

George's mother becomes concerned when instead of barking, her son goes "meow," "quack-quack," "oink," and "moo." A visit to the vet reveals that George has some very unusual items in his belly!

Ways to Present *Bark, George* in Storytime Sessions

Week 1: Introduce *Bark, George.* (dogs)

Week 2: Tell *Bark, George* as a flannelboard story. (animal sounds)

Week 3: Tell *Bark, George* with stick puppets. (farm animals)

Week 4: Encourage multisensory exploration while narrating the story. (exploring the unknown)

Week 5: Interview George and his friends to find out what really happened. (parents and their children)

Week 6: Examine the story from a veterinarian's perspective. (veterinarians and doctors)

Week 1: Introduce *Bark, George*

Read the story aloud.

THEME

Dogs

ITEMS NEEDED

- tray
- towel
- common items to put on the tray, such as a pencil, a mug, a book, a cell phone, a glue stick, and a scissors

SETUP

Place the common objects on the tray and cover them with the towel.

SUGGESTED CONTENT

Focus Text
Read the book aloud.

SONGS AND RHYMES

"Oh Where, Oh Where Has My Little Dog Gone?"
Put up flannel picture of a dog. Sing the song twice. Music can be found here: http://kids.niehs.nih.gov/games/songs/childrens/ohwheremid.htm.

Oh where, oh where has my little dog gone?
Oh where, oh where can he be?
With his ears cut short and his tail cut long.
Oh where, oh where can he be?

"Puppy Dog, Puppy Dog"
Before beginning this song, practice the movements with the children so they know what to do. Movements: turn, sit, beg, stand on leg, "aroooo" (howl), spin in a circle, creep, sleep.

Puppy dog, puppy dog, turn around. (*Everyone turn in place.*)
Puppy dog, puppy dog, sit on the ground. (*Everyone sit on the floor.*)

Puppy dog, puppy dog, sit and beg. (*Everyone make sit up and begging motions.*)

Puppy dog, puppy dog, stand on one leg! (*Everyone stand on one leg.*)

Puppy dog, puppy dog, bark and wail. (*Everyone bark and then say "arooo."*)

Puppy dog, puppy dog, chase your tail! (*Everyone spin in a circle.*)

Puppy dog, puppy dog, into your bed creep. (*Everyone creep.*)

Puppy dog, puppy dog, go to sleep! (*Everyone close eyes and feign sleep on folded hands under cheek.*)

"B-I-N-G-O"

Before beginning this song, explain to the children that each time you sing the song you will take away a letter sound and clap in its place. Music can be found at http://kids.niehs.nih.gov/games/songs/childrens/bingomid.htm.

There was a farmer had a dog, and Bingo was his name-o.

B-I-N-G-O

B-I-N-G-O

B-I-N-G-O

And Bingo was his name-o.

There was a farmer had a dog, And Bingo was his name-o.

(*Clap*)-I-N-G-O

(*Clap*)-I-N-G-O

(*Clap*)-I-N-G-O

And Bingo was his name-o.

There was a farmer had a dog, and Bingo was his name-o.

(*Clap-clap*)-N-G-O

(*Clap-clap*)-N-G-O

(*Clap-clap*)-N-G-O

And Bingo was his name-o.

There was a farmer had a dog, and Bingo was his name-o.

(*Clap-clap-clap*)-G-O

(*Clap-clap-clap*)-G-O

(*Clap-clap-clap*)-G-O

And Bingo was his name-o.

There was a farmer had a dog, and Bingo was his name-o.

(*Clap-clap-clap-clap*)-O

(*Clap-clap-clap-clap*)-O

(*Clap-clap-clap-clap*)-O

And Bingo was his name-o.

There was a farmer had a dog, and Bingo was his name-o.
(Clap-clap-clap-clap-clap)
(Clap-clap-clap-clap-clap)
(Clap-clap-clap-clap-clap)
And Bingo was his name-o!

>> DEVELOPMENTAL TIP

Clapping in place of a word or sound when all else is silent is called *audiation*. This helps make children aware of syllables (the way words are broken down into different sounds). Being able to divide words into syllables is an important building block for learning how to read.

ACTIVITY

What's Missing? Game

When all of those animals were in George's stomach, we couldn't see them. We only knew what they were by hearing the sounds they made. Being able to hear is one of your senses, and it allows you to discover things that you can't see.

Seeing is another one of the senses. Have a look at everything on this tray. I'm going to give you thirty seconds to have a look. *(Remove the towel from the tray and hold it in a way that everyone can see it. After thirty seconds cover it with the towel.)* Who would like to volunteer to tell me what was on the tray? See if you can remember everything! *(Choose volunteers. Pull out objects from under the towel as they are named. When a child has finished guessing, even if they have not named everything, state enthusiastically how many objects they did find: "You remembered FIVE of the hidden objects!" Then return the objects to the tray under the towel while counting each item aloud, and invite another child to try remembering aloud everything on the tray, under the towel.)*

>> DEVELOPMENTAL TIP

Games like these help sharpen your child's observation skills. You can replicate this game at home by placing easily recognizable items on a tray, covering the tray with a dish towel, and trying to remember what is hidden underneath.

BOOKS ABOUT DOGS

Beaumont, Karen (author), and David Catrow (illustrator). 2008. *Doggone Dogs!* New York: Dial Books for Young Readers.

Beaumont, Karen (author), and Jane Dyer (illustrator). 2006. *Move Over, Rover!* Orlando: Harcourt.

Drummond, Ree (author), and Diane DeGroat (illustrator). 2011. *Charlie the Ranch Dog*. New York: Harper.

Gormley, Greg (author), and Roberta Angaramo (illustrator). 2011. *Dog in Boots*. New York: Holiday House.

Johnston, Lynn Franks (author), and Beth Cruikshank (illustrator). 2009. *Farley Follows His Nose*. New York: Bowen Press.

McCarthy, Meghan. 2004. *Show Dog*. New York: Viking.

McDonnell, Patrick. 2009. *Wag!* New York: Little, Brown Books for Young Readers.

Numeroff, Laura (author), and Felicia Bond (illustrator). 2011. *If You Give a Dog a Donut*. New York: Balzer and Bray.

Rylant, Cynthia (author), and Mark Teague (illustrator). 2001. *The Great Gracie Chase*. New York: Blue Sky Press.

Swaim, Jessica (author), and Jill McElmurry (illustrator). 2007. *The Hound from the Pound*. Cambridge, MA: Candlewick Press.

Van Patter, Bruce. 2006. *Farley Found It!* Honesdale, PA: Boyds Mills Press.

Weeks, Sarah (author), and Holly Berry (illustrator). 2009. *Woof: A Love Story*. New York: HarperCollins.

Willems, Mo (author), and Jon J. Muth (illustrator). 2010. *City Dog, Country Frog*. New York: Hyperion Books for Children.

Week 2: Tell *Bark, George* as a Flannelboard Story

Retell the story using flannelboard characters (and script cards, if needed).

THEME

Animal sounds

ITEMS NEEDED

- flannelboard pieces for *Bark, George*
- mother dog
- puppy
- cat
- cow
- pig
- duck
- vet
- boy

Optional: flannelboard letters and clapping hands for "B-I-N-G-O"

- B
- I
- N
- G
- O

PREPARATION

Copy and enlarge these templates for *Bark, George*

- George's mother (figure 9.1)
- George (figure 9.2)
- vet (figure 9.3)
- cat (figure 9.4)
- duck (figure 9.5)
- pig (figure 9.6)
- cow (figure 9.7)
- boy (figure 9.8)

Figure 9.1 George's mother

Figure 9.2 George

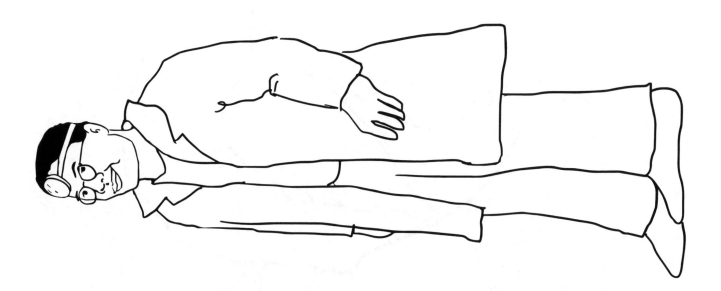

Figure 9.3 Vet

Figure 9.4 Cat

Figure 9.5 Duck

Figure 9.6 Pig

Figure 9.7 Cow

Figure 9.8 Boy

PREPARATION *(cont'd)*

Write out the story of *Bark, George* on notecards to act as cue cards when telling the story with the flannelboard pieces. You can do this by writing out the story word for word, or getting the key plot features down. Write it in whatever way will be useful to you while "telling" the story instead of reading it.

Photocopy and enlarge the templates for the *Bark, George* characters. Color them, cut them out, and use tacky glue to attach them to felt for use on your flannelboard.

Consider making flannel BINGO letters and flannel pieces that show clapping hands. Before beginning the song, put the BINGO letters on a flannelboard. Explain to the children that when you take a letter away, you will all say "bye-bye, —— (whatever letter is being removed)," and you will put up a picture of clapping hands in its place. The picture will show the children when to clap.

SUGGESTED CONTENT

Focus Text

Tell the story using flannelboard pieces. Use cue cards to help you tell and display each flannel piece as it is presented in the story. You can also have children put the flannel pieces on the board as you are telling the story.

RHYME

Use this rhyme in conjunction with the Surprise activity below.

"Jack-in-the-Box"

Climb in the box. *(Pretend to climb in a box and squat.)*
Close the lid. *(Press your hand on your head.)*
Wind yourself up. *(Turn a pretend crank.)*
And here we go . . .

Jack-in-the box
Sitting so still.
Won't you come out?
Yes, I will! *(Jump up.)*

ACTIVITIES

Animal Sounds Simon Says

In the game Simon Says, players only perform the called out action if the caller says "Simon says" first. Players who perform the called action without "Simon saying" are out of the game.

   Once the game has begun and children have the hang of it, call on a different child each turn and have them give a direction saying the phrase Simon says or not.

Simon says, "Moo like a cow."
Simon says "Baa like a sheep."
Neigh like a horse.
Simon says, "Cluck like a chicken."
Simon says, "Oink like a pig."
Simon says, "Honk like a goose."
Simon says, "Crow like a rooster."
Quack like a duck.
Simon says, "Whisper like a rabbit."

Meow like a cat.
Bark like a dog.
Simon says, "Gobble like a turkey."

Continue the game until only one person is left. The winner gets a high five!

Surprise

Surprise is a fun element of Bark, George; *children learn not to judge a dog by its cover!* The Fat Cat *by Jack Kent is a similar story. In this rhythmic read-aloud, the cat gets fatter and fatter by eating everything he sees. When his stomach is cut open, all the animals and people come out. The final picture, showing a skinny cat with two bandages on its stomach, sweetens the ending.*

Homemade Sound Effects

Record the children making the sound of the animals in the book. Read the book aloud again and use the recording as the sound effects. The children will love to hear themselves!

Animal Sounds Matching Game

Use a nonfiction book to show photographs of different animals, and ask the children to make the appropriate sounds.

>> DEVELOPMENTAL TIP

In addition to picture books, be sure to share factual books (or nonfiction books) with your children. Follow their interests, whether in a particular animal, in how things work, about certain vehicles, or anything else that they are curious about. The information in nonfiction books introduces new vocabulary; supporting their curiosity goes a long way in encouraging a love of learning.

Animal Homes Matching Game

Create separate cards for animals and their homes. Ask the children to try to match each animal with the correct home. For instance:

dog—doghouse	*bird—nest*	*duck—pond*
horse—stable	*mouse—mouse hole*	*fish—fish tank*

BOOKS ABOUT ANIMAL SOUNDS

Brock, Lee. 2003. *Oh, Crumps!* Green Bay, WI: Raven Tree Press.

Cazet, Denys. 1994. *Nothing at All!* New York: Orchard Books.

Dodd, Emma. 2011. *Meow Said the Cow.* New York: Arthur A. Levine Books.

Fleming, Denise. 2006. *The Cow Who Clucked.* New York: Henry Holt.

Kutner, Merrily (author), and Will Hillenbrand (illustrator). 2004. *Down on the Farm*. New York: Holiday House.

Macken, JoAnn Early (author), and David Walker (illustrator). 2011. *Baby Says "Moo!"* New York: Disney/Hyperion Books.

Palatini, Marge (author), and Keith Graves (illustrator). 2009. *Boo-Hoo Moo*. New York: Katherine Tegen Books.

Polacco, Patricia. 2005. *Mommies Say Shhh!* New York: Philomel Books.

Root, Phyllis (author), and Helen Craig (illustrator). 1997. *One Windy Wednesday*. Cambridge, MA: Candlewick Press.

Ruddell, Deborah (author), and Robin Leubs (illustrator). 2010. *Who Said Coo?* New York: Beach Lane Books.

Week 3: Tell *Bark, George* with Stick Puppets

Children use stick puppets to dramatize a retelling of the story.

THEME

Farm animals

ITEMS NEEDED

- flannel pieces for
  - › All Around the Farm: cow, horse, pig, chick, sheep
  - › B-I-N-G-O: letters B, I, N, G, O and clapping hands
- *Bark, George* written out on cue cards or paraphrased so you can tell the story without the book
- tongue depressors
- glue
- scissors
- About 10 pictures or colored pages each of 2 dogs (1 George, 1 mother), cow, cat, duck, pig, and a person to be the vet The cartoonlike book illustrations lend themselves well to being color copies and turned into puppets. You may also want to create templates out of figures 9.2 (dog), 9.3 (vet), 9.4 (cat), 9.5 (duck), 9.6 (pig), 9.7 (cow), 9.8 (boy). Add to the story by including more animals, such as sheep.

PREPARATION

Create stick puppets for each character in *Bark, George*. If you anticipate having more children than there are characters, make more than one of each animal. Each picture can be an illustration, a photo, or a colored picture. Cut out each one and glue each to a separate tongue depressor.

SUGGESTED CONTENT

Focus Text

Hand out the stick puppets, one to each child. Explain to the children that you are going to tell the story without using the book. They need to listen carefully: when they hear the name of the animal or person that matches their stick puppet, they should raise their puppet and "dance" it in the air for that part of the story.

>> DEVELOPMENTAL TIP

At home, play a fun game by asking your child to listen to something carefully (a story, a song, etc.) and if they hear a specific word or sound, to react in a predetermined way (such as getting up and dancing or calling out, "I heard it!"). In addition to exercising the sense of hearing, this game develops listening skills and encourages children to practice paying attention, an important skill needed by children entering kindergarten.

SONG

B-I-N-G-O

Repeat this song, with the following variation: give the children instruments such as bells, sticks, or maracas (any sort of shaker item). Have them make sound with their instruments for the missing letters.

ACTIVITIES

Animal Charades

We were able to use our sense of hearing to figure out the animals coming out of George by the different animal sounds he was making. *(Choose children to volunteer to be George, to come up to the front of the room and make an animal sound that has not been used yet. The child who correctly guesses the animal gets the next turn.)*

Animal Movements

How does a dog move? On all fours! See if you can move like a dog.
How does a snake move? On its belly. See if you can move like a snake.
How does a bird move? It flies! See if you can flap your wings and fly.
How does a frog move? It hops. See if you hop high into the sky.

>> DEVELOPMENTAL TIP

Learning different types of movement has many benefits for children. For example, tiptoeing helps develop good balance skills. Show your children how to walk on tiptoes (not on the sides of their feet), and make a game out of tiptoeing to bed!

Painting a "George" Box

After this session, if time and space permit, you may want to ask the children to help you prepare something for the following week. Spread a disposable plastic tablecloth or newspapers out on a tabletop or floor. Set out plates with brown paint and brushes. Place a medium-sized cardboard box (about as big as a microwave) next to the paints, and ask the children to help you by painting the box.

You may want to recommend that they turn their shirts inside out first, or supply aprons if possible.

As soon as the painting is complete, move the box in a nonpublic area to dry. Clear up the paints and hand out wipes (or invite parents to help their children wash their hands in the rest room).

HANDOUT FOR PARENTS

Help your child develop all five senses by playing fun guessing games at home.

Looking at illustrations of animals or playing charades and naming the animal involves using the sense of *sight*.

Making an animal sound or guessing the animal's name after hearing the sound engages the sense of *hearing*.

Guessing what an object is only by feeling it involves the sense of *touch*.

Guessing what certain foods are simply by eating them involves the sense of *taste*, and by smelling them involves the sense of *smell*.

Playing these games in a fun, nonstressful way helps children learn about making deductions based on limited information supplied by their senses. Being able to check if they are right while feeling no pressure or sense of failure if they are wrong encourages them to try to decipher clues in the future, strengthening both observation and reasoning skills.

BOOKS ABOUT FARM ANIMALS

Cutbill, Andy (author), and Russell Ayto (illustrator). 2008. *The Cow Who Laid an Egg.* New York: HarperCollins.

Edwards, Pamela Duncan (author), and Megan Lloyd (illustrator). 2006. *The Mixed-Up Rooster.* New York: Katherine Tegen Books.

Emberley, Rebecca (author), and Ed Emberley (illustrator). 2009. *Chicken Little.* New York: Roaring Brook Press.

Fox, Mem (author), and Jan Thomas (illustrator). 2010. *Let's Count Goats!* New York: Beach Lane Books.

Himmelman, John. 2006. *Chickens to the Rescue.* New York: Henry Holt.

McPhail, David. 1993. *Pigs Aplenty, Pigs Galore!* New York: Dutton Children's Books.

Meadows, Michelle (author), and Ard Hoyt (illustrator). 2011. *Piggies in the Kitchen*. New York: Simon & Schuster Books for Young Readers.

Meng, Cece. 2009. *Tough Chicks*. New York: Clarion Books.

Palatini, Margie (author), and Barry Moser (illustrator). 2002. *Earthquack!* New York: Simon & Schuster Books for Young Readers.

Urbanovic, Jackie. 2007. *Duck at the Door*. New York: HarperCollins.

Willems, Mo. 2011. *Happy Pig Day!* New York: Hyperion Books for Children.

Wilson, Karma (author), and Marcellus Hall (illustrator). 2010. *The Cow Loves Cookies*. New York: Margaret K. McElderry.

Week 4: Encourage Multisensory Exploration while Narrating the Story

Act out the story by using a cardboard "George" box.

THEME

Exploring the unknown

ITEMS NEEDED

- "George" box painted brown with items of different textures inside, such as a rubber ducky, a washcloth, a spoon, a key, a little plastic flashlight, a rubber ball, a piece of Duplo, a plastic bug, a jump rope, a little teddy bear, and a cup Be sure to have enough objects so there is at least 1 per child.
- cue cards for *Bark, George* story
- stethoscope and/or child-size white coat

PREPARATION

- Use the cue cards from week 2 with the story of *Bark, George* on them.
- Gather objects listed above and place them in the "George" box for the retelling of the story.
- To create the "George" box, use the painted brown box from the week before, or another brown box. Attach construction-paper floppy ears on top. Draw eyes and a nose. Cut out a big hole (large enough for a child's hand) underneath the nose. Cut a few strips of white or yellow paper and attach them to top of the mouth from the inside of the box. They will look like teeth, but will provide a flap through which children can stick their hands yet will prevent them from seeing what is inside the box. Once the objects have been placed inside the box, seal the top with tape. This is "George."

SUGGESTED CONTENT

Focus Text

Introduce the box "George" and begin telling the story. Embellish the story by telling the children that this time George had a REALLY BIG appetite and ate lots of different things. However, some of the items don't make sounds, so the vet won't be able to tell what they are until he reaches his hand into the dog's mouth.

Invite the children to come up one by one. Put the stethoscope around their neck or the white coat on them. Ask them to choose one object and guess what it is by the way it feels. You may want to say "George swallowed a bunch of things today. Stick your hand inside and tell us what you find!" You may want to ask questions regarding why the child has guessed that particular thing that will encourage observation skills and descriptive vocabulary: "Does it feel round? Is it squishy? Is it cold?"

Once the vet makes a guess, ask that child to pull out the object and show everyone what it is. Place it on a tray and invite the next vet to come up and help George. When all of the items have been pulled out, hold each item up one at a time and let the group name the object. Once it is named, George "swallows" it again. When all the objects are back in George's tummy, it is time for storytime to end!

›› DEVELOPMENTAL TIP

In this game, instead of relying on their eyes, children are using their sense of touch to determine the object that is hidden. You can play a similar game at home by taking turns putting familiar objects into a paper bag (or on a tray covered by a dish towel) and asking each other to guess what's inside by using the sense of touch only. This activity exercises hand coordination and matching skills while developing the sense of touch.

RHYME

"Hey Diddle Diddle"

Traditional rhyme with animals who also do unusual things!

Hey diddle diddle,
The cat and the fiddle,
The cow jumped over the moon.
The little dog laughed to see such sport,
And the dish ran away with the spoon.

Consider using American Sign Language with this rhyme. Look up the signs online at the American Sign Language University: www.lifeprint.com/index.htm or www.aslpro.com.

BOOKS ABOUT EXPLORING THE UNKNOWN

Billingsley, Franny (author), and G. Brian Karas (illustrator). 2008. *Big Bad Bunny*. New York: Atheneum Books for Young Readers.

Litwin, Eric (author), and James Dean (illustrator). 2010. *Pete the Cat: I Love My White Shoes*. New York: HarperCollins.

Sadler, Marilyn, and Roger Bollen. 1984. *Alistair in Outer Space*. New York: Prentice-Hall Books for Young Readers.

Scotton, Rob. 2008. *Splat the Cat*. New York: HarperCollins.

Watt, Melanie. 2007. *Chester*. Toronto: Kids Can Press.

Week 5: Interview George and His Friends to Find Out What *Really* Happened

Pretend to be a television announcer. Interview storytime children to hear different impressions of the story from a wide range of viewpoints—the sillier the better.

THEME

Parents and their children

ITEMS NEEDED

- empty water bottle
- screen
- copy of the Weston Woods film *Bark, George* in 16 mm film, video, or DVD format
- film projector, video player and television screen, or DVD player and LED projector
- cue cards with *Bark, George* written out

SUGGESTED CONTENT

Focus Text

Show the video Bark, George, *produced by Weston Woods. The running time of the original Weston Woods film on video or DVD is 6 minutes (Gene Deitch, John Lithgow, and Jules Feiffer. 2003.* Bark, George, *Norwalk, CT: Weston Woods). It is also in the Scholastic Video Collection, on* Bark, George—and More Doggie Tails. *Follow with pretend television interviews.*

We have a very special guest here today. It is a television news announcer from W-LIB! He is here to interview George's mother. Who would like to be George's mother? *(Choose a volunteer. Be sure to choose someone who has been at the previous storytimes and knows the storyline of* Bark, George. *Hold an empty water bottle up to your mouth as if it is a microphone.)*

Hello, George's mother. We are very happy to have you here on our show today.

Tell me, George's mother, when did you first notice that George was having a problem barking? *(Hold microphone up to child's mouth—or have another "microphone" available for the child to hold, and pause for an answer.)*

What was the first sound he made? *(Pause for an answer.)*

What did you think was causing it? *(Pause for an answer.)*

Well, thank you, George's mother, for being on our show!

Now it's time to interview the vet. *(Choose a volunteer.)*

Tell me, vet, what happened when George arrived at your office? Were you scared to reach deep down inside George? *(Pause for an answer.)*

What did you think when you discovered that there were many different animals inside of George? *(Pause for an answer.)*

Is there a way to keep George from eating everything in sight again? *(Pause for an answer.)*

Thank you very much, friendly veterinarian.

Now I'd like to interview one of the animals that was inside of George. *(Choose a volunteer.)*

Welcome to our show, Mrs. Cow.

How did you and George first meet? *(Pause for an answer.)*

What was it like inside of George's stomach? *(Pause for an answer.)*

What is it like to be out of George's stomach? *(Pause for an answer.)*

Thank you very much, Mrs. Cow.

Now I'd like to interview George. *(Choose a volunteer.)*

Hello, George. Thank you for coming to our show today.

So, what exactly happened that day when you were unable to bark? *(Pause for an answer.)*

I understand that your mother took you to the vet, and he had to put on gloves in order to pull the animals out of your stomach? *(Pause for an answer.)*

Has anything like this ever happened to you before? *(Pause for an answer.)*

Are you hungry now? *(Pause for an answer.)*

What is your favorite food? *(Pause for an answer.)*

Thank you very much, George!

ACTIVITIES

The Veterinarian Says

Play an adapted version of Simon Says.

Freeze Game

Maybe one reason those animals got eaten by George is because they were all moving around and attracted his attention. If they saw George coming and were able to stop and freeze, he might not have noticed them and would have moved on.

Let's play our own freeze game. I'm going to play some music and I'd like everyone to move to the music. But when the music stops, FREEZE! *(Play some lively recorded music as background for a freeze game. You may decide to hand out colored scarves for this as well. Or, after each "Freeze," ask the children to pretend that their scarf is a different animal being retrieved from George's belly. The scarves can slither like a snake, hop like a frog, fly like a bird, run like a dog, etc.)*

>> DEVELOPMENTAL TIP

The ability to stop and think before acting impulsively is called a *self-regulation skill*. It is this skill that enables a school child to hold up his hand and wait until called upon to answer a question, and to settle conflicts with words rather than fists. Learning how to self-regulate most often occurs in the earliest years of life.

BOOKS ABOUT PARENTS AND CHILDREN

Bunting, Eve (author), and Sergio Ruzzier (illustrator). 2011. *Tweak, Tweak.* Boston: Clarion Books.

Durand, Hallie (author), and Tony Fucile (illustrator). 2011. *Mitchell's License.* Somerville, MA: Candlewick Press.

Feiffer, Kate (author), and Jules Feiffer (illustrator). 2011. *My Side of the Car.* Somerville, MA: Candlewick Press.

Guarino, Deborah (author), and Steven Kellogg (illustrator). 1997. *Is Your Mama a Llama?* New York: Scholastic.

Hoberman, Mary Ann (author), and Marla Frazee (illustrator). 1997. *Seven Silly Eaters.* San Diego: Harcourt Brace.

Kasza, Keiko. 2000. *Don't Laugh, Joe!* New York: Puffin Books.

Penn, Audrey (author), Ruth E. Harper (illustrator), and Nancy M. Leak (illustrator). 2006. *The Kissing Hand.* Terre Haute, IN: Tanglewood Press.

Plecas, Jennifer. 2011. *Pretend!* New York: Philomel Books.

Plourde, Lynn (author), and Greg Couch (illustrator). 1999. *Wild Child.* New York: Simon & Schuster Books for Young Readers.

Rex, Michael. 2009. *Runaway Mummy: A Petrifying Parody.* New York: G. P. Putnam's Sons.

Rosenthal, Amy Krouse (author), and LeUyen Pham (illustrator). 2010. *Bedtime for Mommy!* New York: Bloomsbury.

Willems, Mo. 2004. *Knuffle Bunny: A Cautionary Tale.* New York: Hyperion Books for Children.

———. 2007. *Knuffle Bunny Too: A Case of Mistaken Identity.* New York: Hyperion Books for Children.

———. 2010. *Knuffle Bunny: An Unexpected Diversion.* New York: Balzer and Bray.

Willis, Jean (author), and Tony Ross (illustrator). 2008. *Cottonball Colin.* Grand Rapids, MI: Eerdmans Books for Young Readers.

Woodson, Jacqueline (author), and Sophie Blackall (illustrator). 2010. *Pecan Pie Baby.* New York: G. P. Putnam's Sons.

Week 6: Examine the Story from a Veterinarian's Perspective

Explore medical instruments.

THEME

Veterinarians and doctors

ITEMS NEEDED

- doctor's bag
  Include a white coat, stethoscope, tongue depressor, fake or nonbreakable thermometer, eye chart (easy to make), blood pressure cuff (ask ahead of time if a parent or library staffer has one that they don't use anymore), and Band-Aids. Get a first aid kit and put the gauze, cold pack, and anything else interesting into the doctor's bag.

- 5 monkey flannel pieces or finger puppets
- dog/puppy flannel piece
- maracas or shakers of some sort
- "George" box

SUGGESTED CONTENT

Focus Text

Display the pictures in the book while the children tell the story. Explain that items in a doctor's bag are also called instruments, even though they are not for playing music. Then pull out each item in the doctor's bag and ask what its name is and what it is used for. Give the answer if no one knows. If a child gives an incorrect answer, don't say, "You're wrong." Simply say, "This is a ——" and give the correct name and use.

If your storytime children can handle practicing each instrument without chaos, give them time to do so. Or bring back the "George" box from last week. After showing and naming all of the items in the doctor's bag, have a very hungry George swallow the entire thing!

Enlist the help of the children one by one to help by finding an instrument in George's belly, naming it, and pulling it back out.

Read the story aloud. Pause before turning each page and encourage the children to predict what is going to happen next.

Encourage discussion by asking the following questions:

What do you think a veterinarian usually does?

What do you think a vet might usually find in a dog's stomach?

How do you think the vet felt when he found all the animals that George had eaten?

>> DEVELOPMENTAL TIP

When your children have happy experiences, they want to repeat them. Starting kindergarten can be seen as an extension of our informal library "classes." Children who have had joyful experiences in the public library often approach school with a positive attitude, ready and excited to learn.

SONGS AND RHYMES

"Five Little Monkeys Jumping on the Bed"

Use five monkey flannelboard pieces, a monkey puppet, or five monkey finger puppets. To use flannel pieces, put all five monkeys on the flannelboard. Pull off each monkey one at a time as monkeys "fall off." To use finger puppets, put all five puppets on your fingers and remove them (or just lower each finger) as monkeys fall off the bed. There are also actions that can be used. See below.

Five little monkeys, jumping on the bed, *(Bounce five fingers.)*
One fell off and bumped his head. *(Bump forehead with fist.)*
Mama called the doctor, and the doctor said, *(Pretend to make a phone call.)*
"No more monkeys jumping on the bed!" *(Shake finger no.)*

Repeat actions, counting down number of monkeys jumping on the bed until there is one left.

Last verse:
One little monkey, jumping on the bed,
She fell off and bumped her head.
Mama called the doctor, and the doctor said,
"Put those monkeys back to bed!"

"The Lady with the Alligator Purse"

A lovely illustrated version of this song can be found in Nadine Bernard Westcott's 1988 book The Lady with the Alligator Purse *(Boston: Joy Street). The recorded song can be found on Nadine Bernard Westcott and Mary Ann Hoberman. 2001.* Sing-Along Songs: The Lady with the Alligator Purse, Miss Mary Mack, Skip to My Lou. *Boston: Little, Brown. A list of CDs including this song appears in the text box. Plus different versions can be downloaded from iTunes.*

Miss Lucy had a baby,
His name was Tiny Tim.
She put him in the bathtub,
To see if he could swim.

He drank up all the water,
He ate up all the soap.
He tried to eat the bathtub, but it
Wouldn't go down his throat.

Miss Lucy called the doctor,
Miss Lucy called the nurse.
Miss Lucy called the lady
With the alligator purse.

"Mumps!" said the doctor.
"Measles!" said the nurse.
"Nothing!" said the lady
With the alligator purse.

Miss Lucy pushed the doctor.
Miss Lucy pushed the nurse.
But Miss Lucy paid the lady
With the alligator purse.

CDs with "The Lady with the Alligator Purse"

Downing, Johnette, and George Izquierdo. 2001. *Silly Sing Along*. Johnette Downing.

Jam, Jeff. 2009. *Elephant Shoes*. Toy Jam Music.

Landau, David, Greg Dierks, Patrick Logterman, Kurt Kellesvig, John Purnell, and Al Byla. 2005. *Kids and Kitties*. Milkbreak Music.

BOOKS ABOUT VETERINARIANS AND DOCTORS

Beaty, Andrea (author), and Pascal Lemaitre (illustrator). 2008. *Doctor Ted*. New York: Atheneum Books for Young Readers.

Charlip, Remy (author, illustrator), and Burton Supree (author). 2001. *Mother Mother I Feel Sick, Send for the Doctor, Quick Quick Quick*. Berkeley, CA: Tricycle Press.

Cole, Babette. 1994. *Dr. Dog*. New York: Dragonfly Books.

Cousins, Lucy. 2007. *Maisy Goes to the Hospital*. Cambridge, MA: Candlewick Press.

Dodd, Lynley. 1999. *Hairy Maclary's Rumpus at the Vet*. Milwaukee, WI: Gareth Stevens Children's Books.

Harvey, Alex. 2011. *Olivia Becomes a Vet*. New York: Simon Spotlight.

Huneck, Stephen, 2004. *Sally Goes to the Vet*. New York: Harry N. Abrams.

Lee, Chinlun. 2004. *Good Dog, Paw!* Cambridge, MA: Candlewick Press.

Lloyd, Sam. 2008. *Doctor Meow's Big Emergency.* New York: Henry Holt.

Parish, Herman (author), and Lynn Sweat (illustrator). 2002. *Calling Doctor Amelia Bedelia.* New York: Greenwillow Books.

Steig, William. 1982. *Doctor DeSoto.* New York: Farrar Straus Giroux.

Yolen, Jane (author), and Mark Teague (illustrator). 2003. *How Do Dinosaurs Get Well Soon?* New York: Blue Sky Press.

chapter 10

Series 8
The Little Old Lady Who Was Not Afraid of Anything

Focus Text: *The Little Old Lady Who Was Not Afraid of Anything*

by Linda D. Williams and Megan Lloyd
(New York: HarperTrophy, 1986)

A little old lady on a walk encounters noisy shoes, wiggly pants, a shaky shirt, applauding gloves, and a polite hat. After losing her wits when presented with an enormous pumpkin head, she ultimately finds a creative solution.

Ways to Present *The Little Old Lady Who Was Not Afraid of Anything* in Storytimes Sessions

Week 1: Introduce *The Little Old Lady Who Was Not Afraid of Anything*. (clothing)

Week 2: Repeat the story using props and signs. (pumpkins)

Week 3: Put yourself in another person's shoes. (little old ladies)

Week 4: Take a nut-and-herb walk. (overcoming fear)

Week 5: Build a scarecrow and watch a movie starring storytime children. (scarecrows)

Week 6: Encourage children to dramatize the story, guided by book illustrations. (autumn)

Week 1: Introduce *The Little Old Lady Who Was Not Afraid of Anything*

Introduce selected book and read it aloud.

THEME

Clothing

ITEMS NEEDED

- bag or storage bin
- items that can be worn on or around the body, such as mittens, sunglasses, socks, toothbrushes, hair clips, earmuffs, belts, bracelets
- small table

PREPARATION

Fill a bag or storage bin with items that can be worn on or around the body.

SUGGESTED CONTENT

Focus Text

Before beginning this story, practice the movements associated with each article of clothing. Demonstrate the movement and then have the children do it with you. For example, when the two shoes go "stomp, stomp," stomp your feet and have the children perform the same motion. Do this for all incorporated movement.

Read the book aloud with audience participation. Since this story is cumulative, once you have established a rhythm to the story, have the children call out the articles of clothing and their actions while you read.

SONGS AND RHYMES

"My Hat Has Three Corners"

Traditional German rhyme. Tune can be found here: www.songsforteaching.com/folk/ myhatithasthreecorners.php. Practice the movements and singing beforehand and become familiar with them. Movements are as follows:

my—finger pointing to self
hat—hand on head
three—hold up three fingers
corners—point to bent elbow
had it not—shake finger no
it would not be—shake finger no

My hat it has three corners.
Three corners has my hat.
And had it not three corners,
It would not be my hat.

Sing the song repeatedly, each time substituting a hum for a word while still including the movement. Begin by removing "My" for the first round, "My" and "hat" for the second round, and so on. Continue until the entire song is hummed with movements, rather than sung aloud.

"If You're Wearing . . ." (to the tune of "If You're Happy and You Know It")
Have children perform the actions in the song if they are wearing the mentioned color.

If you're wearing red today, nod your head.
If you're wearing red today, nod your head.
If you're wearing red today, go ahead and nod away!
If you're wearing red today, nod your head.

If you're wearing green today, pat your back . . . go ahead and pat away!
If you're wearing white today, stomp your feet . . . go ahead and stomp away!
If you're wearing blue today, shout hooray . . . go ahead and shout hooray!

>> DEVELOPMENTAL TIP
It takes time to learn how to get dressed by yourself and involves much more than simply putting on and taking off clothes. Children exercise cognitive skills when they decide which clothes to put on first, second, and third. Gross motor skills are activated when children put on pants by standing on one leg and then another. Pulling up zippers and fastening buttons use fine motor skills. What we do as adults seems almost effortless, but remember that there are many steps involved in children getting dressed by themselves, and it may take time!

ACTIVITY

What Do We Do with This?
Open the bag of props and pull out an item.

What's this? *(Pause for answers.)*
Where do you wear it? *(Pause for answers.)*
Touch the part of your body that wears this item! *(Pause while children do so.)*

Place the item on a table next to you and repeat with the next item.
Once all the items have been displayed, ask the children to say the relevant body part and touch it at the same time when you hold up an item. Do this briefly.
Once the children know what to do, choose three or four items that correspond to parts of the body not near each other. Hold up each one in rapid succession, mixing up the order, and have children try to keep up with you. Laughter will quickly ensue!

BOOKS ABOUT CLOTHING

Billstrom, Diane (author), and Don Kilpatrick III (illustrator). 2008. *You Can't Go To School Naked!* New York: G. P. Putnam's Sons.

Brooks, Eric K. 2000. *Practically Perfect Pajamas.* New York: Winslow Press.

Chodos-Irvine, Margaret. 2003. *Ella Sarah Gets Dressed.* San Diego: Harcourt.

Crunk, Tony (author), and Scott Nash (illustrator). 2001. *Grandpa's Overall's.* New York: Orchard Books.

Dodds, Dayle Ann (author), and Jill McElmurry (illustrator). 2002. *The Kettles Get New Clothes.* Cambridge, MA: Candlewick Press.

Dormer, Frank W. 2010. *Socksquatch.* New York: Henry Holt.

Fox, Mem (author), and Patricia Mullens (illustrator). 1990. *Shoes from Grandpa.* New York: Orchard Books.

Kuskin, Karla (author), and Marc Simont (illustrator). 1982. *The Philharmonic Gets Dressed.* New York: Harper & Row.

Litwin, Eric (author), and James Dean (illustrator). 2010. *Pete the Cat: I Love My White Shoes.* New York: Harper.
Encourage the children to participate in the story by calling out the color they think the shoes will turn.

Monsell, Mary Elise (author), and Lynn Munsinger (illustrator). 1988. *Underwear!* Niles, IL: Albert Whitman.

Nedwidek, John (author), and Lee White (illustrator). 2008. *Ducks Don't Wear Socks.* New York: Viking Children's Books.

Parr, Todd. 2005. *Underwear Do's and Don'ts.* New York: Little, Brown.

Plourde, Lynn (author), and Christopher Santoro (illustrator). 2009. *Grandpappy's Snippy Snappies.* New York: HarperCollins.

Rao, Sandhya (author), and Nina Sabnani (illustrator). 2006. *My Mother's Sari.* New York: North South Books.

Schertle, Alice (author), and Curtis Jobling (illustrator). 2003. *The Skeleton in the Closet.* New York: HarperCollins.

Schrawz, Viviane. 2007. *Timothy and the Strong Pajamas.* New York: Arthur A. Levine Books.

Taback, Simms. 1999. *Joseph Had a Little Overcoat.* New York: Viking.

Tafolla, Carmen (author), and Amy Cordova (illustrator). 2008. *What Can You Do with a Rebozo?* Berkeley, CA: Tricycle Press.

Willems, Mo. 2009. *Naked Mole Rat Gets Dressed.* New York: Hyperion Books for Children. This book is best read in dramatic fashion as it is written. Familiarize yourself with the text beforehand to be comfortable in reading it during storytime.

Week 2: Repeat the Story Using Props and Signs

Incorporate music and the printed word along with this dramatization.

THEME

Pumpkins

ITEMS NEEDED

- clothing and objects for *The Little Old Lady Who Was Not Afraid of Anything* (most of these can be purchased inexpensively at a secondhand store):
  > pair of child's shoes, with the laces tied together
  > child's pair of pants
  > child's white shirt
  > 2 gloves
  > tall black hat (or a black hat of any kind)
  > large plastic pumpkin head (the kind children use when they are trick-or-treating)
  > basket
- enlarged photocopies of figures 10.1–10.8, printed on copy paper and laminated, or printed on tagboard. Each sign has a picture of an item and the phrase associated with that item.

Figure 10.1 Shoe sign

Figure 10.2 Pants sign

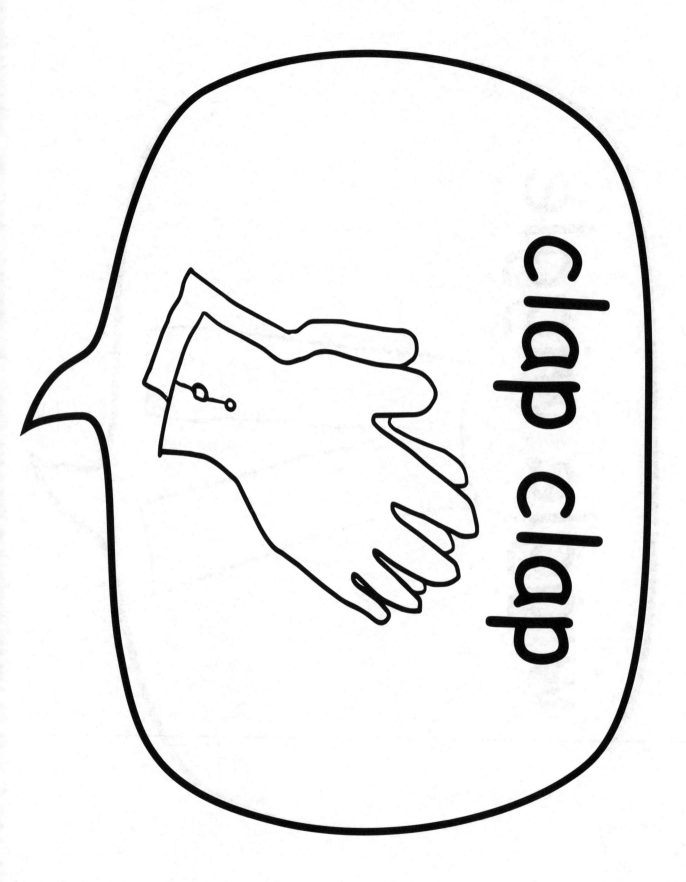

Figure 10.3 Gloves sign

Figure 10.4 Shirt sign

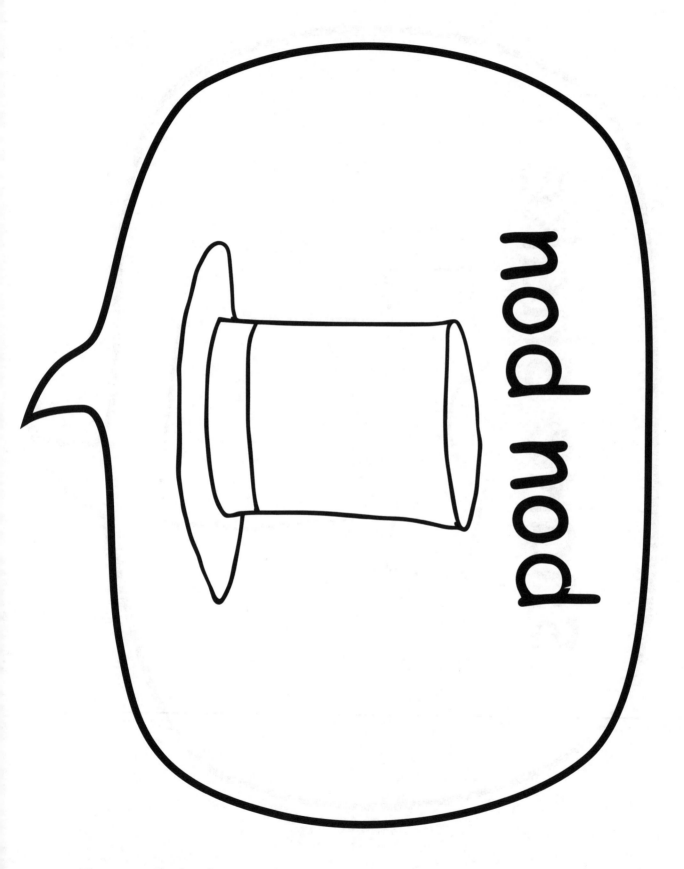

Figure 10.5 Top hat sign

Figure 10.6 Jack-o-lantern sign

Figure 10.7 Door sign

Figure 10.8 Little old lady sign

SUGGESTED CONTENT

Focus Text

Pick a child to be the little old lady. Hand the child the basket as well as the card that says, "Go Away." Choose another child to hold the pants in one hand and the sign in the other. Choose volunteers to be the shirt, the hat, the glove, the shoes, and the pumpkin head. Each of these children gets one item and one sign. Stand them in a row in front, in the order in which they appear in the book. Everyone together can practice the movements the clothing and items make.

Begin reading the story aloud. Point to each volunteer when that volunteer's turn comes to shake an object, say a word, or raise a sign. Do this for the entire story.

RHYME

"Five Little Pumpkins"

Recite the rhyme as a fingerplay. You may want to visit DLTK's Growing Together website—www.dltk-teach.com/minibooks/halloween/felt.htm—to print out a "Five Little Pumpkins Mini Book" or the single-sheet poem for the children to take home. There are also black-and-white or color templates that can be printed and used as stick puppets or flannelboard templates.

Five little pumpkins
Sitting on a gate.
The first one said,
"Oh, my, it's half past eight!"
The second one said,
"There are witches in the air!"
The third one said,
"Good folk, beware!"
The fourth one said,
"We'll run and run and run!"
The fifth one said,
"Let's have some fun!"
OOOOOOOH, went the wind
And OUT went the light.
And the five little pumpkins
Rolled out of sight.

"Five Little Pumpkins" lyrics and sound clip can be found on the album Music with Mar: Songs at My Fingertips *by Mar Harman, or at www.songsforteaching.com/childrens songslyrics/artists/marharman/fivelittlepumpkins.mp3 or at www.kididdles.com/*

lyrics/f042.html. A "Five Little Pumpkins" video clip presented by Sally Trigg features spooky music, clear annunciation, and bright illustrations at www.youtube.com/ watch?v=9U8ZZugvw9o.

ACTIVITIES

Musical Instruments

Pass out a variety of musical instruments. Play them along with the movements in the story. See how different they sound when shaken vigorously. Follow along with story musically; in place of a "nod," move instruments slowly up and down; in place of a "stomp," tap the instruments to your knees; and so on.

>> DEVELOPMENTAL TIP

Using musical instruments to reenact the story gives children the opportunity to experiment with expressing ideas and concepts through music. Try this at home by reading or telling a story and asking your child to use music or dance to illustrate it.

Math and Science Activity

On the Scholastic website, instructions for "Measuring Pumpkins and Our World" by Jan Tankey includes questions for discussion, simple ways to explain estimation and circumference, and an easily implementable method for measuring pumpkins with string. www.scholastic.com/teachers/lesson-plan/measuring-pumpkins-and-our-world.

HANDOUT FOR PARENTS

Go to www.makinglearningfun.com/themepages/PumpkinsFiveLittleRhyme.htm, print out pictures of the gate and the pumpkins, and give them to parents as a take-home activity with the following explanation.

> In storytime today, we recited a rhyme called "Five Little Pumpkins." Here are some props to help you repeat the rhyme at home with your children. Cut out the pumpkins (or supervise your child cutting them out) put them on the gate, and ask your child to use them as you recite the poem together.

BOOKS ABOUT PUMPKINS

Bunting, Eve (author), and Eileen Christelow (illustrator). 1997. *The Pumpkin Fair*. New York: Clarion Books.

Cooper, Helen. 1998. *Pumpkin Soup*. New York: Farrar Straus Giroux.

Grant, Judyann Ackerman (author), and Sue Truesdell (illustrator). 2008. *Chicken Said "Cluck!"* New York: HarperCollins.

Hall, Zoe (author), and Shari Halpern (illustrator). 1994. *It's Pumpkin Time.* New York: Scholastic.

Hills, Tad. 2009. *Find a Pumpkin.* New York: Schwartz & Wade.

Kimmel, Eric A. (author), and Steven Haskamp (illustrator). 2001. *Pumpkinhead.* New York: Winslow Press.

Levinson, George (author), and Shmuel Thaler (photographer). 1999. *Pumpkin Circle: The Story of a Garden.* Berkeley, CA: Tricycle Press

Mantle, Ben. 2010. *Five Little Pumpkins.* Wilton, CT: Tiger Tales, 2010. Board book.

McKy, Katie (author), and Pablo Bernasconi (illustrator). 2006. *Pumpkin Town.* Boston: Houghton Mifflin.

Mortimer, Anne. 2011. *Pumpkin Cat.* New York: Katherine Tegen Books.

Ray, Mary Lyn (author), and Barry Root (illustrator). 1996. *Pumpkins: A Story for a Field.* San Diego: Harcourt Brace.

Rohmann, Eric. 2003. *Pumpkinhead.* New York: Alfred A. Knopf.

Scott, Michael. 2003. *Five Little Pumpkins.* New York: Hyperion Books for Children.

Serfozo, Mary (author), and Valeria Petrone (illustrator). 2001. *Plumply Dumply Pumpkin.* New York: Margaret K. McElderry.

Sloat, Teri. 1999. *Patty's Pumpkin Patch.* New York: Putnam.

Yaccarino, Dan. 1998. *Five Little Pumpkins.* New York: HarperFestival.

Yacowitz, Caryn (author), and Joe Cepeda (illustrator). 1998. *Pumpkin Fiesta.* New York: HarperCollins.

Week 3: Put Yourself in Another Person's Shoes

Children help retell the story in front of a camera.

THEME

Little old ladies

ITEMS NEEDED

- bag of clothes including the items from the *Little Old Lady* story
  - 2 shoes
  - white shirt
  - pair of pants
  - 2 gloves
  - tall black hat
  - pumpkin head
  - flip camera

Go Away
I'm not afraid of you!

SUGGESTED CONTENT

Focus Text

Open a dress-up bag and hand out the clothing pieces for the story, choosing children other than the ones who held the signs the previous week. Have all children practice the motions from the story. Explain that while you are telling the story the children who have the corresponding item of clothing should perform the motions described in the story, say their words, and hold up the sign.

Ask a parent or child to record the presentation using a flip camera and upload the movie to a computer. Save the movie to show as a special presentation at a later session. Repeat enough times so that every child has a chance to act out a story character and be in a movie.

SONGS AND RHYMES

"Grandma's Glasses"

These are Grandma's glasses, *(Encircle eyes with fingers.)*
This is Grandma's hat, *(Imitate placing small hat on head.)*
This is the way she folds her hands, *(Fold hands compactly in front of you.)*
And lays them in her lap. *(Gently lay hands in lap.)*

Louder voice:
These are Grandpa's glasses, *(Encircle eyes with fingers.)*
This is Grandpa's hat, *(Imitate placing larger hat on head.)*

This is the way he folds his arms, *(Gruffly fold arms across chest.)*
Just like that. *(Tap folded arms against chest with much emphasis.)*

>> DEVELOPMENTAL TIP
Talk with your children about their clothing choices! Ask them to name colors, sizes, and types of clothing. Discuss the connection between the weather and what to wear by asking questions such as, "It's very wet outside; what would be best to wear on your feet if there are going to be lots of puddles?"

"She'll Be Comin' 'Round the Mountain"
Music can be found here: http://kids.niehs.nih.gov/games/songs/childrens/mountainmid.htm.

She'll be comin' 'round the mountain when she comes—toot, toot!
   (Pull imaginary train whistle.)
She'll be comin' 'round the mountain when she comes—toot, toot!
   (Pull imaginary train whistle.)
She'll be comin' 'round the mountain, she'll be comin' 'round the mountain,
She'll be comin' 'round the mountain when she comes—toot, toot!
   (Pull imaginary train whistle.)

Additional verses:
- She'll be drivin' six white horses when she comes—whoa, back! . . .
   (Pull on reins.)
- Oh, we'll all go out to meet her when she comes—hi there! . . .
   (Wave enthusiastically.)
- Then we'll all have chicken and dumplings when she comes—yum, yum! . . .
   (Rub stomach.)
- Oh she'll wear her red pajamas when she comes—scratch, scratch! . . .
   (Scratch sides.)
- Oh, she'll have to sleep with Grandma when she comes—snore, snore! . . .
   (Make snoring noise.)

ACTIVITIES

Creative Movement
Ask everyone to stand up and walk around in a circle. Then ask them to pretend they are very tall with very long legs and to take giant steps around the circle. Next, pretend to be a little old lady. Ask questions about how she might walk, such as "Would she run?

Would she shuffle? Would she stand up tall? Would she be a bit stooped over? Would she take big steps or little steps? Would her hands be moving back and forth? Would she be holding a cane?" Once you have determined how the little old lady might walk, put on some music and take a stroll around the circle.

There is a song called "Little Old Lady" with words and music by Hoagy Carmichael and Stanley Adams from a 1936 musical by Vincente Minnelli called The Show Is On, *which is great for the stroll and can be downloaded from iTunes. Don't confuse this with the rock 'n' roll song called "Little Old Lady from Pasadena," written by Jan Berry, sung by Jan and Dean, which goes at a much faster pace.*

Acting Out the Story

If you have another adult who is willing to be the scarecrow, you can be the lady and act out the story.

BOOKS ABOUT LITTLE OLD LADIES

Alsenas, Linas. 2007. *Peanut.* New York: Scholastic.

Bee, William. 2008. *Beware of the Frog.* Cambridge, MA: Candlewick Press.
Encourage children to make the sounds along with you during the story.

Best, Cari (author), and G. Brian Karas (illustrator). 2005. *Are You Going to Be Good?* New York: Farrar Straus Giroux.

Bunting, Eve (author), and Donald Carrick (illustrator). 1989. *The Wednesday Surprise.* New York: Clarion Books.

Cruise, Robin (author), and Stacy Dressen-McQueen (illustrator). 2006. *Little Mama Forgets.* New York: Farrar Straus Giroux.

Fox, Mem (author), and Julie Vivas (illustrator). 1985. *Wilfrid Gordon McDonald Partridge.* Brooklyn: Kane/Miller Book Publishers.

Galdone, Paul. 1984. *The Teeny Tiny Woman.* New York: Clarion Books.

Hester, Denia (author), and Jackie Urbanovic (illustrator). 2005. *Grandma Lena's Big Ol' Turnip.* Morton Grove, IL: Albert Whitman.

Johnston, Tony (author), and Tomie DePaola (illustrator). 1995. *Alice Nizzy Nazzy, the Witch of Santa Fe.* New York: Putnam.

Johnston, Tony (author), and Yuri Morales (illustrator). 2009. *My Abuelita.* Orlando, FL: Harcourt.

Leijten, Aileen. 2009. *Hugging Hour.* New York: Philomel Books.

Parr, Todd. 2006. *The Grandma Book.* New York: Little, Brown.

Zolotow, Charlotte (author), and James Stevenson (illustrator). 1984. *I Know an Old Lady.* New York: Greenwillow.

MUSIC ABOUT LITTLE OLD LADIES

Carmichael, Hoagy. 1993. "Little Old Lady." Track 4 on *Hoagy Carmichael*. CD. Smithsonian Collection of Recordings.

Mann, Manfred, Terry Stafford, and J. Frank Wilson. 1989. "Little Old Lady from Pasadena." Track 4 on *Billboard Top Rock 'n' Roll Hits 1964*. CD. Rhino.

Week 4: Take a Nut-and-Herb Walk

Face your fears and learn about herbs.

THEME

Overcoming fear

ITEMS NEEDED

- nuts and herbs (actual or pictures)
- smelly herbs in small containers (thyme, rosemary, mint, parsley)
- 2 flashlights

PREPARATION

Use pictorial representations of popular nuts and actual herbs. Find pictures in magazines, in discarded books, or on the Internet; or print out coloring pages and make your own. Use nuts that children might be familiar with such as peanuts, cashews, and almonds. Do the same for herbs. Preschool children most likely are not familiar with many (if any) herbs. So find fresh herbs, dried herbs, or pictures of different herbs such as parsley, rosemary, thyme, and mint. USE ONLY NUT PICTURES IN CASE ANY CHILD MIGHT HAVE A NUT ALLERGY!

SETUP

Place the nuts and herbs around the storytime area. You will be taking the children on a nut-and-herb walk, so keep that in mind as you place the items around your space.

SUGGESTED CONTENT

Focus Text

Read the story using one or two flashlights with the lights off. Leave out key words and pause so the children can fill them in. Wave the flashlight around for spooky effects.

The little old lady did not seem to be afraid of anything, but most people are afraid of things. Some things can be very scary. Can you tell me about some things that scare you? *(If no one volunteers anything, mention going to the doctor, being in the dark, watching a scary movie, seeing people fight, knowing you did something wrong and are afraid someone will find out, etc.)*

What kinds of things can you do to make your fears easier, or to make them totally go away? *("Have someone come into the doctor's office with you, use a flashlight, don't watch a scary movie, walk away when people are fighting, admit that you did something wrong and apologize.")*

Walking in the woods in the dark is not safe and is very scary, but taking a walk in the woods with your family or friends can be lots of fun. Let's take a walk just like the little old lady did.

ACTIVITIES

Nut-and-Herb Walk

Explain to the children this walk is just like one taken by the little old lady in the story. Everyone should be on the lookout for nuts and herbs. When a child locates a nut or an herb, stop and talk about what kind it is and let each child smell the item (if real).

>> DEVELOPMENTAL TIP

Even if you live in the city, you can help sharpen your child's observation skills by taking a nature walk near your home. Collect small items such as pieces of wood, leaves, pebbles, acorns, or shells. Compare them by noticing size, shape, and color. While learning about the characteristics of each item, your child will find no two items in nature are exactly the same. Observing nature up close in this way helps children gain critical understanding about their world.

Musical Instruments

Hand out musical instruments. Play different types of music and ask the children to play along and tell you how the music makes them feel. Fast, lively music may make some children happy. Slow, somber music may make some children feel sad. Lullabies may make children feel sleepy. Ask the children to try playing their musical instruments in a way that shows how they are feeling.

HANDOUT FOR PARENTS

Even if you live in the city, you can help sharpen your child's observation skills by taking a nature walk near your home. Collect small items such as pieces of wood, leaves, pebbles, acorns, or shells. Compare them by noticing size, shape, and color. While learning about the characteristics of each item, your child will find no two items in nature are exactly the same. Observing nature up close in this way helps children gain critical understanding about their world.

If you bring the items home, you can play matching games with your child. These build math skills, and increase vocabulary at the same time.

Ask your child to put the pebbles in one pile and the leaves in another pile.

Ask your child to put everything that is heavy in one pile and light in another pile.

Ask your child to match things by colors.

Ask your child to match things by texture: smooth items in one pile, rough items in another.

Ask your child to put fragile items that can break (such as leaves) in one pile, and sturdy items that can't break in another.

If your child enjoyed playing these games, expand the activity by using nonfiction books from the library to learn more about the items. See if you can identify any of them!

BOOKS ABOUT OVERCOMING FEARS

Browne, Anthony. 1995. *Willy the Wimp*. London: Walker Books

Dubosarsky, Ursula (author), and Andrew Joyner (illustrator). 2009. *The Terrible Plop*. New York: Farrar Straus Giroux.

Frazee, Marla. 2003. *Roller Coaster*. San Diego: Harcourt.

Greene, Rhonda Gowler (author), and Joseph A. Smith (illustrator). 2002. *Eek! Creak! Snicker, Sneak*. New York: Atheneum Books for Young Readers.

Helakoski, Leslie (author), and Henry Cole (illustrator). 2006. *Big Chickens*. New York: Puffin Books.

Kirk, David. 1994. *Miss Spider's Tea Party*. New York: Callaway Editions.

Lester, Helen (author), and Lynn Munsinger (illustrator). 2003. *Something Might Happen*. Boston: Houghton Mifflin.

Mathews, Judith, and Fay Robinson (authors), and Alexi Natchev (illustrator). 1994. *Nathaniel Willy, Scared Silly*. New York: Bradbury Press.

Mayer, Mercer. 1976. *There's a Nightmare in My Closet*. New York: Puffin.

———. 2005. *There Are Monsters Everywhere*. New York: Dial Books for Young Readers.

McBratney, Sam (author), and Ivan Bates (illustrator). 1996. *The Dark at the Top of the Stairs*. Cambridge, MA: Candlewick Press.

Powell, Polly. 1996. *Just Dessert*. San Diego: Harcourt Brace.

Salley, Colleen (author), and Janet Stevens (illustrator). 2009. *Epossomondas Plays Possum.* Boston: Harcourt Children's Books.

Schrawz, Viviane. 2007. *Timothy and the Strong Pajamas.* New York: Arthur A. Levine Books.

Watt, Melanie. 2008. *Scaredy Squirrel.* Toronto: Kids Can Press.

Williams, Linda (author), and Megan Lloyd (illustrator). 1986. *The Little Old Lady Who Was Not Afraid of Anything.* New York: HarperTrophy.

Wilson, Karma (author), and Jane Chapman (illustrator). 2008. *Bear Feels Scared.* New York: Margaret K. McElderry.

Week 5: Build a Scarecrow and Watch a Movie Starring Storytime Children

Children work together to build a scarecrow and then enjoy watching themselves in action.

THEME

Scarecrows

ITEMS NEEDED

- items to make a scarecrow:
  › rope
  › markers
  › tape (duct tape will work best)
  › lots of plastic bags (1 to stuff for the head and lots to stuff the body)
  › an old long-sleeved shirt (don't buy anything new: use old stuff or ask for donations)
  › 1 pair of old pants
  › 1 old pair of gloves, an old hat
  › 1 old pair of suspenders
  › two 4- to 6-foot-long bars or handles of some kind. You need something to be the length of the body and something to be the arms. Old handles from brooms, mops, shovels, rakes work well; you can also purchase dowels inexpensively.
- bag of dress-up clothes from week 3
- computer with movie from week 3 uploaded
- projector
- screen
- flannel scarecrow (figure 10.9)

Figure 10.9 Scarecrow

Focus Text

Screen the movie(s) created in week 3! Ask the children to make the sounds and motions along with the movie.

SONG

"Silly Scarecrow Dance" (to the tune of "Alouette")

Display a flannel scarecrow on the flannelboard. The tune can be found on many You-Tube videos or here: http://kids.niehs.nih.gov/games/songs/childrens/alouettemid.htm.

Silly scarecrow, *(Sway side to side in rhythm.)*
Silly dancing scarecrow.
Silly scarecrow,
Dance around all day!

First you flop your arm like this, *(Flop arm.)*
Then flop your other arm like this. *(Flop other arm.)*
Arm like this, arm like this . . . oh-oh-oh-oh *(Flop one arm, then the other.)*

Silly scarecrow, *(Sway side to side.)*
Silly dancing scarecrow.
Silly scarecrow,
Dance around all day!

Additional verses:
First you bend your leg like this, *(Bend knee.)*
Then bend your other leg like this . . . *(Bend other knee.)*

First you nod your head like this, *(Nod head up and down.)*
Then you nod your head like this . . . *(Shake head side to side.)*

ACTIVITY

Build and Dress a Scarecrow

Start with one plastic bag; have children draw a face on it with markers. Then have an adult tie the two wooden rods together to form a cross shape. Next, put the long-sleeved shirt on the top of the scarecrow and stuff it with plastic bags. Then put the pants on and attach the suspenders. You may want to put a belt on the pants to keep the stuffing up in the shirt. Next, stuff the "head" with more plastic bags and slip it on the top of the vertical rod and attach it with duct tape. Lastly, put the gloves on the ends of the horizontal rod. Stand up the scarecrow and admire your creation! When storytime is over, take the scarecrow apart, but don't throw anything away—you're going to use it next week.

▶▶ DEVELOPMENTAL TIP

You are your child's first and best teacher. Spending time together in joyful activities, paying attention to what your child says and thinks, having conversations together and providing lots of love are essential for your child's healthy development. Challenging your children to think and giving them opportunities to use words to express what they are thinking help them to become better thinkers.

HANDOUT FOR PARENTS

Print out a mini book on how to make a scarecrow from the Teaching Heart website: www.teachingheart.net/scarecrow.html. Give the pages to each family with the following instructions. Include the developmental tip (without the title) on the instruction sheet.

Today in storytime, we made a scarecrow. Now your child can create a book about making scarecrows.

1. First ask your child to color in the pictures. Children this age often have difficulty coloring within the lines, so simply adding color to the black-and-white drawings is fine.
2. Cut out the pages.
3. Staple the pages together.
4. Read the book aloud with your child.
5. Ask your child to "read" the book to you by telling the story while looking at the pictures.

BOOKS ABOUT SCARECROWS

Brown, Ken. 2001. *The Scarecrow's Hat*. Atlanta, GA: Peachtree.

Brown, Margaret Wise (author), and David Diaz (illustrator). 1998. *The Little Scarecrow Boy*. New York: HarperCollins.

Cazet, Denys. 1994. *Nothing at All*. New York: Orchard Books.

Dillon, Jana. 1992. *Jeb Scarecrow's Pumpkin Patch*. Boston: Houghton Mifflin.

Martin, Bill Jr. (author), and Ted Rand (illustrator). 1986. *Barn Dance*. New York: Henry Holt.

McGeorge, Constance W. (author), and Mary Whyte (illustrator). 1998. *Waltz of the Scarecrows*. San Francisco: Chronicle Books.

Moulton, Mark Kimball (author), and Karen Hillard Good (illustrator). 2005. *Scarecrow Pete*. Nashville, TN: Ideals Publications.

Preston, Tim (author), and Maggie Kneen (illustrator). 1999. *The Lonely Scarecrow*. New York: Scholastic.

Rylant, Cynthia (author), and Lauren Stringer (illustrator). 1998. *Scarecrow*. New York: Harcourt Children's Books.

Schertle, Alice (author), and Margot Tomes (illustrator). 1994. *Witch Hazel*. New York: HarperCollins.

Vainio, Pirkko. 1994. *Don't Be Scared, Scarecrow*. New York: North-South Books.

Williams, Linda (author), and Megan Lloyd (illustrator). 1986. *The Little Old Lady Who Was Not Afraid of Anything*. New York: HarperTrophy.

Yolen, Jane (author), and Bagram Ibatoulline (illustrator). 2009. *The Scarecrow's Dance*. New York: Simon & Schuster.

Week 6: Encourage Children to Dramatize the Story, Guided by Book Illustrations

Repeat the nut-and-herb walk, discover a scarecrow who needs to be put together, and retell the story through words and movement.

THEME

Autumn

ITEMS NEEDED

- nuts and herbs from week 4
- scarecrow materials from week 5
- flannelboard
- flannel pieces for the story (figures 10.9–10.18)
  - › scarecrow (figure 10.9)
  - › little old lady (figure 10.10)
  - › basket with cover (figure 10.11)
  - › shoe (figure 10.12)
  - › pants (figure 10.13)
  - › gloves (figure 10.14)
  - › shirt (figure 10.15)
  - › top hat (figure 10.16)
  - › jack-o-lantern (figure 10.17)
  - › door (figure 10.18)

Figure 10.10 Little old lady

Figure 10.11 Basket with cover

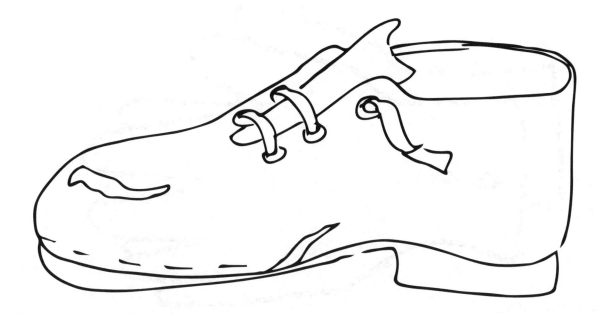

Figure 10.12 Shoe

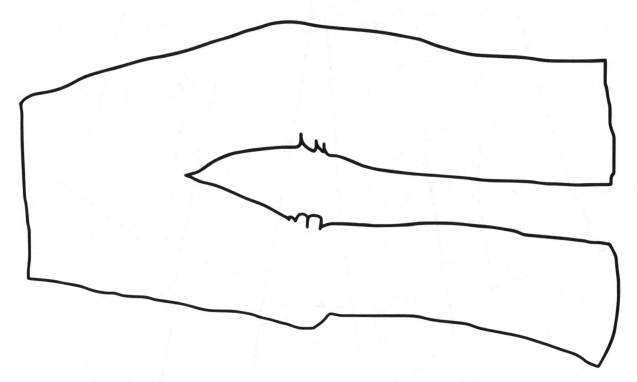

Figure 10.13 Pants

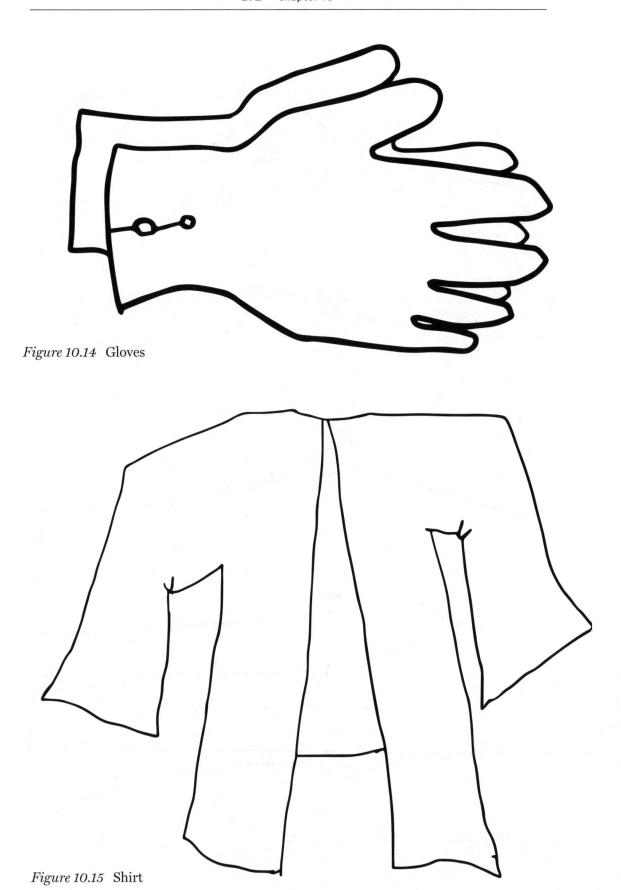

Figure 10.14 Gloves

Figure 10.15 Shirt

Figure 10.16 Top hat

Figure 10.17 Jack-o-lantern

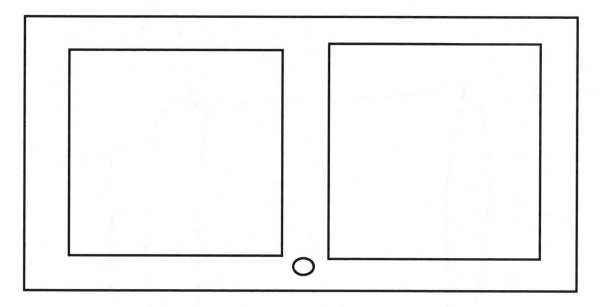

Figure 10.18 Door

PREPARATION

Create flannelboard pieces out of figures 10.9–10.18.

SETUP

Lay out the trail of nuts and herbs as you did in week 4. Along the trail, lay out the different pieces of the scarecrow from week 5.

SUGGESTED CONTENT

Focus Text

By now, the children should be able to tell the story through words and movement. Ask for volunteers to be specific characters and ask them to put on a play for everyone. Ask members of the audience to provide scary sound effects. It does not matter if the story is faithful to the book; however, you may decide to guide the children by simply showing the book illustrations.

›› DEVELOPMENTAL TIP

As you can see, rereading a book and presenting it in different ways has many benefits. After just six weeks of playing with this story, your children have been able to reenact it in creative ways. They have not only heard this book, they have walked it, talked it, made sounds, worn it, drawn it, and reenacted it. The next time they see a scarecrow, it is likely they will be reminded of this book. *The Little Old Lady Who Was Not Afraid of Anything* is going to be a story they will not forget!

Now that you have seen the value in presenting a book in multiple ways, find a picture book that you really enjoy and see how many ways you can share it with your child.

ACTIVITIES

Nut-and-Herb Walk with Scarecrow Assembly

Lead the children on a nut-and-herb walk similar to one from week 4. As they find the items, ask if they remember what they are. Stop and refresh their memories if needed. Also, along the walk, have the children discover the scarecrow pieces. At the end of the walk, gather the scarecrow pieces together, and with the children, remake the scarecrow from week 5.

Leaf Match Game

Assemble a number of different leaves (maple, oak, beech, ivy, poplar). They can be cut from coloring pages, made from an Ellison or Accucut machine, or downloaded from the Internet. Laminate them, if possible. Scatter the leaves along your walk and ask children to pick those up too. Later, encourage the children to play a matching game with the leaves, by type, by size, and by color.

Color Diffusion Craft

Materials
- coffee liners cut into leaf patterns
- plastic tablecloth
- bowls of water
- food coloring in a few colors
- eyedroppers

Setup
1. Cover a table with a plastic tablecloth.
2. Set up a table with a few bowls of water with different colors of food coloring in them, with an eyedropper in each bowl.

Activity
Encourage the child to drop a small bit of "paint" onto their leaf and watch the colors spread.

HANDOUT FOR PARENTS

While exploring the story *The Little Old Lady Who Was Not Afraid of Anything* by Linda D. Williams, illustrated by Megan Lloyd, we have taken a walk in the woods, discovered herbs and nuts, put together a scarecrow, and collected leaves.

If you would like to begin a leaf collection with your child, an online site for identifying leaves through their photographs is www.kidzone.ws/plants/leaf1.htm.

Look for a cookbook in the library that uses fresh herbs. Cook together with your child and taste your new culinary creation!

Plant some herb seeds in an empty egg carton filled with dirt, and watch as your herbs grow.

BOOKS ABOUT AUTUMN

Bullard, Lisa (author), and Nadine Takvorian (illustrator). 2010. *Leaves Fall Down: Learning about Autumn Leaves.* Mankato, MN: Picture Window Books.

Ehlert, Lois. 2005. *Leaf Man.* Orlando, FL: Harcourt.

Florian, Douglas. 2003. *Autumnblings: Poems and Paintings.* New York: Greenwillow Books.

George, Lindsay Barrett. 1994. *In the Woods: Who's Been Here?* New York: Greenwillow Books.

Hall, Zoe (author), and Shari Halpern (illustrator). 2000. *Fall Leaves Fall!* New York: Scholastic Press.

Iwamura, Kazuo. 2009. *Hooray for Fall!* New York: North-South.

Lenski, Lois. 1948. *Now It's Fall.* New York: Random House.

Parish, Herman (author), and Lynne Avril (illustrator). 2010. *Amelia Bedelia's First Apple Pie.* New York: Greenwillow Books.

Plourde, Lynn (author), and Greg Couch (illustrator). 1999. *The Wild Child.* New York: Simon & Schuster Books for Young Readers.

Rawlinson, Julia (author), and Tiphanie Beeke (illustrator). 2006. *Fletcher and the Falling Leaves.* New York: Greenwillow Books.

Sherry, Kevin. 2009. *Acorns Everywhere!* New York: Dial Books for Young Readers.

Tafuri, Nancy. 2007. *The Busy Little Squirrel.* New York: Simon & Schuster Books for Young Readers.

Thompson, Lauren (author), and Jonathan Bean (illustrator). 2007. *The Apple Pie That Papa Baked.* New York: Simon & Schuster Books for Young Readers.

Ziefert, Harriet (author), and Mark Jones (illustrator). 2009. *By the Light of the Harvest Moon.* Maplewood, NJ: Blue Apple Books.

questions
for evaluation

1. Did you feel well-prepared for storytime? Were you comfortable with the plans you made?

    ☐ Yes   ☐ No

_____

2. Were the children engaged? How?

    ☐ Yes   ☐ No

_____

3. Were the activities appropriate for the group?

    ☐ Yes   ☐ No

_____

4. In retrospect, would you change anything to make the program more successful? If so, what?

    ☐ Yes   ☐ No

_____

5. Are children remembering the story from week to week (after week 1)?

    ☐ Yes   ☐ No

_____

6. Did the storytime help develop or strengthen any of the following school readiness skills? *(Highlight or circle all relevant areas.)*

Approach to Learning
- › Desire to learn
- › Encouraging curiosity
- › Problem solving
- › Courage to try new things
- › Creative thinking

General Knowledge
- › Social studies (places and how people live)
- › Geography
- › The natural world

Physical Development and Health
- › Fine and gross motor development
- › Nutrition
- › Personal health habits
- › Exercise

Personal and Social Development
- › Building self-confidence
- › Caring for others
- › Having trust in others
- › Paying attention
- › Following directions
- › Being patient (learning how to wait)

Language and Literacy
- › Print motivation (books are fun)
- › Growing vocabulary
- › Print awareness
- › Letter knowledge
- › Narrative skills
- › Phonological awareness

Mathematical and Scientific Thinking
- › Recognizing shapes and patterns
- › Understanding sequences
- › Forming hypotheses
- › Testing out cause and effect

The Arts
> Appreciation of fine art
> Familiarity with a particular illustrator
> Exposure to different types of music
> Creative expression through music, art, or drama

7. Did the storytime touch upon any of the multiple intelligences? *(Highlight or circle all relevant areas.)*
> Linguistic intelligence (connecting learning with words)
> Logical-mathematical intelligence (connecting learning with numbers or logic)
> Spatial intelligence (connecting learning with pictures)
> Bodily-kinesthetic intelligence (connecting learning with the body or with a physical experience)
> Musical intelligence (connecting learning with music)
> Interpersonal intelligence (learning through social experiences)
> Intrapersonal intelligence (learning with self-reflection or knowledge of one-self)
> Naturalist intelligence (learning through an experience in the social world)
> Emotional intelligence (self-awareness and self-confidence, empathy for others, managing disturbing emotions and inhibiting disruptive emotional impulses)
> Social intelligence (working together as a team)
> Ecological intelligence (awareness of and appreciation for our environment)

Comments:

_____

_____

_____

8. Did the storytime help develop or strengthen any of the following life skills?

Focus and Self-control
> Remembering rules
> Paying attention
> Thinking flexibly
> Taking turns

Perspective Taking
> Figuring out what other people think and feel
> Understanding the intentions of people around you

Communication
> Knowing your own thoughts
> Knowing what you want to say
> Knowing how to communicate
> Understanding how others will interpret your communication

Making Connections
> Determining what is the same and what is different
> Finding ways to connect what is the same and what is different
> Using a solution for one problem to solve another problem

Critical Thinking
> Wondering about the world
> Forming questions
> Looking for alternative solutions
> Discovering accurate answers
> Making decisions based on knowledge

Taking on Challenges
> Embracing a problem
> Tackling a problem

Self-directed, Engaged Learning
> Ways to continue outside of the library program

9. Did the children remember the author and illustrator of the book?
    ☐ Yes   ☐ No

_____

10. Do the children seem to know and love this book?
    ☐ Yes   ☐ No

_____

about the authors

Dr. Betsy Diamant-Cohen is an independent library trainer/consultant specializing in children's programming, early literacy, and partnerships. Diamant-Cohen's experience as children's librarian has been enhanced through her connection with children's museums in the US and abroad. Both institutions have the same mission of serving children, but the different approaches have enriched her repertoire and cemented her belief that the best way to learn is through play. Diamant-Cohen received her master's degree in library and information science from Rutgers University and a doctorate in communications design from the University of Baltimore. She was named a Library Journal Mover and Shaker in 2004 for developing the *Mother Goose on the Loose* early literacy program. Visit her website at www.mgol.net.

While attending graduate school at the University of Arizona, **Melanie Hetrick** envisioned herself as a government documents librarian. However, she had the opportunity to work with children in school libraries and quickly became hooked. She is now the children's librarian in Tillamook County, Oregon. She focuses on early literacy, reading difficulties, and learning differences in children. Her other passion in life is collection development. While at work, Hetrick can often be found in storytimes. She also enjoys working with teachers, tackling summer reading, and finding books for kids who swear they have read everything or don't want to read anything. To keep up with the voracious readers, Hetrick quickly became a voracious reader herself. However, her reading is often interrupted by her two very demanding cats.

index